CITY JOINS FIGHT ON SPEARS

Jury Probe Set As State Acts To Close Clinic

Spears Sanitarium Contagious Disease Deaths Checked

THE DENVER POST—Dec. 4, 1949

Court to Act on Clinic

Spears Held 'Public Nuisance'

THE DENVER POST—Dec. 3, 1949

Move to Close Sanitarium Gets Governor's Okay

THE DENVER POST—Dec. 10, 1949

Chiropractors Ask State Set Regulations for Them

The Denver Chiropractic Assn. last night demanded that the State Health Department set up separate regulations to meet
Obviously preparing to meet outside attacks against their profession, the chiropractors moved to establish a professional

Metzger Considers Two Moves in Probe Of Spears Sanitarium

THE DENVER POST—Dec. 5, 1949

Spears Seeks $3 Million In Suit Against Medics

PRAIRIE THUNDER

DR. LEO L. SPEARS AND HIS HOSPITAL

WILLIAM S. REHM

ASSOCIATION FOR THE HISTORY OF CHIROPRACTIC

Prairie Thunder: Dr. Leo L. Spears and His Hospital
By William S. Rehm

FIRST EDITION

Copyright © 2001 Association for the History of Chiropractic, Inc.

Printed in the United State of America
Printing/binding by Clinch Valley Printing Co.
Cover design and photo insert by Russell W. Gibbons
Graphics by Jo Butz Graphic Design Studio
Editor and project manager: Alana Callender

ISBN 0-9659131-2-0 (hardcover);
Library of Congress Control Number 00-132837

Dr. Leo L. Spears, 1894–1956

PRAIRIE THUNDER

DR. LEO L. SPEARS AND HIS HOSPITAL

Publication of the book has been made possible, in part, through the generosity of the following:

Colorado College of Chiropractic
David D. Palmer Health Sciences Library
Foot Levelers
H.F. Hill and Associates
Life University
Life Chiropractic College West
Northwestern Health Sciences University
Palmer College of Chiropractic
Palmer College of Chiropractic West
Southwest Virginia Community College
Theraquip, Inc.
University of Bridgeport - College of Chiropractic
Virginia Chiropractic Association

Dr. Richard L. Brown
Ms. Alana Callender
Dr. and Mrs. Ted Conger
Dr. and Mrs. Doug Cox
Dr. William Holmberg
Dr. P. Reginald Hug
Dr. Robert Jackson
Dr. Joseph P. Keating
Dr. Mildred Kimbrough
Dr. Arthur G. Lensgraf
Dr. Chuck Masarsky and Dr. Marion Todres
Dr. Jack Mask
Dr. Timothy Musick
Dr. Brian Porteous
Doyle and Linda Rasnick
Dr. and Mrs. Gary Randolph
Dr. and Mrs. Ray Tuck
Col. Nyle Vernon
Jane and John Willis
Dr. and Mrs. Jerry Willis
Dr. and Mrs. Joe Willis
Dr. Ken Young

We are grateful for their support.

Contents

Photo insert follows page 97

Photo credits: Inside covers from *Spears Sanitarium News*, 10 (Jan.) 1950.
All other photos are from author's collection.

AUTHOR'S INTRODUCTION

"I hear they're going to close that place down," the credit manager of Denver Dry Goods department store told me while denying my application for a store charge card. "That place" was Spears Chiropractic Hospital, my new employer. Who "they" were wasn't immediately clear.

It was early November, 1955. I was about to begin my 12-month internship, the capstone of my professional education, at chiropractic's largest and best known hospital. Anticipating that I would be in private practice in a year or so, I thought it would be a good idea to establish credit. But Denver Dry would have none of it.

This brief encounter was my introduction to how the Spears institution was viewed by some in Denver at that time. It was a notion, I would soon learn, surmised by a long-running battle between the hospital's intrepid founder, Dr. Leo L. Spears, and the medical establishment, fueled by an eager, sensational press.

I would also learn that the depth of this acrimony had its roots in the 1920s, well before there was a Spears Hospital. In fact, it had grown out of the singular personality of Dr. Spears himself.

It is no stretch to conclude beforehand that Leo Spears was the best known, most successful and most controversial chiropractor of his era. In the history of Colorado, his story would be among the more colorful chapters.

James Truslow Adams devoted a book to the individualism that opened the American frontier. "The West had jumped across seven hundred miles of the American Desert and a new frontier had come into being to impress again on more Americans those characteristics stamped by all the big and little frontiers that had been coming into existence for two and a half centuries."[1] Mr. Adams would have admired Dr. Spears, if only for his determination to extend the frontier.

No! Spears Hospital was not about to close. Any notion to the contrary was simply foolish and uninformed. Just consider this. Dr. Spears built an 800-bed hospital - one of the largest in the country - and had well advanced plans to almost quadruple that capacity, all without public dollars. When I arrived in 1955 the hospital had been a fixture in the city for more than a decade and was an acknowledged economic asset. There is no question that, at least in Colorado, Spears was one of the most discussed figures of his time; any criticism simply came with the territory.

That Leo Spears held many opinions and was not shy about advancing them in any forum was a given. He had even anticipated the great social debate of gun control by three decades and provoked a flood of response in the Denver newspapers for his views.[2,3] "He could spin theories as fast as he could talk," noted a Colorado colleague. "His convictions usually became prejudices. Unfortunately, there was no way to reason with him. I doubt that he ever accepted advice except from his lawyers and closest family members."[4]

AUTHOR'S INTRODUCTION

But it was toward medicine in general that Spears waxed the hottest and loudest. The public was well aware of the hostility of medicine toward chiropractic and vice versa. In the case of Dr. Spears, this was played out to its maximum decibel in the press, as witness this 1951 account of a civil suit for libel brought by Spears:

> Rarely does a trial in the civil divisions of the district court pack in an audience as in the libel suit contest of Dr. Leo L. Spears vs. Dr. Julian Maier the last couple of weeks.
>
> At many times during the eleven days of jury selection, testimony and argument, Judge William A. Black's division four courtroom was filled nearly to capacity. This would not be rare in a criminal case - a murder trial, for instance. It has even been noted on occasions during a contested divorce. But it is unusual indeed for a suit in libel to pack the uncomfortable courtroom benches.
>
> The reason: Personalities involved and implications of the case. Behind the fact that it was a suit for $300,000 in damages, people could sense a larger struggle - an epic showdown between the medical profession and the chiropractic profession.
>
> On the one side of the courtroom was Dr. Spears, who lost the decision eventually, center of a stormy debate ever since he began to fashion the mushrooming chiropractic hospital in east Denver. And on the other side of the courtroom was Dr. Maier, chief of staff at St. Luke's hospital and one of Colorado's most widely-known physicians.
>
> It has been said of fiction writing that optimum drama exists only when irreconcilable forces of optimum energy clash. That and more were present in this case of the embattled healing arts.[5]

So there you have it, the public's appetite for gladiator contests also feeding its perceptions. It was ever so throughout the very public 35-year career of Leo Spears.

He became the curator of his own legend, beginning early with carefully cafted advertisements he was certain the public would remember.[6] The press responded in kind, often seeming to command the public's indignation. Frequently, a story would outpace the actual facts; a prophecy clamoring for self-fulfillment. Spears was equally guilty for his part. Still, anyone who rated more than 500 news stories and editorials in the Denver press alone, not to mention 19 banner headlines, is worthy of an historical accounting for posterity.

SOURCES AND ACKNOWLEDGMENTS

In April of 1993, on virtually the eve of its demolition, I made my last visit to Spears Hospital. Accompanied by chiropractic educators Drs. Carl Cleveland, III and James Winterstein, and Dr. Charles Kirkpatrick of the National Jewish Hospital, Denver, ours may have been the last group to tour the facility. But it was during that visit that I decided to attempt this book when time permitted. Five years would pass before I finally began the arduous task.

Most of the research for this work, initially funded by a grant from the Association for the History of Chiropractic, was carried out over a $2^1/2$ year period. Visits to the National Archives and the Library of Congress, the Palmer College of Chiropractic Archives, the Denver Public Library, the Colorado Supreme Court Library and the Colorado State Archives provided abundant documentation from the considerable public record.

There would be bumps on the road delaying progress, but none so frustrating and ultimately unnecessary as was caused by a certain indifferent Colorado bureaucracy. Regrettably, a fourth and final research trip to Colorado scheduled in early 2000 was canceled for personal reasons. In the end, 85 percent of the research agenda was accomplished. It can be said, then, this is still a work in progress, perhaps to be completed at a later time by others.

The present work is not a biography of Dr. Leo Spears but rather is an attempt to examine a colorful and important era as a prism for some of chiropractic's most dramatic history. It was decided to write this complex story as a series of essays, allowing the record to speak for itself. To the extent that it succeeds in this objective, I am indebted to several individuals: editor and project manager Alana Callender for her guidance; Russ Gibbons, not only for his critiques of the manuscript and his contribution of the final essay, but for his expert touch in the design of the covers and the photo insert; Walt Wardwell for his welcome manuscript critiques, and Bob Jackson and Joe Keating for their helpful comments on the work in progress.

Special thanks are owed Colorado State Archivist Terry Ketelsen, whose kind considerations helped stretch the research budget, and my attorney, John J. Sweeney, Jr., for the same reasons, as well as his considerable help in rescuing a stalling project.

I would be remiss in not also acknowledging Glenda Wiese, Ron Beideman and fellow intern from so long ago, Ed Kletzel, for their encouragement and help whenever requested.

I have used rather extensively a tape-recorded interview conducted with the late Dr. Dan C. Spears by Brian Greer, then-director of the David D. Palmer Health Sciences Library, in 1983. My own diary while an intern at Spears Hospital in the mid 1950s is also used, though sparingly.

Some who remember the times and events recounted herein might wonder why Dr. Howard M. Spears is not acknowledged as a primary source. Regrettably, Dr. Howard was unable to participate.

SOURCES AND ACKNOWLEDGMENTS

One of Dr. Leo's contemporaries, Dr. Louis O. Gearhart, shared a good bit of useful information on some of the pertinent history of chiropractic in Colorado, and I am thankful. I am mindful, too, of the help of Dr. Harry Swanson and Dr. Anthony Olaiz, as well as another of Dr. Leo's associates who, although preferring anonymity, shared views which I deemed worthy of inclusion.

Finally, I acknowledge with undying devotion my wife, Jean, for her patience and understanding throughout all of this.

There is still a lot to be said about Dr. Leo Spears and his hospital. To those who might continue the research, this volume, considering its sins of both commission and omission, might be a useful start.

William S. Rehm

August, 2000

CHRONOLOGY

1894   **Feb. 7-**Leaston Leo Spears is born in Ivan, Florida.

1917   **Sept.-**Enlists in United States Marine Corps.

1919   **Nov.-**Honorably discharged from Marines with rank of corporal.

1921   **April 25-**Graduates from Palmer School of Chiropractic, Davenport, Iowa.
           July-Begins practice in Majestic building, downtown Denver, Colo.
           Sept. 10-Publishes open letter to President Harding and Congress asking Veterans' Bureau be mandated to provide chiropractic care for disabled veterans.
           Sept. 16-First newspaper interview published, in *Rocky Mountain News.*

1922   **Nov.-**Publicly denounces compulsory smallpox vaccination order for Denver residents.

1924   **Feb. 25.-**Attacks Fitzsimons Hospital and Veterans' Bureau in newspaper advertisement.
           Feb. 28-Charges filed with State Board of Medical Examiners accuse Spears of libel.
           April 18-Medical board finds Spears guilty of "immoral, unprofessional and dishonorable conduct" and revokes license to practice.
           June-National convention of Disabled American Veterans supports Spears' call for "freedom of choice" in health care.
           Sept. 25-District Court rules medical board exceeded its authority in revoking Spears' chiropractic license. Board appeals.
           Expelled from Majestic Building; relocates practice to Steele Building.

1925   Begins teaching and promoting "Spears Painless System" - an adjustive technique.

1926   **June 7-**Colorado Supreme Court overrules trial court and upholds license revocation.
           Publishes first edition of text, *Spears Painless System of Chiropractic.*

1927   **Jan.-**Opens convalescent home at 1828 Lincoln St. for disabled veterans voluntarily choosing chiropractic care.

Dec. 12-U.S. Supreme Court refuses jurisdiction in license revocation matter.

1928 **March 27**-Federal District Court denies Spears injunction against medical board.
April 11-Accepts negotiated one-year license suspension.

1929 **April 11**-Resumes practice after serving suspension.

1931-34 Purchases "Health Creamery" and operates network of emergency free food distribution centers during the Great Depression. Is denounced by some mainline charities.

1932 **Jan. 5**-New charges of "unprofessional conduct" against Spears are filed with Board of Medical Examiners over certain advertising.
July 11-Medical Board dismisses charges.
Aug.-Begins operating free clinic for indigent children, becoming model for the profession.

1933 Licensed by newly-created Colorado Board of Chiropractic Examiners.
Nov. 22-Nonprofit Spears Free Clinic and Hospital for Poor Children is incorporated.

1936 Begins daily "Health Chats" radio program.

1937 Sells Lincoln St. property and purchases "Gaylord House" at 2209 E. 13th Ave.
Nephew Dan C. Spears, D.C., joins practice.

1938 **Oct. 28**- State Supreme Court rules that certain real property owned by Spears Clinic is not exempt from local taxes.
Nephew Howard M. Spears, D.C., joins practice.

1939 Visits lepersarium in Hawaii.
Purchases undeveloped acreage in east Denver for construction of hospital.

1940 **April**-Hospital construction begins, using volunteer and nonunion labor. Building site vandalized.
Dr. Dan Spears begins operating mobile clinic through rural eastern Colorado to promote coming hospital.

1941 **Dec. 8**-United States enters World War II.
Mobile clinic discontinues operation for duration of war.

CHRONOLOGY

1942 **May-**Dr. Dan Spears enlists in Navy.

1943 **Jan.-**Planned opening of 136-bed hospital is announced. Difficulties with Board of Health over licensing begin.
May 2-Spears Hospital opens without license.
Denver Medical Society demands confiscation of hospital for military use in the "public interest." Federal government reportedly offers $300,000 for building.
Dr. Dan Spears receives medical discharge from Navy; re-joins practice.
May 4-Hospital license refused by Board of Health.
May 22-Spears sues in attempt to obtain hospital license. Charges State Board of Health and Denver Health Department lack constitutional authority to refuse license.
June 11-District Court dismisses Spears' petition.
June 14-Drs. Leo and Dan Spears arrested and charged with manslaughter in death of patient in the hospital. Hospital ordered closed by city district attorney.
June 18-Leo Spears marries Laura Ellen Lyle.
July-Dr. Howard Spears enlists in Army.
July 31-Amended hospital license application is filed.
Sept. 6-District Court orders Board of Health to issue license to Spears Hospital.
Sept. 27-Board issues "temporary, provisional permit" to operate sanitarium.
Nov. 10-Directed verdict clears Drs. Leo and Dan Spears of criminal indictments.

1945 **Sept. 2-**Foundation work begins on Unit 2, again with non-union labor. Cancellation of contracts, shortages of building materials and picketing of site impede progress.

1946 **May 8-**Attorney General rules Spears Sanitarium cannot say it is a hospital. Spears files suit for "malicious prosecution" against health officials who caused arrest.
June-Files antitrust suit against members of Board of Health et al. Case dismissed when not prosecuted in timely manner.
Nov. 19-Board of Health acts to revoke permit for alleged violations. Spears obtains stay.
First issue of *Spears Chiropractic Sanitarium News* published.

1947 **Jan. 9-**Sues in District Court to set aside permit revocation.
March 12-City Council rejects Spears' proposed charter amendment to permit indigent to receive chiropractic care.

CHRONOLOGY

May-Clinic moves from Steele building to Gaylord House.
Negotiations with Chiropractic Research Foundation falter.
Master Plan for hospital expansion announced. 2,600 beds and chiropractic school envisioned. Neighborhood group files protest.

1948 **March-**Mayor vetos Spears rezoning bill.
July 27-City Council okays Spears expansion.
Aug. 23-Spears Clinic establishes as nonprofit, tax-exempt corporation. Dr. Leo Spears "retires" from private practice.
Nov.-Hospital inaugurates one-year residential internship and three-year nursing programs.
Dec. 18-District Court upholds Board of Health's right to revoke temporary, provisional license of Spears Sanitarium.

1949 **March 14-**Spears appeals trial court's decision to Supreme Court.
May-Spears postgraduate seminars inaugurated.
Sept.-Spears Chiropractic Sanitarium Guild, a lay fund raising and public relations organization, is established.
Nov. 6-Unit 2 (600 beds) opens.
Nov. 29-Attorney General declares Spears Sanitarium a "public nuisance" and orders closing. Spears obtains stay.
Nov. 30-District Court rules Spears Sanitarium is a hospital for insurance purposes.
Dec. 3-*Rocky Mountain News* publishes old charges of "criminal neglect" against sanitarium (the Maier case).
Dec. 4-State Senator Neal Bishop denounces Board of Health, charging conspiracy to destroy Spears and the chiropractic profession.
Dec. 6-Spears answers Board's accusations.
Colorado Chiropractic Association denounces arbitrary actions of health board and demands fairness.
Dec. 10-Spears files antitrust suit against Colorado Board of Health and Denver Medical Society.
Dec. 18-Attorney General asks District Court to place sanitarium under direct supervision of Board of Health.
Spears, labor reach accord on future building plans.

1950 **Jan. 5-**Spears' antitrust suit against Board of Health dismissed. Files appeal.
Jan. 11-Malicious prosecution suit against city and state health officials refiled in District Court.
Jan. 14-Files $300,000 libel suit against Julian Maier, M.D.
Jan. 26-Unit 2 formally dedicated as D.D. Palmer Memorial Building.
March 12-Refiles antitrust suit against Colorado Board of Health et al.

May 22-Arguments before Supreme Court in license revocation appeal are heard.

July 1-Colorado Supreme Court unanimously finds that the Board of Health conspired to put sanitarium out of business. Rules that profession may operate its own hospitals. Sanitarium permit invalidated. Board of Health ordered to issue unrestricted hospital license in accordance with chiropractic practice statute.

Oct. 14-Board of Health issues license to Spears Hospital.

Second edition of *Spears Painless System* is published.

Dr. George A. Wilson is named director of research.

1951   **May**-Inaugural issue of *Spears Sanigram.*

May 24-Spears sues *Collier's* magazine, its owners, editors and a staff writer for libel, asking $24 million.

June 8-New Spears mobile clinic crashes in New Mexico on maiden trip.

July 13-Spears loses antitrust suit in federal court.

July 14-Spears files $25 million libel suit against American Broadcasting Co., columnist-broadcaster Walter Winchell et al.

Sept. 7-Libel suit against Julian Maier begins.

Sept. 20-Spears' libel claim rejected by jury.

Oct.-Wilson releases report on "First 211 Cancer Cases Treated at Spears Hospital."

Nov.-Blue Cross rejects hospital's application for membership. Spears charges discrimination.

Spears Cancer Research Fund is created.

1952   **Jan.**-First Chiropractic Cancer Symposium at Spears Hospital.

May 10-U.S. Court of Appeals rules against Spears in anti-trust suit of Colorado Board of Health.

Aug.-National publicity campaign is launched.

Sept. 11-Laura Lyle Spears is granted uncontested divorce.

Dec. 19-Groundbreaking for 2,150-bed Unit 3 (Pioneers building).

"Chiropractic Proof" film is produced.

1953   **April**-Offers $100,000 to anyone who can disprove claims of discovering cause and cure of cerebral palsy and mental deficiency.

May/June-Spears testifies in Washington, D.C. before U.S. Senate subcommittee hearings on medical monopoly in military (the Langer hearings).

Aug.-Langer hearings shift to Tenth U.S. Circuit Court, Denver, and to Spears Hospital. Unit 1 dedicated to Dr. Willard Carver.

Sept. 21-Supreme Court rules against Spears in Maier case.

Nov. 22-Spears claims blood test for cancer.

Dec.-Testifies at U.S. Senate inquiry on juvenile delinquency; presents theories on cause and cure.

Press-medical "code of cooperation" charged.

1954   **Jan. 19-**Ailing Pope Pius XII is invited to Spears.

Feb. 4-Denver grand jury probe on "medical quackery" opens.

April 6-Food and Drug Administration agents seize Neuromicrometer devices from hospital. Charge unsupported treatment claims and misbranding. Spears accuses state of illegally using attorney general's office.

July-Federal court hears misbranding charges.

Leo Spears threatened for "contempt" in refusing court-ordered medical and psychiatric examinations in conspiracy suit.

April 12-Grand jury subpoenas records of Spears Hospital.

May 13-Grand jury report hits Spears' advertising.

May 20-Spears sues Denver Better Business Bureau and some 80 other defendants for alleged conspiracy, asking $10 million damages.

June 29-Grand jury adjourns while returning no indictments against Spears, but again denounces testimonial advertising.

July 21-Clinic files $1 million conspiracy suit against Better Business Bureau, later joined to suit brought by hospital.

Oct. 14-Longevity Research Study underway.

Dec.-Mobile cancer education program launched in Rocky Mountain region.

Loan fund to assist graduate D.C.'s proposed by Spears.

1955   **March 14-**Loses *Collier's* suit in New York federal court.

April-ABC-Winchell suit settled out of court.

Oct. 13-Suit against Better Business Bureau and *Post* dismissed. Spears appeals.

Sept. 12-Conspiracy trial begins.

Oct. 14-Court rules that evidence fails to back conspiracy claim.

Dec.-Spears denounces Ford Foundation decision to withhold grant to hospital.

Dec. 22-Conspiracy suit appealed to Supreme Court.

1956   **Jan. 18-**Suit against ex-health officials thrown out of court.

Feb.-Launches new $500,000 national publicity campaign.

May 16-Dr. Leo Spears dies from heart attack at age 62.

Board of Trustees reorganizes.

Work on Pioneers Building is halted.

Sept. 9-Hospital featured on ABC-TV "Cavalcade of Progress."

CHRONOLOGY

1957 **July 10-**Hospital loses appeal of antitrust suit.

1958 **Aug. 18-**State affirms ban on chiropractic hospital care for old age pensioners.
Oct.-University of Colorado studies purchasing unfinished Pioneers Building.

1959 **Feb. 16-**Suit filed to prevent city from taxing unfinished building and undeveloped acreage.
Nov. 8-Sen. William Langer dies at age 73.

1960 **April 12-**Colorado Supreme Court rules that city of Denver has no authority to tax hospital's unfinished Unit 3 or three blocks of undeveloped land.

1963 **Feb.-**Industrialist Andrew J. Sordoni, longtime friend of Dr. Leo and hospital, dies at age 77.

1966 **July 24-**Unfinished Pioneers Building (Unit 3) is sold for private development.
Proposal to merge Lincoln Chiropractic College with Spears Hospital fails to materialize.

1967 **July 7-**Attorney General Burt Keating dies.

1975 **May 7-**Attorney Charles Ginsberg dies at age 81.

1976 **Nov. 18-**Spears Hospital featured in favorable *Denver Post* story.

1980 **May 20-**Former state senator Neal Bishop, D.C., dies at age 79.

1983 **Sept. 27-**Roy L. Cleere, M.D., former state health director, dies at age 77.

1984 **April-**Spears Hospital closes.

1988 **Dec. 13-**Dr. Dan C. Spears dies at age 72.

1993 **Jan.**-Remaining hospital property sold to private developer.
July-Razing of original buildings underway.

Prologue

Leo L. Spears was born February 7, 1894, in a one-room log cabin on the family homestead at Ivan, Florida, just south of Tallahassee. He was given the name Leaston Leo, which he so disliked that he later had it legally changed to Leo L. His father was a non-ordained Baptist preacher, crop farmer, blacksmith and craftsman of wood furniture lathed in his own workshop. His mother was strictly a housewife. The family ancestry was English and Scotch and had been in Florida for two generations. Leo was the fourth of eight children, all of whom survived into adulthood.[1] As it was not uncommon in rural America of those times for children to also labor on the family farm, formal education was often minimal. Leo had completed the sixth grade but told a *Rocky Mountain News* reporter that he was actually illiterate until he was 18 years old. "The advantages of life are not thoroly [*sic*] appreciated until the disadvantages have been experienced," he said.[2]

At 18, he left home to work in the fruit groves of Terra Ceia, near Tampa. There, he said, he had his first opportunity to study, from a wholesale seed catalog. His employer, perhaps recognizing an untapped ability in need of tutoring, urged Leo to complete his basic education and pursue a meaningful trade. Taking the advice, he went to Jacksonville a couple of years later and studied stenography and English at a business school while also completing requirements for a high school certificate.[3]

In 1915, when he was 21, he was hired as secretary to the head claims agent of the Seaboard Airline Railway, headquartered in Jacksonville. Later transferring to Norfolk, Virginia, Leo continued with the railroad until June 1917, then enlisted in the Marine Corps when it appeared the United States would enter the World War.[4]

After basic training at the Parris Island Marine Corps Barracks in South Carolina, he was assigned to the Quartermaster Corps at command headquarters in Washington, D.C. Early in his military service, Leo received special permission to attend night classes at George Washington University for courses to improve his reading and writing skills. It was while attending these classes that he developed appendicitis requiring emergency surgery, and two additional operations for complications. Convalescing at the Naval Hospital in

1

Bethesda, Maryland., and still seeming not to improve substantially, another patient recommended to Leo that he see a Washington chiropractor named Dr. Hod Norton, which he did, reportedly improving "dramatically."[5]

The First World War ended with the armistice of November 11, 1918. After serving 27 months, Corporal Leo Spears was honorably discharged from the Marines in September 1919. He returned to Florida to ponder what to do next as his former position with the railroad had been abolished. Because he was entitled by his military service to receive educational benefits, he recalled his good impression of Dr. Norton and his associate Dr. Charles Shellhorn, and their recommendation that he consider entering the Palmer School of Chiropractic (PSC) in Davenport, Iowa, after his discharge.[6] And so with funds borrowed from relatives, he made the long bus trip to Davenport for the fall term beginning September 22, 1919.[7] It was said that Leo continued to wear his government-issue clothing at the PSC because he was too poor to afford anything else, and indeed a 1921 photograph of the student body does picture him in Marine uniform.[8] To supplement his meager government allowance, Leo gave ballroom dancing lessons, and wrote and printed several small booklets that he sold to students, one of which was entitled "The Shortest Road to Success."[9]

Leo Spears was graduated from the Palmer School on February 25, 1921.[10,11] For the class yearbook he penned a simple but provident essay:

> I never stopped doing a thing because somebody else said it was wrong. Nor did I keep on because somebody else said it was right - I did my own thinking! I always persisted when I knew I was right, and when I found I was wrong I acknowledged it. Above all, I always kept my word. When I said I would do a thing, I did it; when I thought I couldn't do it, I said so. I always tried to treat other people as I would have them treat me. I never wasted any time, but put every minute to good use. In the last analysis, I never made excuses, I made good.[12]

Through the years, Leo continued to employ his talent for composition, in such ways as writing popular music that found its way to the dancing pavilion at Elitch Gardens, and at least one play performed on the Denver stage. If his efforts in the performing arts were less than financially rewarding they are still regarded in Denver as examples of merit in local popular culture.[13] He also wrote at least two best-selling books of interest to the chiropractic profession.

Having chosen to cast his lot in Denver, Colorado, the 27-year-old Spears arrived there in the early summer of 1921 and opened his practice on the 5th of July. His license was issued by the State Board of Medical Examiners, which at the time had statutory authority to regulate chiropractic.[14]

His first office was in the Majestic Building at 16th and Broadway, the business crossroads of the city. This building was a favorite of the medical fraternity and doctors' signs could be seen from the street on all sides. It was also the high rent district and Leo had wagered borrowed capital on immediate success.[15]

To begin with, he advertised regularly in the local newspapers, an activity then frowned upon and generally regarded by mainline medicine as the telltale mark of an incompetent or a quack. Later, he broadcast daily "Health Chats" on radio.[16] But Spears was doing exactly as he had been taught by his chiropractic mentor, Dr. B.J. Palmer, the autocratic leader of the Palmer School regarded by many at the time as the very apotheosis of chiropractic thought.

Spears persuaded Dr. Charles Mathis, a school chum from the PSC and fellow Floridian, to join the practice. Although the partnership apparently lasted only one week--Mathis preferring to return to Florida--the familiar corporate name Spears & Mathis remained unchanged for a number of years.[17]

The practice flourished beyond all expectations.

1.

Early Controversies

"I Will Not Be Vaccinated"

Smallpox, after years of steady decline in America, reemerged as a significant threat in the early 1920s.[1] Public health officials were satisfied no one was naturally immune to the contagion and that susceptibility of a large population was determined by its history of vaccination, considered the safest and most reliable preventive.[2] Not to be vaccinated was regarded as selfish and antisocial.[3]

In the city of Denver, the situation had become one of extreme urgency with more than 200 deaths reported between August 1921 and November 1922, among the highest tolls in the nation. Of the city's 300,000 residents, at least two-thirds were believed to be either unvaccinated or inoculated too long ago to be considered immune.[4] No one who had succumbed to the disease was thought vaccinated.[5]

On November 21, 1922, a compulsory vaccination order went into effect. With the authority of the municipal code, City Health Commissioner William H. Sharpley, M.D., also known as Manager of Health and Charity, issued the emergency proclamation with a warning that failure to immediately comply with the order would result in quarantine and fines up to $200. Residents, including transients, were informed that the only exceptions would be evidence of inoculation within the past five years, such as a vaccination certificate or recent inoculation scar.[6] Free vaccination centers were set up throughout the city.[7]

Dr. Leo Spears believed that inoculation of "pus off a sore on a sick calf's belly"[8] should not be forced upon the public, epidemic or not. Others opposed to compulsory vaccination pointed to government figures in the U.S. and Britain linking the high incidence of tuberculosis to the variola toxoid.[9,10]

Through a succession of advertisements in the three major newspapers, the *Times, Post* and *Rocky Mountain News,* Spears staged his own Wittenberg-style protest, urging city residents to join his resistance, and even offered legal assistance should it be necessary.

[Nov. 22, 1922]
I WILL NOT BE VACCINATED

I regret to violate a city ordinance, but when such is necessary in order to prevent flagrant violation of my person and my personal rights and liberties, then I do it with no mental scruples.

During the world war I fought for life, liberty and the pursuit of happiness. Now I settle down in good old Denver to enjoy those rights only to find that the fight is not yet finished.

I say, let those who want to be vaccinated have their choice. Let those who want medicine have it. And I say with equal emphasis that those who do not want either SHALL NOT have either FORCED upon them. I am free born and 21. My life is my own. My blood is clean. I am no menace to those who are vaccinated, according to the vaccination theory. Those who do not want to be vaccinated are not afraid of me. Therefore, I am not a criminal subject to a fine for refusal to permit anyone to trample on my rights.

An ordinance that presumes to violate one's person; to restrict one's LIBERTY OF CHOICE in matters pertaining to one's personal welfare is beyond all bounds of reason and good judgment.

This may be construed as a flat refusal to be vaccinated and a defiance of the ordinance requiring it. Also to those who feel as I do, I pledge both personal and financial support in the protection of their RIGHTS.

If you don't want to be vaccinated, you don't have to be.

SPEARS & MATHIS, Chiropractors

[Nov. 23, 1922]
STILL NOT VACCINATED.
CITY HEALTH DEPARTMENT MAKES ANOTHER BAD MISTAKE.
CALLS TO ARREST ME BUT HAS NO WARRANT.

What a great time we had. The inspector wanted to know if I had ever been vaccinated. I showed him a scar about fifteen years old, but he said it looked young and unsophisticated to him. "Yes," says I, "I was vaccinated while in the service but it didn't 'take.'" As a matter of fact, I washed it out with soap and water. If we find that a fifteen-year-old scar on me is satisfactory to the health department, then why vaccinate others who have been vaccinated during the past fifteen years?

No, I am not against vaccination for those who want it. But I am totally against compulsory vaccination, deliberate assault on the bodies of those who do not want it. I find that there are many thousands in Denver who are with me and behind me. I want to thank the hundreds who called me today and pledged their support to the limit. And the thousands who would have called had I possessed a hundred phones, and the additional thousands who will prove they are with me when the assault is made.

The inspector called me a quack and intimated that I had no support on my stand. I venture to predict, however, that at least a hundred thousand will absolutely refuse vaccination.

Mr. Lawyers, prepare yourselves. If the health department keeps up its nerve, I may need all of you to protect those whom I have promised and again pledge my support.

I want to announce also that in case my fifteen-year-old scar proves unsatisfactory and the warrant is not forgotten again, it may be necessary for me to take care of my patients in jail. I don't love the thought of jail, but my fight shall be to the finish. I am standing on principle and it SHALL NOT PERISH.

SPEARS & MATHIS, Chiropractors

EARLY CONTROVERSIES

[Nov. 24, 1922]
OUR FIGHT HAS BEEN WON

You need not worry - it is a sure thing that your body will not now be assaulted. I am still out of jail and still unvaccinated. That isn't all. If need be I will continue to fight for the right.

Thanks to the many hundreds who have offered to pay my advertising bill, and the many thousands who have offered hundreds of thousands of dollars to back me. I am glad to say that due to a most wonderful practice I am able to fight at my own expense.

Let me say again that OUR fight has been won, but that MY fight is still on. Therefore, for evidence in case of further exhibition against me, my attorneys, Spaulding & Seydel, Foster Building, request the following information: Names and addresses of persons who have been injured by vaccination, or who have had smallpox after vaccination, and the names of doctors who vaccinated such persons. Also any information that you have along these lines. Send the information to me personally.

SPEARS & MATHIS, Chiropractors

Spears' own claims of public support notwithstanding, the *Denver Times* reported that indeed a sense of resistance was noted, especially among the city's substantial number of transients: "Several cowboys living outside the city had been stopping at the house (apparently a brothel), the manager of health said, and flatly refused to be vaccinated. The police were ordered to prevent any one from leaving the house until the vaccination order was complied with." [11]

At the request of Health Commissioner Sharpley, the U.S. Public Health Service dispatched an assistant surgeon general to Denver to supervise the compulsory vaccination order.[12] Sharpley had been under considerable pressure from the county medical society for not acting sooner. The osteopaths agreed, the county and state associations jointly passing a resolution favoring a vigorous vaccination campaign as the only effective method of curbing the epidemic.[13] Sharpley told the press that "antivaccination propaganda by certain nonmedical groups and individuals" was partially responsible for his request that the government take supervision in the city.[14]

The smallpox epidemic was declared under control before Christmas of 1922 with more than 200,000 residents complying with the vaccination order. Deputy Surgeon General Thomas Parran, satisfied that the health threat had ended because of compulsory inoculation, expressed his dismay that any resistance had been offered, noting that even the Christian Scientists had complied because it was the law.[15] Whether any legal consequences resulted for resisters is not clear.

Grassroots opposition to compulsory vaccination gained a threshold in the legislature in 1927 and the law was repealed.[16] While Spears' continued activism might well have had some influence, he had been presured to gag his public criticism because of personal difficulties with the State Board of Medical Examiners.[17] These problems will be examined next.

7

State Board v. Spears

Charles H. Culbertson, an Army veteran gassed and seriously wounded at Chateau-Thierry, had been a patient at Denver's Fitzsimons Army Hospital for about two years. During part of that time, surreptitiously, he had also been receiving chiropractic care at Spears' downtown clinic. Apparently seeing in his relationship with Culbertson an opportunity to showcase what he believed to be true, that many disabled war veterans would seek and benefit from chiropractic care in government hospitals and clinics if it were available to them, Spears drafted a petition to this effect which Culbertson was able to circulate among other Fitzsimons patients. It was addressed to the President and the Congress. Some 300 signatures had been obtained before the petition was "discovered" and Culbertson was allegedly "thrown out" of the hospital as punishment. He died of kidney failure on February 20, 1924, "a victim of government tyranny," Spears believed.

Convinced that a grievous wrong had been committed, Spears had Mr. Culbertson's widow recount the circumstances of her husband's alleged mistreatment at the hospital. Her statement, as well as those of other patients who said they witnessed the events take place, were published by Spears on February 22, 1924 in full-page advertisements in Denver's major daily newspapers. "Take this not lightly, for, even tho [*sic*] you may think me a fool, I am not foolish enough to make statements I cannot prove," he wrote.[18]

The main text of the lengthy article was a description of Mr. Culbertson's history of alleged neglect and an attack on Fitzsimons Hospital and the Veterans' Bureau. His specific accusations were:

■ Charles H. Culbertson died a victim of greed.

■ The fact that Culbertson sought relief through chiropractic was regarded and treated as an offense by the authorities of the Fitzsimons General Hospital and the officials of the Veterans' Bureau.

■ Culbertson died because he attempted to save his own life after medicine had failed, because he signed a petition, because he asked for the privilege of using freedom of choice, and because of the prejudice and greed of the medical system.

■ He was told "a lot of you birds are going to get kicked out of this place" (for signing the petition).

■ He was thrown out of Fitzsimons Hospital.

■ He suffered from tuberculosis of the lungs.

■ He had petitioned the Veterans' Bureau to fix his teeth.

■ The Veterans' Bureau refused to fix his teeth.

■ He was not offered hospitalization when he returned to Denver about six weeks prior to his death.

■ The Veterans' Bureau refused to bury Culbertson because he chose a doctor outside of the Bureau.

■ The officers of Fitzsimons General Hospital falsified their records in order to suppress the truth in regard to Charles H. Culbertson.

Just how seriously the charges were taken are obvious from the high level of quickly exchanged communications:

February 23, 1924

Surgeon General M.W. Ireland
United States Army
Washington, D.C.

My Dear General Ireland:
I am enclosing herewith an advertisement by one Leo L. Spears who as you note is a Chiropractor, and who was educated at the expense of the United States Government under the vocational training. I am wondering whether you may see any way clear to the hospital and clip this young man's wings relative to the Government and its handling the case of Charles H. Culbertson. We note that in the reported statement of the wife that he had "two of the same kind of convulsions that killed him" the day before he was kicked out of the Hospital. I also call your attention to the beautiful X-ray photograph of his teeth given in the article.
Leo Spears is one of the most aggressive and unprincipled men we have in the Chiropractic profession and if there is some way to get his goat we would be very pleased.

Cordially yours,
David A Strickler, M.D.
Secretary-Treasurer
Colorado Board of Medical Examiners

February 26, 1924

My Dear Dr. Strickler:
Of course the whole thing is contemptible, but there is nothing this office can do about it. However, I am sending the paper to the Director of the Veterans' Bureau to see if he is inclined to take the matter up. It may be that their Legal Department will find some way in which to sue Spears, who of course has made a mass of untruthful statements. I have no doubt that the man Culbertson was discharged from the hospital because he refused to abide by any of the rules promulgated to insure the welfare of the patients and prevent the unruly ones from jeopardizing the welfare of other patients in the institution. However, the Veterans' Bureau is in a position to make a very complete investigation of this whole matter. If they are not able to take action I do not know anyone else who can.

Very sincerely yours,
M.W. Ireland, M.D.
The Surgeon General

Spears' outburst found immediate support in two letters to the *Rocky Mountain News*, one from a disabled ex-veteran who said he knew Culbertson well and was with him a few hours before he died; the other from the national executive committeeman of Disabled American Veterans for Colorado, Wyoming, Utah and New Mexico, who seconded Spears' call for veterans' rights in choosing health, although he stopped short of endorsing the most vociferous of the charges.[19,20] On February 29, Spears was served notice at his office that a complaint against him had been filed by a concerned citizen with the State Board of Medical Examiners and that a hearing on the possible revocation of his license to practice chiropractic in Colorado would be held in the Senate Chambers of the Colorado State House, Denver, on the afternoon of Tuesday, April 1, 1924. He was advised to seek counsel if he wished to defend himself against accusations of "unprofessional, dishonorable and immoral conduct."[21]

The complainant was one Nathan Golden, a district officer in the Veterans of Foreign Wars (VFW) who, later testimony would reveal, was chosen after hurried discussions between the medical board and the VFW.

Although one month seemed precious little time for either side to prepare, the trial was mounted. Spears would be represented by the Denver firm of Carle Whitehead, Albert Vogl and Floyd Miles.

Dr. Spears appealed to the public to judge for themselves the merits of the charges against him:

> [*Rocky Mountain News*, March 16, 1924]
>
> If you want to know the truth of my statements (which the complaint says are false), be at the trial. I wish the whole world could be there and see and hear the evidence that I shall present. I have nothing to hide but much to reveal, and that is why I want you there... (for) an afternoon of heartrending entertainment.

The prosecution -- complainant Golden, the State Board of Medical Examiners, Fitzsimons General Hospital, the Veterans' Bureau, the VFW, and the American Legion -- would be represented by a host of lawyers, one even dispatched from Washington by the War Department to assist the Veterans' Bureau.[22]

Thirty-two witnesses would be subpoenaed, including a number of Fitzsimons patients who knew Culbertson.[23] Also subpoenaed was widow Theora Culbertson, whose legitimacy of marriage had even been investigated by the skeptical prosecutors.[24,25]

It was already March 27 when the defense, rebuffed by government red tape from seeing Culbertson's and other records of the case and threatening to ask for a continuance, were finally given the opportunity to examine the evidence.[26]

Trial began at 2:30 p.m. on April 1, 1924. Defense attorney Carle Whitehead in his opening statement said: "The legislature has no power to confer authority upon this board to deny a physician the right to advertise his business, so that if the complaint in this case is as the complaint says it is, the Supreme Court has said that the board has nothing at all to do with that. (This) is an attempt to get around that constitutional provision and have this man punished for publishing something which they state is a libel without being given his constitutional privilege of a trial before a court and jury."[27]

After the opening statement, the decidedly pro-Spears gallery demonstrated for several minutes, ignoring calls for order by Chairman Charles Haines. Mr. Whitehead finally appealed to the spectators to remain quiet: "Friends, I am going to request you on behalf of the board and on behalf of all parties interested in these proceedings, that you refrain from any expression of your feelings. We are going to have a rather extended hearing; there are gentlemen here from out of town who have come a long distance, and under these circumstances I think you will respect the request that I have made and refrain from any applause or other expression of your feelings. It will be necessary to have the room cleared unless we can have quiet so as to proceed in an orderly way."[28]

The demonstrations obviously pleased Dr. Spears:

> [Community Herald, April 5, 1924]
> ### A THOUSAND THANKS
> Such enthusiastic attention and cooperation are undeniable evidence that the public will soon rise up and demand justice and freedom of choice for their disabled veterans in matters of health the same as religion and politics. The trial will be continued at 9 a.m. next Tuesday at the same place. And to say that volumes of interesting evidence is going to be produced is putting it mildly.
>
> You are again extended a cordial invitation.

Testimony continued April 8-11, the final session recessing at 2 a.m. All of the proceedings were observed by representatives of the Colorado and Denver chiropractic societies, the Universal Chiropractors' Association, the Colorado and Denver medical societies, and the American Medical Association.[29]

Several documents produced on behalf of the complainant and corrobated by witness testimony clearly showed that Charles Culbertson had requested his release from Fitzsimons Hospital, which was granted October 5, 1922 with instructions that he be observed by the outpatient department of the Veterans' Bureau because of chronic parenchymatous nephritis and cardiac enlargement. There was no indication from his records that Culbertson ever suffered "convulsions" related to his illness, as alleged by his widow.[30]

On the final day of testimony, Dr. Spears was questioned about the purported statement given to him by Mrs. Culbertson, saying that it was taken verbatim but that he talked it over with her before typing it for publication.[31]

Q. "State whether or not she read it over after it was written."

A. "She did."

Q. "State whether or not she signed it."

A. "She did."

Q. "At the time you wrote this ad were you aware of the statement in Mr. Culbertson's discharge that he was discharged at his own request?"

A. "Yes sir. I was also told a number of times that he had not requested his discharge since he had been taking chiropractic; that he wanted to stay in the hospital."

Q. "In other words, do I get from you that his request for discharge was prior to August 11, 1922?"

A. "That is what he told me, that he had asked a number of times before that time. If he asked after that time he didn't tell me."[32]

Final arguments were heard on April 16 at the offices of the Board of Examiners. Each side was allowed 50 minutes. At 10 p.m., the board adjourned to executive session.

The board's judgment was released in a three-page resolution in which all of Spears' charges were judged to be "false and defamatory." While Spears had been given great latitude in presenting his defense, the board dismissed much of his evidence as "immaterial and irrelevant," and witness testimony as "so unreasonable, inconsistent and improbable that their uncorroborated testimony is not worthy of credence."[33] The resolution concluded, " That by reason of said false statements contained in said advertisement, said advertisement was falsely defamatory and derogatory toward the Officers of Fitzsimons General Hospital and the Officers of the Veterans' Bureau, and said false statements were made without reasonable and probable cause, but were made with wanton and reckless disregard of the truth for the purpose of unjustly discrediting said Officers, and for the purpose of increasing the practice and income of the respondent as a chiropractor."

That the conduct of said Leo L. Spears in causing the publication of said advertisement was immoral, unprofessional and dishonorable.

> WHEREFORE, it is ordered that the license of said Leo L. Spears to practice chiropractic in the state of Colorado be, and the same is hereby revoked.

Dr. Spears was officially notified of the board's action on April 17, 1924. At the same time, the board ordered the Clerk and Recorder of Denver County to remove his name from the license registry, and that a copy of the order be transmitted to Dr. Spears by the sheriff.[34,35]

Although the press covered the public hearings daily, it had been unusually silent, until now. At least one columnist found the results to his liking and minced no words:

> Leo L. Spears got what was coming to him. The state board of medical examiners took away his license to practice as a chiropractor. The board is to be commended.
>
> Spears has shown himself to be an undesirable citizen. Denver and Colorado can get along very nicely without him. He has been a troublemaker for several years, but this time he went too far.
>
> The board found him guilty of "dishonorable, immoral and unprofessional" practice. He caused to be published in the foreign-owned newspapers of Denver advertisements

charging that an ex-serviceman had died thru the neglect of officers of Fitzsimons hospital and the United States Veterans' bureau. The medical examiners found the statements in these advertisements were "falsely defamatory and derogatory" and that they "were made without reasonable or probable cause and were made with wanton and reckless disregard to the truth."

In short, it is the judgment of the board that Spears is a liar.

The state medical board did a fine job when it revoked Spears' license. Its decision should be a lesson to him and others of his ilk. It should be taken as a warning that Colorado will not tolerate dishonorable and unethical conduct in its professional men. The people who treat our sick must behave themselves, regardless of how much or how little they know.

Let's hope we have heard the last of this man Spears who so overrated himself that he thought he knew more than the whole United States.[36]

On the very day of the verdict, Spears began a legal process that would keep his license revocation in abatement for the next four years.

His first step was to file suit on a writ of certiorari in the District Court, charging that the medical examining board had no jurisdiction in cases of alleged slander and had exceeded its authority in revoking his license. Remaining in character, he purchased advertising space to explain where he stood:

The attempted action of the medical board to revoke my license is under consideration by the Courts which I am confident will set aside the action of the board. But in any event until the Courts have taken final action, I shall continue to practice my profession as before.[37]

In District Court, Judge Charles C. Butler did in fact agree with Spears' contention that the matters complained of were outside the jurisdiction of the Board of Medical Examiners and ordered their action annulled.[38]

The medical board immediately sued out a writ of error in the Colorado Supreme Court, asking that the lower court's ruling be set aside.

It was now July 1925 and for the first time the chiropractic profession was heard from, in a letter from the president of the Colorado Chiropractic Association to the president of the Board of Medical Examiners asking that the charges against Spears be dropped "lest it appear to be persecution."[39] The board's response is not known.

Almost a year later, the Supreme Court returned its findings, that the lower court erred in that Judge Butler had examined the facts of the case.[40] (See Appendix A.) Reports in the *Rocky Mountain News* and *Denver Post* that Spears' license revocation had been upheld were apparently the last accounts about the matter published in these newspapers even though the issue was still far from settled.[41,42]

As expected, Spears appealed to the United States Supreme Court which, on December 12, 1927, denied his petition for a rehearing in that no federal question was argued in the state court.[43]

He next filed suit in Federal District Court for a permanent injunction against the medical board and the district attorney on the grounds that the board lacked the constitutional authority to suppress freedom of speech.

"Apparently, Speers [sic] has the financial ability and the disposition to appeal from the Federal District Court in case of a decision adverse to him. It is possible in this new suit he may obtain a record entitling him to a review by the United States Supreme Court," wrote Samuel H. Crosby, counsel for the Board of Medical Examiners. "It seems very unlikely that Judge Symes will grant either a temporary order or a permanent injunction. We believe he will sustain the validity of the Medical Practice Act, the alleged unconstitutionality of which is the sole basis of the attack."[44]

A temporary injunction was granted, however, on January 23, 1928, Judge Symes expressing from the bench his "grave doubts but that the state medical board exceeded its authority in revoking the license of Dr. Spears." Symes added: "I will say, however, that Dr. Spears must understand that I am not passing upon the merits or the law of the case. Any attempt on his part to exploit any remarks the court has made, or the injunction, will lead to a prompt vacating of this order upon motion of counsel, or the court's own motion."[45]

Crosby was matter-of-fact about the ruling: "We were somewhat surprised at the granting of the temporary order but in view of the remarks of the Court we may accept it with complacency as one of the incidents of litigation."[46]

On March 27, the three-judge Federal Court dissolved the temporary restraining order and denied the writ of injunction. Judge Lewis noted that Spears' contention of unconstitutionality of the medical law was immaterial inasmuch as the case was considered on its merits.[47]

Leo Spears' license to practice in Colorado was now legally revoked. Although he could still appeal on constitutional grounds to the U.S. Supreme Court, he chose instead to appeal to the good graces of the Board of Medical Examiners.

On March 31, a supplicant Spears submitted a formal appeal for the return of his license:

> I beg herewith to make application for reinstatement of my license or the issuance of a new one.
>
> My justifications for such a request are fully set forth in the resolution being presented to the Board by the Colorado Chiropractic Association and the Denver Chiropractic Association.
>
> As further evidence of my good faith, and that there may be no impediment to favorable action by the Board, I have dismissed my appeal to the United States Supreme Court for a permanent injunction, knowing full well that such dismissal disbars me from further legal action in this case.
>
> As set forth in the resolution above referred to, I succeeded in canceling my contract for the inside back cover of the Telephone Directory for the coming and future issues. And I am now negotiating cancellation of my street car contract, which negotiation I hereby promise will be consummated at the earliest possible moment.
>
> In addition to pledging my future good will toward, and co-operation with the Board,

if the Board so requests, I promise to cease all manner of advertising and, even though it does not so request, I will certainly do very little of any kind of advertising, and none that can be considered unethical or obnoxious by the most ethical and conservative of either of our professions.

As explained to the Board in person a year ago, my mistake in publishing the ad that resulted in all this confusion was not of the heart but due entirely to improper teaching in my Alma Mater and the inexperience and enthusiasm of youth.

All I ask is the chance that the individual members of this honorable Board would no doubt like to see given their own boys under similar circumstances.

Your obedient servant,

Leo L. Spears[48]

Attached to the letter was a resolution of support jointly agreed to by the Colorado Chiropractic Association and the Denver Chiropractic Society, also signed by the six-member investigating committee appointed to advise him on the acceptable parameters of professional decorum.[49]

At its regular meeting on April 2, 1928, the Colorado State Board of Medical Examiners, after considering what they had been given along with some 200 letters of support from the public and a recommendation from Governor William H. (Billy) Adams, voted 1) to revoke the license of Dr. Spears on statutory grounds and 2) to reconsider their action in one year.[50] Accepting in effect a one-year period of probation, Spears agreed to have no contact with his office or patients and to abstain from all forms of advertising and public comment.[51]

Leo Spears' license to practice chiropractic in Colorado was restored on April 3, 1929. He agreed to accept the counsel of colleagues C.W. Johnson and Leo E. Wunsch in all matters pertaining to strict ethical standards and to never again speak publicly about the case.[52]

When it was over, five years had passed since publication of an offending advertisement ignited the colossal controversy, but now the newspapers were silent.

Could Leo Spears have been reinstated to practice much earlier, avoiding lengthy and expensive litigation? The answer seemed to be hinted in the board's response to an overture by the Colorado Chiropractic Association in July 1925: "If the action of the Board is sustained by the Supreme Court of the United States, the Board will not reinstate the license of Dr. Spears unless a majority of its members are convinced that the public interest will not suffer if they do so."[53]

It had become obvious as well that members of the board had grown weary of the situation and seemed ready to agree on a settlement.[54]

A small controversy that occurred in mid-January 1927 indicated that a significant segment of the chiropractic profession also had become frustrated by the ongoing controversy, to the point of questioning Spears' sincerity.

On January 16, just days after he had apparently pledged in writing to refrain from seeking publicity, Spears took out an advertisement in the *Rocky*

Mountain News to ventilate his opinions on, of all things, divorce. Taking strong exception to advertisement, Charles W. Burgess, D.C., of Denver, saw fit to dispatch the following letter to Dr. Spears:

Sir:-

In light of your written pledge to the Chiropractic Associations of this state and city to abstain from obnoxious publicity bringing discredit and undesirable notice of the public and especially the medical profession upon us, can you imagine the shock I sustained in reading your article in yesterday's papers? There could have been no other thot [*sic*] in your mind in writing such an article than publicity and notoriety. But you answer that you did not advertise in the article anything regarding Chiropractic. True. Your face in the paper over articles of an unethical, flamboyant, and obnoxious nature, has been so commonly displayed in connection with Chiropractic that regardless of any article you may write, especially where superimposed with your picture, whether you do or do not say anything relative to Chiropractic will always be, in this locality at least, linked to the profession.

It seems to me that the exercise of the slightest amount of discretion would have forbade your writing the article you published yesterday. At the expense of their time, and risk of their integrity and reputation, certain gentlemen met Dr. Strickler by appointment and made an impassioned plea for your reinstatement clinching it with your written pledge not to besmirch or in otherwise cast reflection upon our profession, and to adhere strictly to the by-laws, constitution, and code of ethics of our association. Not twenty-four hours had elapsed before you totally forgot and ignored your pledge, and publicly dragged us thru the quagmire and filth of your mind by openly declaring that the great American institution, known as the home, is instituted solely and purposely for the gratification of passion.

Even if your were invited to write on the subject, inasmuch as you can but express yourself in the above language, would it not have been infinitely better for you to have conducted such correspondence privately and not thru the press?

I feel that your article will jeopardize your chances of reinstatement, for from the start the board were not over enthusiastic, as far as we could learn, about reinstating you, and the Chiropractors who interceded for you took on a difficult task. You have by your own act greatly increased their burden and, in my judgment, lessened your chances to an amazing degree for reinstatement, to say nothing of the fact of having flung in our faces a defy, and made null and void your pledge to abstain from obnoxious and unethical publicity. Furthermore, you are not mature enough in years to give pronouncement and make final disposition of so momentous a question as the regulation and government of human relations; to say nothing of some very pertinent questions that could be put to you regarding your own conduct along these very lines.

I feel so concerned over this matter that I am sending a carbon copy of this letter to the members of the committee who waited upon Dr. Strickler in your behalf, and I feel that it is incumbent upon you to in some way reassure that committee and each member of it that you meant what you said in signing your pledge, and until you see fit to do so, I propose to wash my hands of any action in your favor.[55]

In a letter to board secretary Strickler, Burgess said, "We as Chiropractors collectively (are) unalterably opposed to other than strictly conservative and ethical behavior. The committee who waited upon you feel that it is right and proper that I should hand you a copy of this letter, which places us on record." [56]

His Own Counsel

A solitary letter in the files of the Colorado State Archives reveals that within months of his reinstatement to practice, the Board of Medical Examiners was again becoming concerned about Dr. Spears' advertising. The letter was written by Frank R. Spencer, M.D., a member of the Board of Examiners, to Major Alphose Ardourel of the Colorado National Guard, an apparent confidant of Governor Adams:

> As soon as we gave Leo L. Spears his license back last April he began broadcasting over different radio stations such as KOA and KLZ. His newspaper advertisements were not quite so objectionable. Doctor Wunsch, who was on the Chiropractic Committee of the State Chiropractic Society, succeeded in getting Leo to stop broadcasting. He suggested that he use his mailing list instead. A great many complaints have been made by M.D.s and laymen. Members of the Colorado Board of Medical Examiners have been criticized for giving him back his license, even after punishing him by not allowing him to practice for one year. All we ask of Dr. Spears is that he be decent and refrain from objectionable, rank advertising and criticisms of others.
>
> I was selected by the Colorado Board of Medical Examiners to talk to him at the April meeting of this year before we reinstated him. He gave me his word of honor he would go straight if we would give him back his license. While he has not done anything very bad he gives me the impression he is going to crowd the dividing line just as much as he possibly can without putting his foot in a trap. We know that men who do this, in any walk of life, sooner or later get into serious trouble. My only suggestion is that he try to be honorable with all his fellow-men whether they be lawyers, merchants, dentists, chiropractors or what-not, because, we as a Board do not want to have to revoke his license a second time. If we do, it is doubtful if succeeding boards will ever reinsate him.[57]

During the early part of January 1932, a complaint was filed with the medical board about a booklet being advertised and circulated by Dr. Leo L. Spears and Associates. What particularly concerned the board about the 48-page tract of testimonials entitled "A Pleasant Way to Health" were a two-page introduction claiming "new discoveries and revolutionary developments" and a chart summarizing the results of a purported but unidentified national survey concluding that chiropractic care for insanity was superior to standard medical care.[58]

Spears was notified that a hearing was to be held to determine if he had caused publication of the booklet, if it constituted unprofessional and dishonorable conduct, and if his license should be revoked.[59]

At the April 5, 1932 hearing, he read the following statement in defense of his publication:

> 1-When my license was returned to me, Mr. Haines made the statement to the Board that it could not be returned with any strings on it. If it was returned to me it would have to be with the same privileges afforded all other Chiropractors.
>
> 2-I stated to the Board that I did not intend to stop advertising but I would faithfully promised that I would publish only those kinds of advertisements that come within the ethics of our profession.
>
> 3-Dr. C.W. Johnson and Dr. L.E. Wunsch kindly volunteered to be my sponsors for the purpose of seeing that I did not step beyond the bounds of Chiropractic ethics in my advertising.
>
> 4-After my license was returned we had a talk and it was agreed that before publication they were to OK all copy referring direct to Chiropractic to be run in newspapers or other publications - but that all office and mailing literature were of a personal nature and would not

require their perusal and censorship.

5-Testimonial advertising is the generally accepted method of Chiropractic advertising throughout the country. It is the method employed by the "Chiropractic Educator" put out monthly by the Palmer School and the "Health Builder" put out by Burton Shields Company, both for general use by Chiropractors throughout the country. Thousands of these testimonial circulars are put out in Denver each month by Chiropractors. Not only this, but they are far more critical than my booklet.

6-Since neither our State or National associations have condemned testimon-ial advertising and since many other Chiropractors in Denver are using this method, and since I understood that I was allowed all privileges that any other Chiropractor is allowed, and since no kick has been made against the advertising of any other Chiropractor, I didn't dream that there would be any objection to my booklet. The testimonials published are those of patients and most of the booklet has been in use for several years. I have original testimonials and many X-rays in my files to back them up.

7-Since the return of my license I have never published in a newspaper or other publication any Chiropractic ad without the OK of my sponsors. In fact, I have published very few indeed, and have even refused to allow several news items that I could have had in connection with Chiropractic.

8-I have tried to live up to my agreement with the Board in every detail and am even now unable to see where I have failed. If, however, I have failed in any respect, I am deeply sorry.

9-Since this matter has come up, rather than cause my sponsors any embarrassment, this is to ask that the Board kindly relieve them of their obligations and I will take the consequences of the Board's decision. Responsibility for my acts must not fall upon any living soul but myself.[60]

Several among the eight-member board had again expressed their "weariness" with Spears and their desire to dispose of the new complaint quickly; some were concerned about the possibility of new litigation.[61] On July 13, 1932, the board secretary advised:

At our meeting last Monday (July 11) we failed to take action on the complaint against Leo L. Spears, Chiropractor, who had been cited before the Board for unethical advertising. I am advised by Mr. Haines that in view of the decision of the Supreme Court in the Sapero case that we ought to dismiss this complaint against Spears. If such action meets the approval of all members of the Board I will enter on the minutes of the July meeting that such action was taken.[62]

Not until August 19 was Spears told that disciplinary proceedings had been dismissed and that he was "not required to give further attention to the matter."[63] The action taken by the board was reflected in minutes of the meeting of July 11, 1932, to wit:

Mr. Haines next reported to the Board that he had been informed that Leo L. Spears, Chiropractor, had discontinued circulating the pamphlet upon which the resolution of the Board adopted on January 5, 1932 concerning him had been based and recommended that proceedings under that resolution be dismissed without prejudice to new proceedings on a new resolution to the same effect if Dr. Spears should again circulate the same or a similar pamphlet, and that the question as to whether the circulation of the pamphlet constitutes unprofessional and dishonorable conduct be left for determination until that time.[64]

2.
An "Astounding" Practice

Sometime in the spring of 1924, during his early standdown with the Board of Medical Examiners, Spears was told that his Majestic Building lease would not be renewed. As it turned out, his eviction was fortuitous. He quickly found new space only a few blocks west, in the Steele Building at 16th and Welton, where he was offered more than twice the square feet for his growing practice.[1] The move was undoubtedly beneficial in another respect, providing a ready-made cause to advertise.

It was also at this time that he developed a strong relationship with Dr. Roy Babcock, an associate who remained loyal through thick and thin and allowed Leo needed flexibility to deal with growing legal problems while maintaining his practice.[2]

The Free Children's Clinic

In August 1932, Dr. Spears began operating the first large-scale free children's clinic in chiropractic. The demands became so great, he reported, that soon he was forced to employ six chiropractors at $1 an hour to take care of the increasing patient load which had grown to more than 300 children a day. The free clinic operated from 6 to 8 p.m. on Monday, Wednesday and Friday. Using federal relief guidelines, any indigent child under the age of 12 was eligible.[3]

The clinic was incorporated on November 23, 1933 as the nonprofit Spears Free Clinic and Hospital for Poor Children (*see Appendix B*). Spears, Frank Seydel and Dr. A.A. French were the named incorporators. The new corporation became in fact the legal designation for what would become known as Spears Chiropractic Sanitarium and Hospital. The private practice, now known as Dr. Leo Spears & Associates, remained a separate and distinct entity, although both practices operated in the same suite of offices in the Steele Building.

Dr. Leo had introduced the profession to his concept of free children's clinics at the annual meeting of the National Chiropractic Association (NCA) in Hollywood, California, in August of 1935. The idea was so enthusiastically received he wrote monthly columns for several years in *The Chiropractic Journal*. Entitled "Children's Clinics," the columns were a nuts and bolts guide for a movement that within the first year saw 125 free clinics established nationwide.

> The best way to gain the good will and respect of the public is to be a Good Samaritan in your neighborhood. There is nothing quite so effective as the establishment of Free Clinics for Poor Children. Nor is there any better way to educate the public to the efficacy of Chiropractic, or to convince legislators and public officials that Chiropractic is necessary to the health of the people. Where the curing of a child whose parents are able to pay for his treatments will go unnoticed, the curing of indigent and unfortunate children will attract attention, and win the love and good will of mankind.[4]

Advertising was the key to growth, he maintained, especially free care for poor children.

> My clinic is still growing. The advertising of its thousands of beneficiaries is doing more to ingratiate Chiropractic in the hearts of the people and our political authorities than all the commercials we have ever run. It is indeed the talk not only of Denver but all of Colorado and surrounding states. The public does not ignore the fact that the man who loves children and who spends his money and his energies for their benefit when they are unable to pay is deserving of the patronage of those who are able to pay.
> That which we justly earn will come back to us. Four cases so far this week have transferred from my clinic to my day practice and started paying for their treatments. When times get better, the thousands who are now treating free will do the same.[5]

As remarkable as the children's clinic turned out to be, the paying practice, usually referred to by Dr. Leo as the "commercial practice," was a phenomenon. Having expanded to 27 rooms, the office was staffed by five full-time doctors and four attendants and operated 5 days, generally seeing about 1,400 patients.[6] Spears wrote matter-of-factly of his success:

> Chiropractors have journeyed from many states to see what we are doing... and they have been greatly amazed. And after viewing with surprise the happy crowds that flock to the children's clinic they sometimes sit for hours in my office to witness a commercial practice that completely astounds them. They invariably ask, "How do you do it?"
> When I started to practice fifteen years ago, I started on a shoe string. I vowed that I would put 50% of every dollar I collected back into advertising until I needed no more business. I did exactly that thing with the result that I had all the business I could handle in less than a year. And I have never lacked for business because I believe in spending whatever is necessary of my earnings in order to keep my office filled. It is needless to say that while I still advertise, I am now reaping a greater harvest than ever from the money that I spent in advertising years ago. How many of you have the courage to pledge 50% of all your earnings for the promotion of your science and your practice for at least a year?[7]

Nothing had ever been revealed about Spears' personal wealth until he was forced into a financial disclosure during 1954 divorce proceedings, admitting to peak earnings of $90,000 to $100,000 annually during the 1920s and 1930s, before "retiring" from private practice.[8] It was a phenomenal income by any standard of the times; more than the President earned, even more than the New York Yankees gladly paid Babe Ruth. His income was certainly a good deal more than the average medical practitioner.

The Health Creamery

Not since the Civil War had the nation endured as severe an infliction as the Great Depression of 1929-1939. Historians estimate joblessness at the height of this calamity to have been anywhere from 25 to 50 percent.[9] But such statistics lost most meaning in the midst of utter despair, when all pleas for government help fell on deaf ears. An ineffectual and palpably out of touch Hoover administration remained steadfast in its refusal to grant any sort of relief except to big business. To the desperate average citizen, it was a bitter symbol of Hoover's "complete indifference to the poor." [10]

Lack of any apparent foresight and initiative in Washington shifted the burden of dealing with the nation's new poor to charities and local government. An inward migration to the cities saw several millions leave rural America in search of anything better, and the beleaguered cities responded as best they could.

In the early 1930s, Denver saw many thousands of such refugees from throughout the Southwest flood into the city and tax local services almost to the breaking point. It was a time for innovations. A comprehensive study of the period, *Trials and Triumphs: A Colorado Portrait of the Great Depression*, reminisces in great detail about such innovations, especially private initiative.[11] But nowhere in this recounting is it even hinted the genuine contributions of Denver's "prodigal son," Dr. Leo L. Spears.

Rex suggests that Spears had saved $125,000 from sales of a textbook he had published in the mid-1920s, enough to begin construction of the chiropractic hospital he had hoped to see up and running by the mid-1930s.[12] But for the Depression, it might have happened.

Leo made an arrangement with a dairy store called The Health Creamery, located at 2145 Court Place, downtown, to supply bread and milk to a network of free distribution stations set up throughout the city. For several years, thousands were reportedly served every day, each given one loaf of bread and a quart of fresh milk.[13] Within his own practice, he estimated giving away 70,000 quarts of milk to needy children in 1933 alone.[14]

It soon became clear that his funds could not sustain the effort very much longer. An agency was set up - the Emergency Free Milk and Bread Fund – with the sponsorship of a number of public-spirited citizens and a radio station, KFEL, to appeal for donations, even as little as a dime dropped into milk bottles placed at strategic locations. The Community Chest came forward, but even it could not collect enough money to keep the free milk stations open. Finally, Leo appealed directly to service organizations typically aided by the Community Chest to forgo such assistance temporarily, only to be denounced as a "headline seeking meddler" by some.[15]

With the Health Creamery facing shutdown, he purchased the facility with his personal funds. There was an agreement that he would operate the store as a business and keep the milk stations open if the dozen or so employees would accept a temporary wage cut, which they were happy to do. Thus, they managed to stay employed and keep the operation afloat, selling products from the store at slightly above cost.[16]

About 1935, with the hunger crisis mostly under control, the Health Creamery was sold as a going business. The operation from beginning to end had cost Leo far in excess of the $125,000 he had originally committed.[17]

For reasons known only to themselves, no Denver newspaper ever mentioned Spears' genuine charity during the darkest days of the Great Depression until after his death in 1956.

"Spears Painless System"

Leo was sure he had perfected the technique of spinal adjusting to the level of a revolutionary breakthrough, "the greatest development since the discovery of the science thirty-six years ago."[18] He called his technique "Spears Painless System." Releasing his textbook of the same name in 1926, it was an instant best-seller.[19] He also urged those who had mastered the technique to become itinerant "missionaries" as a way of publicizing both themselves and the technique.

Leo Spears and B.J. Palmer

Dr. Leo's entrepreneurism -- promoting a chiropractic technique he claimed to be superior to all others -- would obviously have chagrined Dr. B.J. Palmer, but perhaps not more so than what happened next.

Dr. James N. Firth, a revered faculty member at the Palmer School of Chiropractic who had recently resigned from his position in protest of certain policies of Dr. Palmer, had agreed to go on a six-month teaching tour for Spears Painless System. While on tour, Firth received word that fellow PSC faculty H.E. Vedder and S.J. Burich had also resigned from the school faculty and were actively discussing the formation of a new chiropractic school. Firth fulfilled his agreement to teach the Spears technique, then joined his colleagues in forming what became Lincoln Chiropractic College (LCC) in Indianapolis, opening in September of 1926. Along with A.E. Hendricks, who had also bolted from the PSC in protest, the LCC founders became known in chiropractic as the "Big Four."[20]

As the Lincoln College represented independence from the Palmer dogmatism that lately had become a professionwide issue, it seemed natural that Spears would throw his support behind the dissidents. Leo allowed the new Lincoln College to teach his technique and sell his textbook to sudents.[21] But there was even more to the issue of his apparent break with Palmer, and it would surface six years later.

Revocation of Leo's license had been threatened again in 1932, as already discussed. However, he was not the only Colorado D.C. so threatened at the time, as evidenced by the following revelations of L.M. Rogers, D.C., in the *Journal of the National Chiropractic Association*:

> At the January, 1932, meeting of the (medical board), no less than six Chiropractors faced the Board on such charges (so-called mixing). Twenty-two such cases are pending. One case was dismissed, one case postponed, five chiropractic licenses were revoked. And now the cat comes out of the bag! We find letters, some dating back several months before these cases were tried, from Dr. B.J. Palmer to the Secretary-Treasurer of the Colorado State Board of Medical Examiners, William Whitridge Williams, as part of the record of these cases. Letters from B.J. Palmer to a Medical Board encouraging them in their prosecutions and offering and giving his aid.
>
> Do you wonder that we are convinced there is grave danger when a so-called Chiropractic leader is found fraternizing with a Medical Board in an effort to revoke Chiropractic licenses?[22]

More than anything, it was the last straw in bringing down a once close friendship between Spears and Palmer. Leo would refer four of his nephews to Lincoln Chiropractic College for their training. Daniel C. Spears was graduated from Lincoln in 1937 and his younger brother, Howard M. Spears, in 1938.[23,24] Two other nephews, Perry McClellan and Paul Grant, went on to graduate from Lincoln in 1940 and 1953 respectively.[25,26]

Drs. Dan and Howard Spears assumed leadership roles in the clinic operation and as Leo's closest associates would be equally responsible for all the success to come to the burgeoning practice and, soon, to the hospital.

Building on Success

Spectacular financial success in practice undoubtedly bolstered Leo's determination to build a chiropractic hospital as soon as possible. It also allowed him the luxury to speculate a bit in real estate.

He reportedly purchased a tract of land in the early 1920s.[27] The site was in an area called Sand Creek, some six miles northeast of downtown.

Mayor Ben Stapleton, almost from the time he took office in 1923, had been thinking of a municipal airport, and the site he favored over all that were suggested was Sand Creek. Virtually undeveloped prairie land, the principal occupant was a dairy farm. But Sand Creek was controversial. Critics complained it was too far from the city, too close to the city, the soil too coarse to support runways. But mostly, it was the perception of cronyism.[28]

After several years of study and bickering, the City Council approved the purchase of the Sand Creek site in March 1928, eventually costing a less-than-expected $143,000. The *Denver Post*, no friend of the mayor or his airport plans, called the airport project "Stapleton's Folly." [29]

The new Denver Municipal Airport was dedicated in 1929 and re-named Stapleton in 1944.[30] It isn't known how much Spears was paid for his small slice of the pie.

In 1929, Leo purchased a large frame and stucco house at 1828 Lincoln St. (now the site of one of the city's tallest office towers) and had it remodeled for five apartments. Leaving his comfortable quarters in the Shirley Savoy Hotel, he occupied one of the units himself and allowed four disabled veterans to live in the others without charge. These men, with full knowledge of Fitzsimons Hospital, had chosen to put themselves under Dr. Leo's care.[31] In a sense, the Lincoln Street house was the predecessor of the coming hospital.

The Lincoln Street property was sold in 1937 and another one, at 2209 E. 13th Ave., corner of Gaylord St., was purchased with the proceeds. It was a Spanish-style mansion with 22 rooms on two floors, and a full basement with a regulation length bowling alley. Called the "Gaylord House," it had been built with some attention to extravagance by a Denver banking baron in the 1890s.[32] Although its market value was said to be $92,000, Leo purchased the property for just $12,500 owed the city in defaulted taxes.[33]

He moved into the first floor living quarters, which included a 40-foot-long library. The second floor was converted to three apartments while the large basement was reserved for future use. It is uncertain if he continued to take in veterans as house guests.

In 1944, Leo sold the Gaylord House to the nonprofit Spears corporation for the original $12,500 purchase price and thereafter paid rent for his living quarters.[34]

A decision was made in 1947 to close the office in the Steele Building and relocate the practice to the Gaylord House. The thinking behind the move was a very practical one: the basement provided ample space for the clinic. What it lacked in comparative spaciousness to downtown was more than compensated in reduced overhead.

Just as the Depression meant financial ruin for many, it was also an opportunity to cash in on real estate at rock bottom prices. Residences in tax default throughout the city, both grand and modest, flooded the market. Those fortunate enough to have survived the economic blitzkrieg with almost any disposable funds could now take advantage of an unprecedented buyers' market.

The Spears corporation looked into a number of such properties, including a handsome estate house on Colorado Blvd. once owned by Baron von Richthofen, the famed World War I German flying ace.[35]

But the best opportunity by far was a residential development zone in east

Denver called Montclair, and in 1939 they purchased six city blocks (15 acres). Most of it was available for back taxes, while the remainder of the tract was purchased at depressed market value.[36] Here, Spears Chiropractic Hospital would soon rise.

The Mobile Clinic

With the decision made to move forward with the hospital, Dr. Leo came up with a unique idea for increasing clinic income and promoting the coming hospital. With a 21-foot house trailer hitched to a 1939, 12-cylinder La Salle touring car, they fashioned a clinic on wheels which Leo named the Chiropractic Mercy Trailer. The mobile clinic traveled a 500-mile loop each week through rural eastern Colorado, stopping at 28 towns. The usual work week ran from Monday morning through noon on Saturday.[37]

The 140-square-foot trailer housed a hi-lo chiropractic table bolted to the floor, a desk and chairs, portable lavatory and cold water tap, and a folding cot. Heated by a kerosene stove, power was supplied by the car battery.[38]

Unmarried 24-year-old Dr. Dan Spears was the sole clinician. He recalled that he frequently worked from 4:30 in the morning till 11 o'clock at night, adjusting about 400 people weekly, most paying $2. "It was strictly a straight chiropractic operation and Spears Painless System was used exclusively. I usually arrived in a town to the sound of a cow bell or exhaust whistle to announce that Dr. Spears was here. Whenever possible, I would try to refer patients to a local D.C., but most often I was their only contact with a chiropractor."[39]

The mobile clinic continued its regular schedule for 18 months before discontinuing with the onset of World War II. "By that time I was worn out," Dan said. "This was not something for a married man, but it was an invaluable experience."[40]

Dan Spears enlisted in the Navy in 1942, served stateside as a pharmacist mate and was honorably discharged for medical reasons (bleeding duodenal ulcer) in the spring of 1943.[41]

Howard Spears enlisted in the Army in 1943, headed the physical therapy departments at several military hospitals in Europe and was honorably discharged in 1946.[42]

3.
The Hospital: Unit 1

Produce trucks heading to market swayed on dusty roads and cows still grazed on prairie grass when Spears purchased six city blocks in east Denver. The site was five blocks from the city's main east-west thoroughfare (U.S. 40) and three miles from the municipal airport. At the time, in 1939, only one dwelling existed within several hundred feet of the property. "It was open prairie for many blocks around." [1]

Two structures were initially designed by Denver architect Walter H. Simon – the 150-bed "Healthhaven Hospital" and a free-standing boilerhouse, both of concrete and brick construction.

As saving money was crucial, a decision was made to proceed with non-union and volunteer labor. With good weather, the four-story, 29,000 square-foot hospital could be finished in eight months at a cost of about $100,000. And if war were imminent, the hospital would at least be finished, or so they hoped. Construction would begin in April of 1940.

About those uncertain early days, Dr. Dan Spears recalled: "We started with a four-man pick and shovel brigade. They dug the foundation. We built as we could and paid as we went. Laborers were paid $4 a day; bricklayers received $6. When funds ran out, we ceased building until we could recoup finances." [2]

At one point, their outnumbered work force was beaten up at the construction site by a gang of thugs, who also pulled down steel window frames and much of the brick facade just rising to the second level. It was a serious, costly setback to be sure, but the work continued. As the construction crew thereafter displayed firearms (obtained by police permit), there would be no further trouble with vandals.

Workers fasioned some of their own tools and materials and relied on lots of plain ingenuity, such as rigging a vintage Star automobile as a power source for hoisting as the building rose. When materials became scarce they scoured the country for whatever was available, such as soil pipes and fittings found in Tennessee. "It was a penny-pinching, shoestring operation from start to finish."

Although the country had been on a wartime footing for almost two years, the United States entered World War II on December 8, 1941, with the Japanese attack on Pacific fleet at Pearl Harbor. The federal government now controlled virtually all consumerism through the Office of Price Administration and Civilian Supply and the War Production Board. Strict rationing was established and heavy manufacturing shifted entirely to the war effort. This compounded the difficulties already experienced by Spears, as essential hospital equipment such as autoclave sterilizers and X-ray could not be purchased new. Even installation of an elevator had to be put on hold for the duration of the war.

By January 1943, the building was nearing completion. It had taken almost 36 months at a cost of $200,000. Anticipating opening in early April, an application for a license to operate was filed with the State Board of Health, as required by law. Having obtained the necessary permits and city/county approvals, they believed state inspection should be a routine bureaucratic exercise. It would be everything but that.[3]

In Colorado, the Board of Health was vested with the authority to provide public policy oversight of all health regulations, including hospital inspection and licensing. The eight members of this quasi-legal arm of the State Department of Public Health were appointed by the governor. The state health director was a permanent member of the board and served as executive secretary.[4] Dr. Roy L. Cleere was appointed state health director in 1935. A native of Texas, he had received his medical degree from the University of Texas in 1929 and his master's degree in public health from Johns Hopkins in 1936.[5]

"Dr. Cleere despised Dr. Leo and the hospital," Dr. Dan Spears once related.[6]

The initial license application was considered by the Board of Health at its regular meeting, February 1, 1943. The minutes noted that Dr. Spears had stated in his application that patients might select their physicians and methods of healing – "(it) will not be operated as a closed shop." [7] But a medical staff had not been designated nor was a supervising registered nurse indicated. It was decided to table the application until the board had a report from state hospital inspectors.

Three months would pass before the Board of Health again considered the application to license "Healthhaven Hospital." Interim reports from Mildred East, Hospital, Maternity and Convalescent Home Inspector of the Division of Public Health, indicated that inspection had been attempted in February and twice in April, noting each time "building and equipment incomplete." [8]

One of the major alterations the hospital was forced to complete was bricking in of the elevator well openings, which had been barricaded with studs and plywood. "What else could we do?" said Dr. Leo Spears, lamenting about the added cost.[9]

When it became obvious that the April opening would be impossible, a new date - Sunday May 2, 1943 - was announced in the newspapers:

[*Rocky Mountain News*, April 25, 1943]
DR. LEO SPEARS PLANNING TO OPEN CITY'S NEWEST HOSPITAL NEXT SUNDAY

Denver's newest hospital - Spears Clinic - a non-sectarian institution open to all recognized branches of the healing arts, will be opened next Sunday.

Hospital officials will conduct "open house" in the hospital building and on the grounds at E. 10th Ave. and Jersey St.

Treating rooms, colon therapy departments, operating and maternity rooms, chemical and X-ray laboratories and other therapeutic departments will be open for inspection.

Dr. Leo Spears, Denver chiropractor and founder of the hospital and clinic, said profits of the hospital and clinic would be used to operate a free hospital and clinic for underprivileged children of Colorado.

The hospital also will be open to adults and to children who can afford to pay for treatment, and patients will choose their own doctors and method of treatment, Dr. Spears said.

Open house was held as announced and the first patients were admitted. Without a license, Spears Hospital had opened for business. An amended application for a license was filed the next day.[10]

A few days later, the Denver Medical Society demanded that the facility be confiscated in the "public interest" and converted to military use,[11] the federal government reportedly offering $300,000 for the building.[12] In response, Dr. Leo offered the government free use of the building for the duration of the war, after which nothing further was heard.[13]

May 4 was a regularly scheduled meeting of the Board of Health. Without any Spears representatives present, the board unamimously rejected the application for various reasons of non-compliance with state regulations, which were spelled out: lack of an approved medical staff and nursing staff, inadequate record keeping, lack of provision for laboratory and X-ray needs, inadequate sterilization equipment and isolation, inadequate surgical and maternity facilities, and unsatisfactory food arrangements.[14]

The rejection surprised Spears: "Some few pieces of equipment have not been obtainable because of wartime restrictions, but they are on order and I am sure they will be delivered within a short time." He said a need for additional hospital facilities in the Denver area was recognized by the federal government when "priorities were given for material to complete the unit." As to the board's staffing concerns, Spears said, "We feel that if (chiropractors) are qualified to treat patients outside the hospital, certainly we are qualified to treat them inside."[15]

Attorney Francis Mancini told the press that it was desired if possible to meet all requirements, but indicated that an appeal to the courts was contemplated if Dr. Spears found it impossible to meet with all of them.[16]

On May 22, Spears Clinic and Hospital for Poor Children filed a petition in District Court charging that, since the state had no regulations in place for chiropractic hospitals, the board had exercised arbitrary powers. The petition asked the court to order immediate licensing of the hospital and to cease further interference with its operation. City Manager of Health and Charity Carl P. Schwalb was also named in the petition for failing to act on Spears' request in early May for a local license.[17,18] A hearing was scheduled for June 9.

The board met again on June 4 to consider an amended application, this time inviting Spears and his attorneys, Frank Mancini and Charles Ginsberg. Also present were state hospital and plumbing inspectors and Assistant Attorney General Duke Dunbar. The amended application eliminated the practice of obstetrics and surgery, and substituted the name "Spears Hospital" for Healthaven.[19]

Questioning of Dr. Spears quickly turned to the reported recent opening of the hospital.

"When did you open?"

"We haven't opened yet."

"Have you got some patients?"

"We got a few out there."

"Have you administered treatment?"

"No other treatment than we are allowed."

"You care for them in this institution?"

"Yes."

"You have advertised and carried on as operating a hospital?"

"No, not since we were denied a license."

"How many patients have you had out there... since the license was denied?"

"About 28."

"You have no license?"

"We have none. We are operating at the present time but not seeking or soliciting any patients."

"Since the license was denied you have admitted cases and have treated patients in this institution?"

"Yes, we have had to do it; we have had cases that had to be treated."

"What did you do for such cases prior to the opening of the hospital?"

"We have not opened the hospital."

"You treated them in your office or at home, is that correct?"

"Yes. I think you will find all probably but two who are out there are from out of town. They had no other place to go."

"They came in response to advertising or correspondence that you were going to open the hospital on a certain day?"

"Before we had our license denied. We anticipated no trouble."

When questioning turned to the kind of treatment the facility would provide, or became excessively redundant about what constitutes chiropractic vs. medical care, to the obvious annoyance of his attorneys, Spears had difficulty confining his answers. From time to time his attorneys attempted to respond for him only to be told to let Dr. Spears speak for himself. Once, when his client was led into a discussion of the "germ theory," Mancini shouted, "Now just a minute. Dr. Spears has repeatedly stated that he will abide by the law (on contagious diseases)."

State inspectors delivered their latest reports, now forcing Dr. Spears to explain the various deficiences noted, some of them of a minor housekeeping nature. Again and again he was asked to explain the obvious, that the major shortcomings were due to the war emergency and would be corrected when materials and equipment became available.

After two and a half hours of interrogation, the witnesses were excused and the board went into executive session.

Members of the board decided quickly and unanimously to reject the application for licensing, adding the unauthorized opening of the facility to its list of particulars.

In court on June 9, District Judge Robert E. Steele dismissed the Spears petition while urging the Board of Health to adopt regulations appropriate for a chiropractic hospital.[20] There was now at least some hope for a compromise.

Attorney Charles Ginsberg tried to persuade the board to that logic:

> There has been an institution built out there at great expense and it is our desire to utilize that institution in the best way possible.
>
> We realize we have never had a similar institution in this city or in the state, for that matter. We are willing to conform to any reasonable regulations you want to make if we know what they are. There are some things in which an institution of this type is not identical with a regular hospital.
>
> Some time ago, we made the suggestion to the members of your board that they might formulate a new set of rules entirely applicable to a chiropractic hospital. We are not here to prescribe what those rules should be but are very anxious to open this institution. There is great expense incurred, nurses being employed and being paid, etc.
>
> We are not here in any hostile attitude toward this board. We have tried to comply as far as we understand them, the requirements. If there is anything lacking, if there are rules the board wants to propose, we are willing to be reasonable.
>
> We want to bring this thing to a conclusion; it cannot go on indefinitely.

We would like very much, if we can, to have the board say just what they think ought to be done. If there are any limitations upon types of cases, it is up to the board to say so. There are no rules now made to exclude any type of cases; if there are any, we will do our best to comply.[21]

One board member, L.K. Likes, M.D., seemed to find the process annoying: "He should have thought about these things... I do not propose spending hours at every meeting on Dr. Spears... I know of no hospital in the country trying to open now... I believe Doctor Spears should wait until he can get it in proper shape."

But another, Charles G. Grover, M.D., in a more conciliatory frame of mind, suggested: "I believe the only thing that can be done for Spears, if he so wishes, is to come as close as he possibly can to meeting the requirements, then come before this Board again and say he has done his best to meet the requirements, then we can consider a license. That is all we can do."

Mr. Duke Dunbar went so far as to suggest the whole matter could be resolved if Dr. Spears proposed a convalescent home instead of a hospital. "I will not!" snapped Spears. "We are built and equipped as a hospital. We are not interested in a convalescent home."

After all the discussion, the board's decision remained inflexible: the rules and regulations of Colorado must apply to all hospitals without exception.[22]

On June 17, 1943, Ginsberg wrote to Gov. John C. Vivian, saying, in part:

> It is not sufficient in our opinion that we be referred to rules applicable to medical hospitals, being the only type covered by the rules of the Board, and obviously many of the requirements for medical and surgical hospitals are not required for a chiropractic hospital, to which the Board agrees; and in view of that, it would seem that the simplest, just procedure would be a definite clear statement of what is required for obtaining such a license, and if there is a definite intention of not issuing a license in any event. A statement to that effect would certainly serve to clarify the issue.[23]

The Governor immediately offered advice to Dr. Roy Cleere :

> I am sure you would want to give these people a clear picture in writing of just what they must do to conform to the requirements of the board in this connection.[24]

A Charge of Manslaughter

A damaging but not unexpected setback to the hospital's quest for licensing occured June 14, 1943, when Drs. Leo and Dan were arrested on manslaughter charges filed by the district attorney. The charges grew out of the death on June 6 of one Marion Daugherty of Hartville, Wyoming. An autopsy disclosed that the patient had died of double pneumonia, which a coroner's jury ruled the result of "gross ignorance, negligence and inattention of Drs. Leo L. Spears and Daniel C. Spears."

The Spearses were taken by a sheriff's deputy and a city policeman to the

West Side Court to be booked. They were released after their attorney, Charles Ginsberg, posted bond of $1,500 each. The next day, they pleaded not guilty when arraigned before District Judge William A. Black.[25,26] At the same time, pending the outcome of criminal proceedings, the court set aside an order by the district attorney closing the sanitarium. A pre-trial hearing was scheduled for Thursday, November 11, 1943.[27]

The case was reportedly brought to light after a Denver funeral director refused to accept Mr. Daugherty's body on the grounds that Dr. Dan Spears had no statutory authority to sign a death certificate. The district attorney's charging documents stated that the hospital "lacked X-ray equipment, an oxygen tent and other equipment to diagnose or treat the case."

Almost simultaneously with the criminal arraignment, Judge Steele in the civil division entered a bench order closing the sanitarium and removing 30 patients to Denver General Hospital. The injunction stipulated that the hospital would remain closed until the State Board of Health granted it a license or the courts decided it might operate.[28]

The abatement order resulted from an investigation by the district attorney of reports that the hospital had been operating without a license. An inspection by city and state health authorities revealed that the hospital was operating and that is was "not properly equipped or staffed." For these reasons, the city complaint cited, the hospital represented a threat to public health.

Charles Ginsberg said he would appeal to the Colorado Supreme Court, if necessary, in an attempt to reopen the hospital: "We were operating the hospital only because we understood the authorities would cooperate with us until our difficulties were straightened out." Ginsberg charged that the case represented an attempt by the medical profession to "maintain a monopoly to the exclusion of chiropractors."[29]

At the hearing on November 11, the defendants testified that Mr. Daugherty had been refused treatment at Denver General Hospital and was in terminal condition upon arrival at Spears. According to a statement by the decedent's brother, treatment was refused at the city hospital because of his non-resident status and lack of sufficient funds to pay for care in advance. Only later that night did they come to Spears Hospital.[30]

Dr. Dan Spears testified that he made a diagnosis of interstitial pneumonia and the patient was given penicillin on the prescription of a consulting osteopathic physician. "Everything possible was done for Mr. Daugherty under the circumstances. We stayed with him until the end."

When the coroner was questioned in court about "interstitial pneumonia," he admitted that the condition would indeed be considered terminal.[31] Judge Black then dismissed the charges for lack of any evidence of criminal wrongdoing.[32]

How and when Charles Ginsberg and Leo Spears became acquainted is unclear but their lawyer-client relationship was like a natural bond for the similarities they shared. Early in his 60-plus-year career, Ginsberg was suspended from practice for a year over ethics violations, but he built a reputation as an outstanding defense attorney. He became known for his verbal and physical outbursts in the courtroom. While defending a man fighting extradiction to California in 1932, he knocked down a deputy sheriff in the governor's office. In 1958, he was fined for contempt after calling the presiding judge in a criminal case "a cheap politician." Denver District Attorney Burt Keating, angered by Ginsberg's courtroom charges that he needed a mental test, filed a $1 million slander suit, which Ginsberg successfully defended. Over the years, he served as the court-appointed defense attorney in a number of high profile murder cases. Mr. Ginsberg often teamed with his nephew, George L. Creamer.[33-39]

The Board of Health met in executive session on the evening of September 27, 1943 to discuss what had happened--the directive from Gov. Vivian requiring the board's action and Judge Black's bench order. It was decided that a "temporary provisional license" be granted to Spears Free Clinic and Hospital for Poor Children, Inc. to operate a chiropractic sanitarium. It was in fact a pseudo license since the state hospital code made no provision for a "temporary license."[40] The so-called provisional permit, issued without any official signatures, was subject to the following conditions:

1- That maternity cases shall not be received.

2- That surgery shall not be performed.

3- That drugs or medicines shall not be administered.

4- That no contagious or infectious cases will be admitted or treated.

5- That the name "hospital" shall not be used in describing or designating the institution.

6- That this temporary provisional license shall not become effective until the applicant has confirmed in writing his understanding the conditions.

At its regular meeting on October 5, 1943, Secretary Cleere read to the board the letter of transmittal to Dr. Spears and his acknowledgment that the conditions set forth were fully understood by him. The action of the executive committee was then confirmed by the board.[41]

Spears Sanitarium reopened on Sunday, October 3, 1943 – five months after the licensing application was first rejected.[42]

The provisional license seemed to be a guarantee of frequent inspections and indeed state hospital inspector Mildred East reported regularly to the board, noting both deficiencies and progress.

Her reports from time to time noted overcrowding (as many as 230 patients observed even though the sanitarium's license application stipulated the maximum capacity to be 150); "dining facilities wholly inadequate; nursing staff inadequate; housekeeping problems; unpasteurized milk being used." [43,44] In one report, the inspector made the curious comment, "this institution is incorporated in the names of only two people. It is incorporated as a non-profit institution but it is not so." [45]

The most serious allegations concerned possible violations of the four conditions of the sanitarium's provisional license, namely, performing surgery, administering drugs, admitting contagious diseases, and using the name "hospital." [46]

In December 1945, the board directed Dr. Cleere to make an inspection of the facility and, if evidence of violations were shown, be authorized to take appropriate action.

The Board of Health was ready to consider evidence that violations of the sanitarium's license had occurred and called a special meeting on May 7, 1946. In the meantime, Spears had petitioned the board to permit him to add the words "and Hospital" to the name of the institution known as Spears Chiropractic Sanitarium. The first business on the agenda was the petition. Dr. Spears and Mr. Ginsberg were called into the meeting. [47]

Ginsberg explained that insurance benefits were being denied to some patients because Spears Sanitarium was not a licensed hospital. A secondary purpose for needing hospital designation, he said, was to become classified as a Grade A chiropractic hospital by the National Chiropractic Association. This led to a discussion of the number of chiropractic hospitals in existence and their status as state-licensed institutions. [48]

Asked if patients in licensed chiropractic hospitals in other states are denied insurance benefits, Dr. Spears answered, "I can only speak for myself."

Charles Ginsberg stated that he was not present when the "sanitarium" limitation was imposed and did not know why it was made.

Dr. Drinkwater: "I can refresh your memory. When this first came up, I said that under no circumstances could it be called a 'hospital.' Dr. Spears said at that time he had no idea of running it as a hospital."

Mr. Myers: "I believe the terms of the temporary provisional license specifically state that there will be no medical care, no surgery. A request for a name change is merely trying to get the place licensed as a hospital."

Mr. Ginsberg: "It is clearly stated in our petition that we will stay within the limitations."

Mr. Myers: "It was clearly stated at the time of the issuing of the temporary provsional license that this would not come up."

Mr. Ginsberg: "There is no harm in asking. The institution is functioning and it is no handicap to the institution, but it does embarrass some patients in not getting what they have due to them under their insurance policies."

Discussion turned to the definition of "hospital," the board's belief that the term is reserved only for medical institutions, and why Dr. Spears has violated his license in using the term.

Dr. Likes: "Why has the word 'hospital' been used by you?"

Dr. Spears: "It has not."

Mr. Myers: "I beg your pardon. I have seen it and sent it up to Dr. Cleere."

Dr. Drinkwater: "I have seen it."

Dr. Spears: "It has not been used. I have not seen it. Have you, Mr. Ginsberg?"

Mr. Ginsberg: "No."

Dr. Spears: "The institution was to be called Spears Chiropractic Sanitarium and it has been called Spears Sanitarium to shorten the name and we use the term on all of our literature. The terms 'hospital' and 'sanitarium' are the same. I haven't called it a hospital."

Mr. Myers: "Do you read your own ads?"

Dr. Drinkwater: "I have seen it."

Dr. Spears: "I have not seen it."

Mr. Myers: "It is your intent that it be known as a hospital. Is that not right?"

Dr. Spears: "Only as a chiropractic hospital."

Mr. Myers: "When you violate the conditions of the temporary provisional license, I haven't much faith in what you offer now. You have violated these knowlingly and consistently."

At this point, the board went into executive session. Discussion turned to the original agenda of this special meeting – the alleged violations of the sanitarium's license. Assistant Attorney General James Geissinger advised that the board schedule a hearing with enough time to allow Dr. Spears and Mr. Ginsberg to prepare. He cautioned that the charges be spelled out very specifically in a bill of particulars inasmuch as Spears would undoubtedly appeal to the Supreme Court

Spears and Ginsberg were called back into the meeting and advised that the petition for changing the name of the institution had been denied.

Meeting on June 4, 1946, the Board of Health approved a bill of particulars to be served on Dr. Leo Spears within 10 days. A hearing on the revocation question would be held July 9 in the State Office Building. It would be an open hearing with the right to subpoena witnesses and evidence, and to examine and cross-examine witnesses under oath.[49]

At the hearing on Tuesday, July 9, 1946, Spears was represented by Ginsberg, Fred Dickerson, Anthony Zarlengo and Fred Seydel; Assistant Attorney General James Geissinger represented the state. The process quickly became turbulent.

Ginsberg first asked that the hearing be postponed. When his motion was overruled, he argued against the qualifications of board secretary Cleere, and board member Myers, charging that both were engaged in a "conspiracy to destroy the sanitarium." He contested the jurisdiction of the board over the sanitarium, and charged that the hearing was illegal because the board had no right to make specific provisions when the license was issued. After being overruled on all points, Ginsberg proposed that the meeting adjourn to a back room "where we'll lay our cards on the table and settle this thing in two hours." Dickerson chimed in that it would be "a rare opportunity which would save a world of time." Geissinger advised the board that it was a public hearing.[50]

When James Geissinger began to question Spears about the deaths of certain patients at the sanitarium then thrust a sheaf of papers in his hands "to refresh the defendant's memory," Ginsberg objected to the sarcasm and lack of respect shown by the assistant attorney general.[51]

The next exchange in the fracas occurred during questioning of Fred W. Beasley, state vital statistics director, about who signed the death certificates. Responding that the certificates were signed by Deputy Coroner Economy and city vital statistics director Evelyn C. Myers, Fred Dickerson said, "I object to a record signed by two laymen, one of whom is an ex-hack driver." Dickerson tried to have board member Ray L. Drinkwater disqualified on grounds that "trying a case before a prejudiced member of the jury is like encountering a fixed judge." Drinkwater, who declared he was not fooled by the subterfuges, declined to excuse himself or to be cross-examined, and was upheld by the board.

Amid shouting, the hearing adjourned in a state of near-confusion and was rescheduled for August 6.[52]

At a deposition hearing on July 31, a district court judge ordered Drinkwater to provide testimony to be used in the upcoming revocation hearing. The deposition was conducted by Fred Dickerson before a notary public.[53-54]

When the license revocation hearing resumed August 6, Dickerson again moved to disqualify Drinkwater on the grounds of prejudice. After a lively exchange of accusations, the board overruled the motion.[55]

The six-month-long battle reached its climax on November 22, 1946, when the Board of Health revoked the temporary license of Spears Free Clinic and Hospital for Poor Children, Inc. to operate the sanitarium, finding that the clinic had violated four of its licensing restrictions. The revocation order was to become effective in 60 days.[56]

As expected, Spears obtained a temporary restraining order in District Court.[57] On December 17, 1948, after much legal maneuvering by his attorneys, which the attorney general criticized as "repeated and unnecessary," District Court Judge William H. Luby upheld the revocation while granting a 60-day stay of execution to permit Spears to file an appeal.[58]

The appeal was filed March 19, 1949, but due to numerous extenions granted to both sides final briefs were not submitted until May 3, 1950. Oral arguments would be heard May 22.[59,60] Survival of the Spears institution was now very much on the line.

4.
The Hospital: Unit 2

V-J Day – August 15, 1945. The Japanese surrendered and World War II was finally over. Dr. Leo had always maintained that construction of Unit 2 would begin as soon as the war ended, and thus a ceremonial groundbreaking took place for the new building that would be dedicated to D.D. Palmer, founder of chiropractic.

The four-story structure would contain some 65,000 square feet--more than twice the area of Unit I--designed to accommodate 400 patients and 200 chiropractic students. Projected costs were $500,000.[1]

It is significant to note at this point that the profession, supportive with platitudes, by and large failed with hard financial backing. Construction bonds offered at just 50¢ a share brought in barely $4,000.[2] It was a treachery of neglect that would always define the uneven pride of chiropractic in its largest hospital.

From the outset of construction, the handicaps were immense. Having denied Spears a building permit until after V-J Day, the War Production Board next refused a priority to purchase building materials. For financial reasons, nonunion workers were again hired, leading to renewed labor problems, cancellation of previous contracts for materials and picketing of the site for the duration. Also having had a sand pit contract canceled, the hospital was forced to locate another, although quite far from the building site. This, in turn, made it necessary to purchase their own trucks (six of them) and turn out their own cinder and concrete blocks. Fortunately, enough steel was already on hand, left over from the earlier construction.[3]

Foundation work began on September 1, 1945, as Dr. Leo, with unbridled confidence, forecast completion of the project by the end of 1946.[4-6]

The original timetable could not be met, of course, but substantial progress had been made by the summer of 1947. "Although materials have been hard to obtain and not one dollar of financial assistance has come in from the field, progress has been satisfactory," noted *Spears Sanitarium News*.[7] By this time, also, a decision had been made not to include a chiropractic school in the new building. It was announced for the first time that the D.D. Palmer Building would contain 600 patient beds, including a new pediatrics unit.[8-10] Equipment and furnishings would be the next hurdle, the estimated cost set at $250,000.[11]

In November 1948, two years later than forecast, the building was ready for occupancy.

[*Spears Sanitarium News*,(6) 1949]
PALMER BUILDING OPEN

We have moved into it by degrees during the past several weeks, to accommodate the overflow from the first building.

The official opening, to which the public will be invited, will come some time in January.

Due to the immensity of this building and the shortage of materials, it has taken longer to complete it than we had anticipated. Even after it appeared to be finished, there were literally hundreds of little things to be done which brought about even further delays. You may rest assured that every little detail will be finished and the entire building in tiptop shape when the official opening is announced. We expect thousands of visitors the opening day.

Dedication ceremonies will be held sometime next summer, probably right after the NCA convention.

Except for plumbing, wiring and specialized installations such as an elevator, X-ray equipment and ornamental ironwork, the Spears corporation had acted as its own contractor, a rather remarkable feat. "We built our own doors, most of our chests and chairs, all of our dining room tables, cabinets, etc. Thousands of other pieces of furniture must yet be made in our woodworking shop, which is one of the biggest in Denver."[12]

Although little money had been contributed by the profession directly toward construction, the building was entirely debt free. Eighteen rooms were furnished through memorial contributions.[13]

The D.D. Palmer Memorial Building was officially opened on Wednesday, January 12, 1949.[14-16]

The Postgraduate School

A state charter issued in 1946 allowed the sanitarium to operate professional schools, inaugurating what was called the Spears Post-Graduate School of Chiropractic. The expected postwar growth of chiropractic "increases the demand all over the country for chiropractic hospitals and sanitaria and makes necessary an institution and school where men can be trained in their building and operation," stated an announcement in *Spears Sanitarium News*.[17] Course offerings would include: "building a practice, advertising, documented diagnosis, bedside technique, hospital routine and the many special requirements for the treatment and care of contagious, bedfast, totally helpless, terminal and other types of hospital cases."[18] It was anticipated that training sessions would be held for four weeks on alternate months, but this plan was modified to weeklong sessions several times a year. Later, the postgraduate seminars would take place during one week in August.[19]

A school of nursing was begun in 1946. The three-year program offered free tuition and room and board for "young, female high school graduates."[20]

The free-standing boilerhouse built with Unit 1 housed the hospital's oil-fired heating plant and a workshop. It was expanded during Unit 2 construction to include two upper floors of housing for student nurses. An immense loft storage area was incorporated into the rear of the building.

Rotating internships for graduate D.C.'s commenced in 1948 and proved to be highly effective in the hospital's diversified approach to caring for hundreds of inpatients.[21] Interns were at first housed in the hospital; later, a "dormitory" -- two motel-like structures – was constructed just south of Unit 1.[22]

The school charter also anticipated construction of a large chiropractic college on the campus.

Master Plan

A campus master plan, designed some years earlier by architect Walter Simon, was made public in the fall of 1947 when the hospital applied for a permit to construct a new building.

The architectural rendering pictured a main quadrangle anchored by four buildings at the corners --Units 1 and 2 and their clones. The centerpiece, occupying two square blocks, would be a 16-story clinical tower with 1,200 beds. Also occupying the quadrangle, an interdemoninational chapel would accommodate 1,200 users at a time.

Situated on four square blocks on the north side of the campus, an eight-story student nurses' residence and a five-story, blocklong, chiropractic students' hall would have a capacity of 800 each. Two five-story staff residences would have 200 units, and a guest hotel would provide 600 units. The second largest building on the campus was the proposed chiropractic college. Eight stories high and a block long, it would have a enrollment capacity for 2,000 students and seat 3,000 in the auditorium.[23]

Completed as envisioned, the campus complex would cost $50 million and employ about 5,000 people.

To allow the expansion, the City Council would be required to rezone six city blocks of the Spears property from residence Zone A, where hospitals are prohibited, to residence Zone C, which a majority of adjoining property owners had already opposed when the plan was announced. To the surprise of many, a bill allowing rezoning passed on first reading January 12, 1948, and again on final reading in late March.[24]

Council President Clarence Stafford brought out the ordinance at a time when the press had left the chambers and no neighborhood residents were present.

On its editorial page, the *Rocky Mountain News* lambasted the council president for the way he brought the once-indefinitely-tabled bill to a vote:

"SLIPPERY" STAFFORD - that's what they are calling the president of our City Council.

He's put over another slick deal - or at least he thinks he has - in a series of efforts to oblige his chiropractic friend, Leo L. Spears... We think the whole deal smells to high heaven![25]

Mayor Newton, agreeing with the protest of the Montclair Improvement Association, vetoed the bill.[26-27]

When the veto came up for a vote in the City Council, opponents of the ordinance sustained the veto by a single vote. Stafford was perplexed: "Everybody knew Spears planned to expand. He went out to what was then prairie and improved it by building a boilerhouse and a sanitarium. Only two other buildings then existed in the area. At the time, hospitals were allowed to build in residence A zones. Three years ago he started a new building now nearing completion. This building was in progress when homes were started in the area."[28]

But Stafford demonstrated there's more than one way to skin a legislative cat. In May, he introduced two ordinances to clear the way for expansion of the sanitarium, taking the chance that at least one would pass. But both passed on first reading. A public hearing was called to sort out the quarrel.[29]

Spears, in the meantime, placed a large advertisement in the Denver newspapers in which he charged that the rezoning "is being vigorously opposed by medically inspired opposition." The ad pointed out that "practically all hospitals and sanitaria in Denver and other cities throughout the country are in residence A zones." In the same district where Spears Sanitarium is located, the ad stated, seven other hospitals are either in operation or under construction.[30]

On July 12, after two postponements had been granted to President Stafford, the City Council killed one of the rezoning measures because "Dr. Spears was asking too much for passage of both measures." After it was learned that one of the protesting neighbors had withdrawn her earlier objection, which would be enough of a discretion to allow the measure to pass by a simple majority quorum vote, the attorney representing the opposition requested another deferment. The request would allow opponents to investigate why this one individual had withdrawn her signature, inferring that Stafford was behind it.[31]

Two weeks later, without explanation, the Stafford ordinance passed, ending the politically-charged fight that had begun almost eight months earlier.[32]

The Sanitarium Guild

A nonprofit organization composed of lay friends of the profession and chiropractic wives, the Spears Chiropractic Sanitarium Guild was organized in October 1949. Headquartered at Spears Sanitarium, the guild anticipated state and district chapters also being formed. Mrs. Helen Olson of Denver was named national director pro tem.[33]

The purposes of the guild were listed as follows:

1- To answer any call that may be made by national or state chiropractic associations for the protection of healing freedom, the promotion of public health and the preservation of chiropractic.

2- To provide funds to assist in the building and operation of the Spears Chiropractic Sanitarium as a national chiropractic health and research center.

3- To promote better health through chiropractic advertising, publicity and other educational methods.

4- To provide means for needed chiropractic hospitalization and treatment for underprivileged children.

5- To seek chiropractic hospitalization and care for veterans of the military services.

6- To secure the right of every person to choose his own system of healing and doctor.

7- To secure for chiropractic research and charitable uses, fair portions of government appropriations for health purposes, and donations by the general public to organizations undertaking the prevention and relief of disease, and to promote in any other manner deemed expedient and advisable to general health and happiness of the people.

8- To do all things necessary, proper and incidental to said purposes.[34]

As nothing further was ever published in hospital literature about the Sanitarium Guild, what, if anything, developed from the organization is unknown.

5.
The Hospital: Unit 3

Plans for the proposed 16-story clinical tower took something of a step forward in February 1951 with the announcement that the huge structure would contain an 80,000-square-foot underground shelter to "withstand any type of bombing attack." The Cold War fault line had now stretched all the way to Denver, Colorado.

According to architect Walter H. Simon, the shelter would actually be a subbasement. It would have a four-foot reinforced concrete roof and would accommodate 2,000 persons in the event of an air raid on Denver. All material for construction of the shelter had been purchased, Simon said, and government approval for its construction was awaited.[1]

Construction costs for the shelter and equipment were estimated at $500,000. Once completed, the site would be back-filled and landscaped until the new tower was under construction. Dr. Spears told the press that he would offer the city four square blocks on which to build similar shelters, should the need arise.[2]

If the city of Denver had any interest in Spears' offer, it wasn't evident when it filed suit in March to recover $1,010 alleged to be owed the city in delinquent taxes. The city was claiming that machinery and other equipment owned by the hospital was taxable because they had been used to build 24 houses later sold to veterans. Spears called the suit "arbitrary" and claimed that all property owned by the hospital was tax-exempt, and further claimed that the city had been unresponsive to his repeated requests for a hearing on the matter, something the city denied.[3]

Spears Clinic and the city had waged periodic war over taxation since 1938, when the Supreme Court ruled that certain income-producing property owned by the nonprofit clinic was not exempt from local taxes.[4]

On January 7, 1952, Dr. Leo called a press conference to announce that he planned to build "the biggest cancer hospital in the world." Not the 16-story tower once envisioned, new plans for Unit 3 called for a massive block-square, six-story structure to accommodate 1,412 beds. It would rise immediately south of the two existing buildings and cost an estimated $14 million. Designed like a double-H, all rooms and wards would have outside exposures, and a central kitchen and two dining rooms situated atop the building would accommodate 1,500 people. According to a news release, this one structure would have more beds than the new $10 million Veterans Administration Hospital, Colorado General and Rose Memorial hospitals combined.[5]

Whether steel and other strategic materials needed for such a large structure would be available in the near future was unanswered, but 60 tons of steel (apparently once intended for the air raid shelter) were already on hand to start the construction. Soil tests already had been made and excavation of the basement was to start as soon as plans were approved by the city.

Dr. Lloyd Florio, Coordinator of Institutional Services for the city health department, said he would only concern himself with food service in the hospital. "I have seen preliminary plans for the kitchen and dining room and as far as I can see they are all right," he said, "but we will want to see final plans." Florio went on to say that the city did not recognize the practice of chiropractic and that the Health Department would not license the hospital unless directed by the City Council to do so. His puzzling comments were, of course, the rhetoric of his own well-known animus.[6]

"We will be our own contractor and will build with our own funds as we make them," Dr. Spears said. "We hope to be able to complete the hospital at a cost of $10,000 a bed, which compares with a cost of $20,000 a bed in the VA hospital." He said the new building would increase the Spears combined capacity from the present 800 beds to a total of 2,200 beds.

Further difficulties with organized labor were apparently averted as Spears and the local building trades reached an agreement on employment of union contractors.[7] The settlement would dramatically affect the cost of skilled labor. Whereas non-union brick layers were paid $6 a day in 1943, the new contract called for union brick masons to receive $12 an hour.[8]

Construction of Unit 3, to be known as the Chiropractic Pioneers Building, symbolically began December 21, 1952 with a ceremonial ground breaking by several present and former cancer patients. But it was a dramatically changed concept from that announced in January. Because of a "greater influx of cancer sufferers," Dr. Spears said it was necessary to add 720 beds. The new building would now rise eight stories and have a capacity of 2,150 beds, bringing the hospital's total capacity to more than 3,000. Included in that this figure were 80 beds recently added in two single-story motel-like structures intended to house interns and hospital visitors. Projected cost now exceeded $21 million.[9] The present buildings and grounds were said to be valued at $8,360,000.[10]

A lobby almost a block long would bisect the ground floor, bronze busts and full-length statues of the profession's past and present leaders lining the area. To be called the "Chiropractic Hall of Fame," state associations would make the selections, and auxiliaries would be asked to stage fund drives to finance the cost of sculpturing and materials.[11]

In February 1953, the city zoning board passed requirements that potentially impinged on construction of the new building. The new ordinance imposed strict setback requirements preventing the building, now envisioned for nine stories with a rooftop heliport, to reach its planned height. Spears asked the City Council to vacate the street (Ivy St.) on the west side of the site, which he said he would develop as a private park. If the council agreed, he would automatically be free to build to the nine-story height. The city would not agree, however.[12]

After several hearings, the board gave permission to build the center portion up to six stories and the north and south wings up to five stories, but no higher.[13] Bed capacity would have to be scaled down to approximately 1,600. The building framework by this time had reached three stories.

Funding of the huge project became the ever-present concern. Over the next three years, with frequent work stoppages, the shell of the building was nearing completion. But construction was forced to cease in the spring of 1956.

An editorial in the *Sanigram* explained the situation this way:

> Start of this great enterprise was apparently the signal for enemies of the institution to launch their campaign of calumny. They succeeded to the extent that the flow of patients was diminished 50 percent.
>
> One hostile enemy, collaborating with Chiropractic's traditional foes, systematically circulated, through its national connections, derogatory reports among prospective Spears patients. In this, they were abetted by certain elements of the press and cunning legal guidance. Public confidence was temporarily undermined.[14]

In 1958, the city and county of Denver placed the uncompleted building and three blocks of undeveloped land on the tax rolls "because they were not being used for charitable purposes." A tax lien of $12,850 was assessed, with payment due February 28, 1959. Spears sued the municipality on the grounds that it was exempt from property taxes and that they still intended to complete the Pioneers Building on which $800,000 had already been spent.[15]

In District Court, Judge William A. Black found for the defendants. As expected, Spears appealed to the Supreme Court which, on April 11, 1960, ruled that the city/county revenue division had no authority to tax the hospital on the property in question, finally ending the long-simmering debate with local government.[16,17]

Although Spears denied that the building was for sale, officials of the University of Colorado said it had been offered to the university medical center for $1,100,000.[18]

6.
War With the State

Precipitating a barrage of sensational newspaper stories, the Colorado Department of Public Health announced on December 2, 1949, a renewed probe of Spears Sanitarium on the basis of new reports of city and state inspectors alleging various violations.[1]

The most serious of the charges, reported by Dr. Ward L. Chadwick, director of communicable diseases for Denver, was an outbreak of scarlet fever on the pediatric floor said to have infected 10 children. Chadwick commented to the press that the outbreak was impossible to contain due to "the lack of cooperation of the chiropractic profession." Apparently, according to the report, the outbreak was traced to a nurse with the disease.[2] None of the cases had been removed from the sanitarium.[3] Other violations pointed to unsanitary conditions in the handling of infant formulas, improper storage and labeling of medications, improperly written orders, inadequate nursing records and an "unusual number of patient deaths."[4]

The Denver Health Department found no problems with overall cleanliness; in fact, was complimentary: "The building was eminently clean throughout the section given over to the care of patients. Wards are well lighted and ventilated properly. There is every evidence of good housekeeping on each of the units. Patients appeared to be receiving adequate care."[5]

State Health Director Roy Cleere had turned the reports over to Attorney General John W. Metzger, information which included a $3^1/_2$-year-old death certificate signed by a Denver physician alleging "criminal neglect at Spears Sanitarium." A photostatic copy of the death certificate had been published in the *Rocky Mountain News*.[6]

The attorney general, with an eye toward possible new action against the institution he now characterized as "operating in the twilight zone under a suspended license," asked for and received an executive order from Governor Lee Knous to take whatever action was necessary to "abate the nuisance." "This is obviously the kind of controversy that can only be fairly and impartially decided in the courts. In justice to all sides and the public interest it must be determined quickly," the governor said.[7,8]

With the executive order, Metzger said he would bypass possible action by the State Board of Health and go directly to the Supreme Court "because of the urgency of the situation."

State Senator Neal Bishop, himself a chiropractor, deplored the action of bypassing the State Board of Chiropractic Examiners, which, he said, is the only state agency legally entitled to investigate charges against the chiropractic profession. "I am not carrying the torch for Dr. Spears," Bishop declared, "but I believe he is being persecuted by Dr. Roy L. Cleere. The reason I am suspicious is that I personally heard Dr. Cleere say that he will exterminate the chiropractors in Colorado. Dr. Spears is our most vulnerable point." [9]

Speaking in the absence of Dr. Leo Spears, who was out of the city, Dr. Dan Spears denied that the sanitarium was ever uncooperative with health officials and charged that statements made by Dr. Cleere were "malicious" and apparently intended to cast suspicion on the institution because of "personal bias." "Spears Sanitarium is not closed and will certainly continue to operate," he said. [10]

Dr. Leo Spears, who had been visiting New York City for almost two weeks, issued a statement immediately upon his return to Denver in which he declared that charges made by Dr. Cleere and the attorney general were "exaggerated beyond belief" and intended to "prejudice the court." [11,12]

About reports of 143 deaths in the sanitarium since it opened some six years earlier, Spears said the figure represents less than two percent of the total number of patients treated. "This is an extremely small death rate, especially since 90 percent of all the patients we have treated came to us as a last resort after having been given up or declared to be hopeless incurables by legitimate practitioners of the profession represented by those who seek to destroy us."

Reacting to Spears' charges, the attorney general said, "We feel it is a slur and a slander on the highest court in the state. In as much as Dr. Spears says our action is designed to prejudice the justices, I feel we should go directly to the Supreme Court." [13] On December 8, 1949, Metzger filed a motion with the court asking that the injunction allowing the sanitarium to continue operation be withdrawn and that the institution be placed under the direct supervision of the Board of Health. [14]

A newly appointed member of the Board of Health from distant southeastern Colorado, who had yet to hear any evidence in the matter, wrote to Dr. Cleere: "I was shocked by some of the reports. I am glad you did not wait until the next Board meeting, but went directly to the Attorney General who seems to have the courage to take immediate action." [15]

In the event the court disallowed direct administrative control of the sanitarium by the State Department of Public Health, an alternate plan of supervision was devised as a practical strategy: supervision by a committee composed of a physician from the staff of the University of Colorado Medical Center, a D.O., an R.N., and a D.C. The city and state health departments and the Colorado and Denver General hospitals would make personnel available according to the wishes of the committee. [16,17]

The seriousness of the situation, not only for the sanitarium but for the chiropractic profession, could not be underestimated, as pointed out by Dr.

WAR WITH THE STATE

Howard Spears in the *Sanitarium News*:

So that you might understand the situation in Denver, we feel it necessary to acquaint you with some of the facts.

In 1946, the Colorado State Board of Health revoked the license of the Spears Sanitarium on the false premise that we were harboring infectious and contagious diseases, calling the Sanitarium a hospital, and practicing medicine and surgery. There is no truth in these accusations.

By court order the Spears Sanitarium has been operating, is now operating and will continue to operate until this matter is settled in the courts, where we are confident of winning.

We had reason to believe that the Spears Sanitarium license would be restored in December, 1949, and reasonable rules and regulations would be established by the State Board of Health.

Now, we have proof that the State Board of Health and the Denver Medical Society have conspired and are conspiring to destroy the Spears Sanitarium. As per news items in this paper, they recently started a "smear" campaign to arouse the public against this institution. However, I do not believe they have been successful in this matter. The public seems very much in our favor.

The State Board of Health gave the Denver newspapers a lot of "trumped up" fantastic falsehoods in the hope that it would close the institution, thereby making it practically impossible for a chiropractic hospital to operate anywhere in the country.

Since 1943, when the Spears Sanitarium opened its doors for business, it has been the target of repeated attacks by our common enemy. So far we have been able to withstand the most vicious, malicious and atrocious attacks that our enemy could conceive. Are we going to give up? No, my friends, we shall fight as long as there is life-giving blood in our arteries.

This is it - the big fight! The outcome of this case will affect every man and woman in our profession. This is the testing ground which will decide whether or not there will be chiropractic hospitals in this country. You may be sure that if Spears loses this battle, Chiropractic will suffer its greatest defeat in history. But we will not lose; truth and justice will triumph. During this testing phase we will have many financial obligations. We are not appealing to you for financial assistance, but we are asking that you send us your problem cases. By doing this, you will help relieve our financial strain.

Keep your eyes on the Spears Sanitarium and remember that the outcome of this case will determine to a great extent whether or not chiropractors will be permitted to own and operate their own hospitals.

I believe that if every chiropractor only understood with what cunning and to what extreme medical monopoly is going to exterminate him and our science, he would do everything in his power to send every patient he possibly can to the Spears Sanitarium, which is fighting his battle as well as ours. Had we been willing to compromise with our medical enemies, and sold out the future right of chiropractors to build and operate their own hospitals, we could probably have lived in peace and comfort. But no such compromise will ever be made. The future of chiropractic and the rights of chiropractors... must never be jeopardized under any circumstances. To the contrary, we must all join hands in the great fight for healing freedom and the survival and success of chiropractic.[18]

On January 5, 1950, Charles Ginsberg and George Creamer pleaded in the Supreme Court for a ruling to overrule the District Court's decision upholding the revocation of the sanitarium's temporary license. Among issues raised was the legality of the health board's governance of any chiropractic institution in the state over the authority of the Board of Chiropractic Examiners.[19]

The court rejected the attorney general's petition in its entirety. Until the Spears suit presently in the court was decided, the stay of execution would continue.[20]

But the high court's opinion was not without dissent, in this instance from Chief Justice Benjamin C. Hilliard. He said he was in disagreement with his fellow justices because he was convinced the attorney general "is not now seeking determination on the merits of the controversy, nor has he said ought that is calculated to work prejudgment."

"He does seek an order that will preserve the status quo. The attorney general does not ask that the sanitarium be closed in the interim, nor that inconvenience be visited upon either the management thereof nor those domiciled therein. Rather, he seeks an order that will promote what he deems to be the public laws of the state while the case is pending."[21]

Landmark Verdict

By a unanimous decision on July 1, 1950, the Colorado Supreme Court ruled in favor of Spears Sanitarium in its seven-year life and death battle with the state. Finding that the Board of Health had acted illegally in attempting to close the institution, the court's lengthy opinion adopted these major legal conclusions:

> 1- The state legislature says that the chiropractic profession is a lawful method of treatment, that chiropractors have a right to be licensed and to build sanitariums under the law.
>
> 2- Any rules and regulations the state health board makes governing chiropractic hospitals must be reasonable requirements not contrary to law.
>
> 3- The law requires that permanent licenses shall be issued to hospitals upon showing fitness to operate the institutions, and that they may be revoked solely by reason of not complying with requirements of the act and rules and regulations of the board.
>
> 4- The board did not issue a license in fact to the Spears institution, but merely issued what amounted to an unauthorized temporary provisional permit, not signed or attested to by anyone officially representing the board of health.
>
> 5- Conditions of such a permit, according to Justice Stone, "are not set up as rules or standards for chiropractic sanitariums generally, but are arbitrary and discriminatory restrictions against applicant alone."
>
> "There is not a sentence in the license issued (to Spears Sanitarium) which follows the statute on which it is based... We cannot apply the rule that where a license contains invalid provisions it constitutes a valid license... Instead of pursuing its statutory authority, the state board of health attempted to usurp the functions of the legislature, and set up law of its own," the opinion declared.[22]

As to the board's contention that Spears Sanitarium had violated state law by permitting surgery, drugs and medicines to be administered, admitting and treating contagious diseases, and using the word "hospital," the court held that the board's interpretation of the law was itself invalid. "Even if the evidence adduced at the hearing on those charges established the truth of all of them, as is asserted in behalf of the board, still no ground for valid revocation was shown. The violation of void conditions could not justify the revocation." The Colorado Board of Health was ordered to issue a valid hospital license to Spears, backdated to September 27, 1943, when the entire matter began.(*See Appendix C.*)

The *Denver Post* was quite thoughtful about the verdict:

> The Colorado supreme court's decision against the state health department in its attempt to keep Leo Spears from operating a chiropractic hospital in Denver is one of those decisions which must from time to time be made to insure freedom in this nation.
>
> The point is not whether the supreme court favors chiropractic, or whether it favors medicine. The point is that the state board of health is authorized to do certain things, and in the Spears case the board far exceeded its legal authority. In effect the board tried to invoke and to twist the law for use against a single individual. If successful this would have been persecution.
>
> Denver's doctors have been warring for a long time against Leo Spears. They are wrong if they try to carry their war past the point where it can command public support. They are wrong if they try to use extra-legal means in their fight against chiropractic in general and Dr. Leo Spears in particular.
>
> The doctors and the board of health should remember, as the court reminded them, that the practice of chiropractic is recognized and authorized by law, and that it must be accepted as a lawful occupation and is in the public interest.
>
> Many people in this state and elsewhere in the Rocky Mountain Empire believe wholeheartedly in Leo Spears. If he wants to convert them to chiropractic, that is his business. If the doctors want to convert them away from it, that is their business. But as long as chiropractic is legal, the board of health has no more business trying to curtail it than has this newspaper.[23]

Post columnist Bruce Gustin had this to say:

> Seldom, if ever, has a Colorado state agency been chastised as severely as the state board of health was spanked by the state supreme court in the Spears case. It was the unanimous decision of the court that the board acted illegally in trying to close the sanitarium.
>
> Furthermore, the court held that "instead of pursuing its statutory authority, the board attempted to usurp the functions of the legislature and set up law of its own." Apparently, the board was influenced by prejudice in the medical profession against chiropractic treatment generally and Dr. Spears particularly.[24]

Spears Sanigram correctly assessed the importance of the verdict to the chiropractic profession:

> The Spears Supreme Court decision has gone into history - history that will be felt in years to come - because it established an all-important precedent, the first of its kind even to be written on the statute books of any state, and a precedent that will be followed more or less in similar matters in all states. To say the least, its influence will be beneficial on all similar matters, no matter the state in which they arise. ... while (the) legal factors are important, we must not overlook two other factors of similar importance.
>
> The first of these is that the boldness with which the (medical profession) branded chiro-

practors as quacks, caused many people to feel it was true and that chiropractic had little if any standing in law.

Second, the suit Dr. Spears has instituted against the vilifying medical doctors and medical organizations which, as a result of the present decision, appears very likely to be won, will deter medical interests in their open vilification of chiropractors in the future.

This will aid in the development of chiropractic on its own merits instead of having to waste so much time in defending itself against groundless accusations.[25]

Now free to call the institution a hospital, trustees chose the name Spears Chiropractic Sanitarium and Hospital. "It has been called Spears Sanitarium for so long it is deemed advisable to still keep the word sanitarium and add hospital at the end of the name," Dr. Leo said. "Spears Chiropractic Sanitarium and Hospital is, in effect, now under the jurisdiction of the State Supreme Court. In other words, if the State Board of Health, at any time in the future, violates the orders of the Supreme Court through restrictive rules or regulations or other outright persecution, the Board will have to answer to the Supreme Court. And, according to our attorneys, (could) be cited in for contempt of court."[26]

The State Health Department quietly bowed to the court order and on October 13, 1950, issued a hospital license to the Spears Free Clinic and Hospital for Poor Children. The action ended a squabble of seven years' duration and almost four years of operating under injunctions.[27]

The Spears Amendment

Early in 1950, *The Denver Post* conducted a survey on the question: "Do you believe in chiropractic treatment for illness?" With some qualification, 61% responded "Yes;" 34% said "No;" 5% had no opinion.[28]

After the landmark Supreme Court decision, Spears employed the same opinion and marketing firm to survey on the question: "Many Colorado counties give welfare and public assistance clients free medical treatment, but no free chiropractic treatment. Is this all right, or should welfare patients have a choice?" Generally, 77% felt there should be a choice, while only 23% felt otherwise.[29]

Based on the results of the poll, a Spears-sponsored petition was circulated throughout the city and county calling for an ordinance which would entitle welfare clients to receive chiropractic hospitalization and treatment at taxpayer expense. Dr. Dan Spears explained to the press, "All this does is assure the indigent patient the right of choice between medical and chiropractic treatment, which certainly should be a fundamental right. We feel that such an action would be of great benefit to the city. As it stands now, the indigent patient must take whatever treatment is offered, without recourse or choice."[30,31]

While the so-called Spears Amendment received sufficient support (at least 17,000 signatures) to reach the November ballot, it failed with most voters on election day.

Blue Cross

Perhaps for the first time in chiropractic, Leo Spears leveled a blast at America's largest hospitalization insurer – Blue Cross – for denying the hospital's application for membership. "By its policy, (Blue Cross) seeks to entrench monopolistic practices, with public health at stake. We believe this to be unfair, unjust and discriminatory." He added that he would be considering legal action "to relieve the situation." [32]

In its formal reply, Blue Cross said a committee appointed to investigate the Spears application met with Dr. Spears and other representatives of the hospital: "At this meeting, facts presented indicated that the institution renders a service so dissimilar to the service rendered by member hospitals in Blue Cross that it would not be feasible to include (Spears Hospital) in this non-profit, voluntary effort of Denver hospitals to make it possible for people to prepay hospital expenses. The average patient stay in Spears Hospital was shown by your committee to be six times as long as the average stay in hospital now by members of Blue Cross." [33]

In apparent answer to the threat of legal action, Blue Cross said, "The right of voluntary Blue Cross plans to reject applicants for membership has recently been upheld by the highest court in Texas in a case which is considered precedent."

Spears replied: "Hardly a day goes by when we don't have to tell several prospective patients, whose premiums are fully paid to Blue Cross, that the Colorado Hospital Association will not pay for care in our institution." He also said "several thousand members petitioned Blue Cross for inclusion of chiropractic in its contracts, but officials claimed they were unaware of such petitions." [34]

A Denver District Court decision on November 30, 1949, (known as the Frankfather case) had already ruled that Spears Sanitarium constituted a "recognized hospital" within the meaning of hospitalization insurance. The case had been brought by a former Spears patient denied reimbursement by Reserve Life Insurance Co. of Dallas, Texas.[35]

7.

Research: Promise and Hyperbole

Tapping into the potential of the sanitarium as an advanced training and research center for the chiropractic profession was almost realized in 1947, when trustees of the Chiropractic Research Foundation (CRF) and Spears Sanitarium announced on August 6 an agreement to merge efforts. According to accounts in the local papers, the CRF would authorize $1.5 million for construction of a new hospital and research center on the Spears campus while also assuming general management of the institution. The same news sources said that Spears trustees would retain the title.[1,2] The foundation, established in 1944, was an independently chartered asset of the National Chiropractic Association.[3]

But politics would dash the hopes of many as negotiations fell apart on the very eve of their consummation. This is how Dr. Dan Spears recalled what happened:

> Dr. Leo helped form this organization and it was proposed that we associate our organization with it. The proposed agreement was that the CRF could appoint four members to our board of trustees. The night before we were to meet for ratification of the agreement, members of the CRF called me and Dr. Howard asking for an audience that evening unbeknown to Dr. Leo, which we accepted. When we arrived, the members of this committee stated that when the deal was consummated Leo Spears would be kicked out of the organization, all advertising would be stopped and they would take control of the hospital. This was certainly a dagger in the back.
>
> We kept this information to ourselves until the following evening, at which time the meeting was held. Dr. Leo was called out of the meeting by my brother, Dr. Howard, and he advised of the meeting of the night before, which infuriated him. Leo returned to the meeting, gave the members the news which he had just received, asked them if it was true and they said, yes. He ordered them out of his office and told them if anyone refused to leave he would throw them out bodily. The trustees who had been appointed to our board were asked to resign. Their letters of resignation are in our files.[4]

Dr. Frank Logic, president of the Chiropractic Research Foundation, issued the following statement about the failed agreement:

> According to the terms of the written agreement to effect later a legal contract ... the Spears Sanitarium was placed under a trusteeship consisting of nine members. Five of these members were named by the Spears Corporation and four by the CRF. This ar-

rangement actually left the Spears Sanitarium in majority control of the Spears Corporation. It is true a Board of Management was appointed by the CRF, subordinate, however, to the above named Board of Trustees. No other arrangement was acceptable.

Under this arrangement, it is evident that the Spears Sanitarium was never under actual control or management of the CRF. Realizing that the CRF could not assume the responsibility for the management and conduct of the Sanitarium unless it actually in control, and since no other agreement could be reached with the Spears Trustees, it was deemed advisable to take immediate steps to cancel the existing agreement, in accordance with the majority opinion. Dr. (Leo) Spears was agreeable to such action.[5]

In subsequent years, Spears Hospital proffered its own research as the profession's standard, a stance that would be problematic. (*See Appendix D.*)

Postmortem Research

Dr. Spears asked in 1953 for authority to conduct autopsies at the hospital. In a letter to Health Board secretary Roy Cleere, he explained that it would be "for the purpose of obtaining certain information necessary in connection with our research and intern training programs," suggesting further, "we have men on our staff amply qualified for this work."[6] For the record, the attorney general ruled in 1941 that chiropractors may not sign death certificates,[7] an opinion upheld by the Supreme Court 30 years later.[8]

Spears' letter was forwarded to Lloyd Florio, M.D., manager of the Denver Department of Health and Hospitals, who concluded: "It is our opinion that autopsies are lawful at the Spears institution or on the premises of mortuaries only if the coroner has been informed of such deaths and has completed his investigation, inquest, or postmortem examination as the case may be, and after the Manager is satisfied that the certificate of death contains a proper certification of the cause of death."[9] The attorney general, while pointing out the relevant statutes and legal discretions, could find no specific prohibition.[10]

And so while the way seemed clear for the state to grant the unusual request, it appears from the public record that nothing further developed.

Cancer

On November 21, 1953, a Spears news release announced that its research department had perfected a blood screening test to determine the existence of cancer. The test, based on evaluation of 7,000 slide specimens, was claimed to be 94.6 to 99 percent accurate, depending on the stages of malignancy. "Its simplicity and accuracy are revolutionary," the release said of the microscopic test which required only a drop of blood and 2-5 minutes to complete, and which would now be offered to medical science for critical evaluation.[11]

A free "world premiere" of the blood test would take place at the hospital during the last week of November for anyone interested in taking part. During the public demonstrations, no diagnosis would be undertaken "other than to indicate a suspicion of or a predisposition to cancer, in which case the subject would be referred to his or her own doctor." [12]

Two-hundred twenty-six people submitted to the test during its weeklong public debut. Spears' research director, Dr. George Wilson, told reporters "it is the most accurate screening test known, the thing the world has been waiting for." A *Denver Post* account noted that while Spears assured everyone that he was not "soliciting business or giving out literature," on the reverse side of a report handed each person who took the test was both a description of the hospital and room rates. [13]

About his willingness to share the new technique, Spears told the *Post* "it can be very easily taught to any doctor but, of course, I don't know how the medical profession will react to our findings."

A letter writer to the *Denver Post* saw some justification to at least examine Spears' claims:

> This Leo L. Spears and his cancer research might well get a good workout as to its merits, outside of unfunny reporting and a quick rejection by cancer experts.
>
> After Spears examines 3,500 patients, of whom 1,500 had cancer and a general pattern of diagnosis of blood grouped itself as cancer positive and identified somewhere around 94.6 pct., surely something happened that warrants further investigation.
>
> The tremendous sums spent on cancer research by the "cliques" that have these funds to spend surely have an obligation to look at any possible discovery until they can at least do something themselves. [14]

A credibility gap soon became apparent as Dr. Spears had to admit to the press that he had no real evidence to support his rather precise claims of accuracy: "During the three years of development we never thought it would come to the point where statistics and blood slides would be needed," he said. Commenting on findings during the public demonstrations, he said he was not prepared to present evidence that any of the persons whose test results were "suspicious" actually have cancer or a tendency toward cancer. He added that he was also unprepared to present evidence that those pronounced "non-cancerous" were actually so. [15]

Not surprisingly, the National Cancer Institute (NCI) declared the Spears blood test to be of no value. "We have the right to say if we believe the concept is good or bad, and we believe it is bad," said Dr. John Heller, director of the NCI, who pointed out a number of possibilities for a false conclusion with the test. "Detailed and careful blood tests, in the hands of competent investigators, certainly can be a means of diagnosis of ill health. (But) cancer, or susceptibility to cancer, would be confused in gross blood testing with a multitude of other factors unrelated to malignancy," he advised. [16]

Heller went further, calling the Spears test a modification of the so-called "Bolen Test for Malignancy," introduced in 1942 by Dr. H.L. Bolen of Massachusetts. "It is nothing new," he said. "The Bolen test, as well as the validity of scores of other experimental 'cancer screening tests' advanced by medical scientists, recently was invalidated to the satisfaction even of their originators by Dr. Freddy Homburger of Tufts Medical College."

Spears denied that his test was an extension of Bolen's work, although his press release used those words. He said that he read details about the Bolen test in a reprint of an article on the subject by Dr. N. Phillip Norman, which appeared in the *Journal of Digestive Diseases* in February 1950. He said he disagreed with Norman's method of interpreting the slides and devised his own grading system. While the Bolen test graded slides only positive or negative, the Spears system grades positive slides 1-9. NCI Director Heller said he could see no value in such grading... "but it's a new idea, all right." [17]

At a press conference on November 30, Spears said 3,500 patients over a three-year period were subjected to blood tests in a screening test experiment. Of those, 1,500 were "positive" for cancer. Then, he made the following points:

1- The number of patients used is an approximation; no exact statistical records were kept. "Actually, the correct number is a lot higher – we said that many just to be conservative."

2- No effort was made to determine how many of the 1,500 "cancer" patients were confirmed by microscopic tissue examination.

3- Records showing the exact number of tests used on individual patients were not arranged statistically for ready reference to investigators.

4- Most of the actual blood smear specimens used in the approximately 7,000 experimental tests were destroyed, thus making it impossible to produce evidence of reliability.

Hospital records and charts of the patients involved were offered to investigators which, Spears said, "would produce significant evidence" in proving his theory and screening test. He added, if interested investigators would send a significant number of new experimental patients--perhaps 1,000--his results would prove his claims. [18]

The blood test was actually a highly subjective interpretation of red blood cell groupings of a dried specimen laid down on a slide in a certain way. Key to obtaining the specimen, requiring excellent technique, was that the blood drop not be smeared. As the specimen dries, it forms into "islands" (cell groupings) and "lakes" (plasma). Under ordinary magnification, the appearance of more lakes than islands suggests a pathological process affecting the cell patterns. [19]

Notwithstanding that Bolen was among the very first to use this method of diagnosis, Spears claimed to have identified the factors affecting cell patterns, and to have developed a more reliable method of preparing slides, called the "gravity spread method." More specifically, Spears believed his research involving cross-mixing of blood serum from the plasma of known cancer patients with that of healthy individuals provided the answers as to how blood patterns develop, something other researchers had not done. [20]

A manual authored by research director George A. Wilson, D.C., presented a quite convincing argument. The test, which Dr. Wilson preferred to call the Pathology Determination Test (P-D), was graded "O" for a chronic condition that could become carcinogenic; Grades 1 and 2, for cancer that is developing; Grades 3 and 4 for advanced cancers. According to Wilson, the real value of the P-D test was its very high degree of accuracy in detecting the presence or absence of cancer in more than 9,000 observations. "We believe this gives us the authority to speak on the question," he wrote.[21]

The *Denver Post* report that Spears graded positive findings 1-9 was apparently inaccurate.

In October 1951, Dr. George Wilson released a "Report on the First 211 Cancer Cases Treated at Spears." The study covered an eight-month period through May 1951.[22] *Spears Sanigram* noted that "it was only last October that Spears began accepting cancer cases of all types and in all stages. Prior to that time, occasional patients with malignancies had been treated with encouraging results; but until the institution was fully equipped with laboratory, technicians, (and) a staff of doctors trained in the Spears technique, no general invitation to cancer sufferers was extended."[23]

Wilson reported that 184 cases of the 211 treated had been "declared incurable by reputable cancer clinics and cancer research centers of the United States and Canada. Practically all of them had received the maximum of medical, surgical, x-ray or radium treatment, or a combination of these."[24]

Fifty patients reported in the study were terminal upon arrival and had either died or were discharged. Of the remainder, 20 or 17% of 161 showed "arrest of all cancer activity;" 37 or 23% of 161 had "relief and prolongation of life;" 73 or 45% of 161 had "satisfactory improvement of their condition." The grand total of these figures --130--when figured on the basis of 161 indicated that 80% had received beneficial results.

The lengthy report, which included detailed pathological descriptions of each case, made no claims of curing cancer. It was published in *Spears Sanigram* in 14 installments.

Associated Press (AP) science reporter Howard Blakeslee wired a digest of the Spears cancer report to member newspapers. One such paper, the *Wichita Beacon*, carried the AP reports as a series on the front page. The National Chiropractic Association *Journal* declined to publish the report because the executive board did not believe eight months was sufficient time for Spears to substantiate the findings.[25]

On the other hand, cancer specialist Charles P. Bryant, M.D., of Seattle, in a letter to Dr. Spears, said:

> I was so pleased to read your report of the miraculous results you are having (with cancer). I know too well the folly of attempting to cure cancer by surgery, x-ray or ra-

dium. I also know that cancer is not a local disease ... Your work ... has accomplished far more than surgery, x-ray or radiation.[26]

George A. Wilson, D.C., was well known in the profession prior to coming to Spears in 1951. He had developed a research laboratory in Salt Lake City in 1948, where he conducted experiments in physiology and bio-electrical phenomena as it applied to chiropractic theory.[27,28]

One of his inventions was the Neuromicrometer, an electrical device for which he claimed, among other things, a capability of diagnosing cancer. Like other researchers before him who dabbled in "electronic medicine," Wilson's claims would face severe scrutiny.

A novel approach to cancer education was set in motion in late 1954 when Spears Hospital again revived the "rolling clinic"-- a newly-built 35-foot trailer to tour throughout the Rocky Mountain West, offering the public free cancer screenings.[29] The Colorado Chiropractic Association said it would investigate the claims made by Dr. Spears for his blood test,[30] but the outcome is unknown.

Cerebral Palsy and Mental Deficiency

The United States Public Health Service (USPHS) had denied Spears' application for funding cerebral palsy (CP) research. The application was filed in May 1954 and three investigators from the USPHS were sent to Denver in what was described as a "more than routine probe" of the hospital's work with CP. Their findings formed the basis of the negative action by an advisory committee, but specific reasons leading to the denial were not explained.

A "tragic blow" is how Leo Spears reacted to the rejection. He said he believed the three investigators gave him a "favorable" report but the committee turned him down because he was not an M.D. "We will go directly to the floor of the Senate and House of Representatives to get the funding," he vowed.[31]

Running concurrently in major newspapers throughout the country was a full-page advertisement paid for by Spears describing a "skull remolding" procedure for correcting cerebral palsy and mental deficiency and offering $100,000 to anyone "who can disprove this to the world." [32]

The Senate Judiciary Committee convened what were called the Hearings on Juvenile Delinquency in the Federal District Court, Denver, in December 1954, co-chaired by North Dakota's Senator William Langer and Senator Estes Kefauver of Tennessee. At Langer's invitation, Dr. Spears testified on his theory that "skull distortions" causing pressure on the brain as being one of the major contributing factors to juvenile delinquency as well as cerebral palsy and mental deficiency. "Correction would not only, I believe, prevent cerebral palsy and extreme degrees of mental deficiencies but would eliminate the possibility of problem children and much of the crime rampant in this country."[33] *(See*

Appendix E)

James Bobo, committee counsel, asked Spears what he had done to get his theory to the people and to public officials:

Spears: "Well, we've tried, for instance to get funds from the U.S. Public Health Service but were turned down. We tried for newspaper and magazine articles on our vital work. And we've invited newspaper and magazine writers to come on out, look at what we're doing and then spread the word."

Bobo: "Have you had any opportunity to examine problem children?"

Spears: "Many hundreds, especially during the first 15 years of my practice when I was a child specialist. I found there were very, very few of these problem children without skull distortions which caused mental deficiency and the inability to tell right from wrong."

Bobo: "Do you feel there is a need for further work in this field?"

Spears: "There certainly is; many young people have been punished and sent to jail at great public expense who didn't deserve such punishment. Because of their physical abnormalities they were unable to distinguish right from wrong."

Senator Langer remarked that he had personally visited the pediatrics department at Spears Hospital and saw 150 children there. "It is certainly a remarkable place and I hope I can get the committee to see it before they leave town."

Langer: "I believe you told me you have a large waiting list."

Spears: "Yes, we have over 5,000 children waiting for treatment. There are 750,000 persons in the United States today who need this type of treatment."

Kefauver: "You don't mean to imply that you have found the solution to the overall problem?"

Spears: "No, sir."

Kefauver: "Isn't it possible that lack of oxygen, mucus in the womb, pathological deficiencies and improper bone structure might be a cause of cerebral palsy?"

Spears: "I don't believe so. The United Cerebral Palsy organization still doesn't know what causes the disease. We believe we know what causes the disease."

Langer: "Thousands of patients with skull distortions have been treated at his chiropractic hospital and corrections of their conditions have been achieved in a fine percentage of them."

Kefauver: "You're probably aware that the main body of medical opinion holds that lack of oxygen, the RH factor in the blood and other conditions cause brain deterioration. Statistics show, I think, according to Dr. Draper in the *Rocky Mountain Medical Journal*, that only four percent of cerebral palsy cases are caused by the formative shape of the head."

Spears: "It might be, but I've never read his works. I have discovered that those other things are not as causative as it is said they are. It is not brain deterioration or brain injury but brain pressure in most cases that causes cerebral palsy. I have seen children with heads as flat as saucers in which doctors had cut as many as four holes looking for tumors. Rather than looking for the tumors doctors should have noticed the skull distortion."

Kefauver: "I don't want to get an argument going between you and the brain specialists of the nation, but you must recognize there is quite a divergence of opinion between you and the main body of medical opinion in this country."

Spears: "That may be true. But I've never seen anything written by a cerebral palsy specialist in which he says he knows what causes the disease. It's not my purpose to raise any questions here or bring about an argument, but to submit my theory for the investigation of your committee and the American Medical Asociation."[34]

The Colorado State Medical Society was not impressed:

> The idea of skull moulding to cure disease is a primitive concept, abandoned centuries ago by the first scientist who developed a real knowledge of human anatomy. It was revived two or three times during the Middle Ages, but finally was permanently proved to be of no value. Furthermore, it was proved to be fraught with danger to the child or even the adult who submits to it.[35]

The Longevity Research Study

In September 1954, Leo Spears announced to the convention of the Nebraska Chiropractic Association that "we may be close to learning the secrets of very old age. If true, it could be possible to live 200 years." He explained that a normal, healthy body creates 140 million new cells every minute, but in old age the rate drops to 10-12 million a minute. He added that he had found a way to stimulate normal cell production through a manual technique he called "nerve and cell goading." "By working with the hands, we can 'goad' nature into creating greater energy and therefore longer life."[36](See Appendix F.)

To test his theory, he said he would invite the oldest people on the planet -- at least 25 of them--to his Denver hospital for a clinical study.

"If it can be determined why these oldsters have maintained good health, the secret of how to make other people live very long lives may be uncovered. I think the oldsters we study will be people who have lived active, unpampered lives."

And so, for the first time to an open audience, details were revealed of what would arguably become the single most publicized enterprise in chiropractic history at the time--the Spears Longevity Research Study.

The study was to last indefinitely. "There's no catch or gimmick," Spears assured in a press statement. Each person accepted and one chaperon would each receive travel and living expenses. Subjects would remain in the study 7-10 days and be paid $200 (the equivalent of $1600 today) at the conclusion of their participation, with all costs borne by the hospital's trustees as a humanitarian gesture. "They (the trustees) consider this the most important project they have ever taken part in," noted the *Wichita Beacon*.[37]

In addition to exhaustive physical and mental evaluations, participants understood that personal information would be released to the worldwide press.

Word of the study got out quickly via the wire services; there would be no need to purchase advertising. At Spears Hospital, an employee was designated just to handle the flood of inquiries, from news organizations to foreign consulates and embassies, each one focused on locating the world's oldest citizens. For press distribution, Dr. Spears prepared a lengthy statement about the study and his theories on longevity.

Steamship companies, airlines and railroads announced their interest in providing special service for study participants. In Washington, Senator William Langer, chairman of the Senate Judiciary Committee, of which the Immigration and Naturalization subcommittee was a part, promised cooperation in securing temporary travel visas for those coming from abroad. In some instances, news organizations offered to undertake sponsorship. Even Communist China's state-controlled Peiping Radio was heard from, claiming a Hong Kong resident, 155, as the world's oldest human.[38]

According to a list supplied to Spears by its embassy, Turkey apparently could lay claim to that honor. One of its citizens was said to be an incredible 167, possibly the oldest person alive. Another was listed at 162, and several others were over 130.[39]

Spears Sanigram reported that among other inquiries received from outside the U.S., a 140-year-old man in Peurto Rico and a 137-year-old Cuban woman were thought to be unable to travel. At least 10 possible subjects from Denmark, one in France and another in Japan, all said to be more than 120, were either unable or unwilling to leave home. Dr. Spears decided he should make an around-the-world trip during 1955 to personally examine these individuals in their own homes, enlisting local help to assist with needed lab work, language interpretation and any unforeseen obstacles.[40]

The longevity study officially got underway in October 1954 with the arrival of the first group of centenarians from the U.S.--three men and one woman ranging in age from 114 down to a mere 102. Spears reported that 10 subjects were expected in the study by the end of the year, including four reported to be the sole surviving Confederate Civil War veterans.[41]

The gathering of so many oldsters for such a study was a natural for the media. Even the usually grouchy *Denver Post*, not known for ever cutting Spears much slack, played this story straight down the middle. Each new subject upon arrival in Denver was given considerable local newspaper and

TV coverage, and considerably more via news wire and news film. It was an awfully good story, although the press seemed less interested in Dr. Spears' dissembling ideas on extending life well past the warranty on the human body, as it was understood.

Capturing most media attention were two men with a shared bond. Both had at one time worked for the legendary outlaw Jesse James.

When 117-year-old John Trammell, who also claimed to have been the "uncrowned bare kunckle boxing champion of the world," told the press about Jesse James, the story he told was quite a tale.

After his boxing career, he said he spent years with the outlaw gang, working as a cook, camp tender, forager and general handyman; perhaps even a gunslinger judging by his several healed bullet wounds.

Official accounts of the Jesse James legend pretty much accept that he met his fate in 1882, shot in the back of the head by Bob Ford. "Not so," said Trammell, "a dirty little coward named Charlie Bigelow tried to but ended up dead himself. It was Bigelow's body that was passed off as Jesse so the real Jesse could escape ... to South America. But he later returned and settled in Texas. I saw him in Austin in 1949, a year before he really died."[42]

John Trammell's saga, bolstered by the Jesse James tale, became one of the great human interest stories of 1954, carried in newspapers and on newsreels around the country and, undoubtedly, the world.

But no story of the Spears centenarians was bigger or more durable than that of Charlie Smith, who came to Denver in July 1955.

Charlie had recently become something of a celebrity in his home-town of Auburndale, Florida, where he was working as an orange picker. His job, of course, required tree climbing, no small feat for someone reputed to be 113 years old. Despite his great age, Smith had been turned down for Social Security benefits. How could this be?

Additional facts unearthed by the local press found that Charlie was born in Liberia in 1842, kidnapped at age 13, transported to New Orleans on a slave ship and sold at auction on July 5, 1855. He had never learned to read or write and therefore had never sought citizenship. He merely assumed that he "belonged" after living and working here for a hundred years.[43,44]

Charlie's face and story soon became familiar to the entire nation. He was called "the world's oldest regularly employed person," a theme picked up by syndicated news features Ripley's "Believe It Or Not"[45] and Hix's "Strange But True."[46]

The Ripley piece acknowledged the Spears longevity study, as did a long story about Charlie in the *Saturday Evening Post.*[47]

The Pikes Peak Journal reported that Charlie also visited Jesse James III at Manitou Springs, the two having known each other years before when James was part-owner of a ranch in Galveston where Smith worked as a hired hand.[48]

RESEARCH: PROMISE AND HYPERBOLE

After two eventful weeks in Denver, Charlie returned to Florida and back to work in the citrus groves. But his celebrity would last for years.

On July 4, 1956, his 114th birthday, he officially became a United States citizen and eligible for Social Security benefits. He would have to stop working in the citrus groves, however, something to which he took a dim view. But he complied and opened a small confectionery store in Bartow, Florida, where he spent the rest of his days.[49]

Adding to his already considerable celebrity, his picture was displayed on a poster in post offices all over the country in the 1960s in a government promotion urging agricultural workers to sign up for Social Security.[50]

During the early years of the Apollo lunar expeditions, Charlie was at least twice an invited special guest of NASA for the liftoff from Cape Canaveral. But he remained a skeptic, figuring flying to the moon was, well, just Hollywood.[51]

In his last years, long since acknowledged as the America's oldest citizen, he could be seen on national TV each July 4th. He told *Newsweek* in 1976 he "feels like a shotgun 'bout ready to shoot its last shell."[52] His last TV interview was about 1978. Charlie, now very infirm from the double ravages of great age and diabetes, summed up his extraordinarily long life this way: "I thinks it's the wrath of God."[53]

Charlie Smith died in a Bartow, Florida, convalescent home on October 5, 1979 at the age of 137. He had only one survivor, his 70-year-old son Chester Smith.[54]

An international incident caused the only known controversy about the study reported in the press. The governor of Puerto Rico, acting on the advice of a government public health official adverse to chiropractic, refused to allow a D.C. acting for Dr. Spears to examine a prospective subject.[55]

The longevity study apparently ended after the departure of Charlie Smith. Dr. Spears did not make his planned trip abroad and nothing further was reported in the *Sanigram* about the study after January 1956. What can be surmised is that the study was quietly shelved because of the costs associated with resuming construction of the stalled Pioneer's building by city order and the costs and pressing nature of various legal entanglements.

From a publicity standpoint, however, the longevity research project was an outstanding success.

8.
The Langer Hearings

Veterans' rights in health care--a freedom to choose--had always been of paramount concern to Leo Spears. His record, by now dating back three decades, was unequivocal. The earliest evidence was an open letter to President Harding and Congress in 1921 pleading that the Veterans' Bureau be mandated to provide chiropractic care to disabled veterans.[1]

The public record of veterans organizations demanding chiropractic be offered by the government as a health care option was equally compelling. U.S. Congresswoman Edith Nourse Rogers had accepted the challenge of drafting the American Legion's 1952 national resolution in a bill (H.R. 54) that would mandate chiropractic care for veterans at government expense. But the measure was making little headway.

Dr. Spears conceived a plan of action that seemed both rational and workable - a demonstration project on chiropractic care for disabled veterans. On March 13, 1953, he dispatched the following proposal to Veterans Administration Administrator Carl R. Gray:

> Because (1) the veterans, whose great sacrifices preserved to this country the liberties we all now enjoy, have individually and through the State and National conventions of the American Legion, Veterans of Foreign Wars and Disabled American Veterans petitioned the government for chiropractic at government expense; because (2) such service had never been granted; and (3) because many veterans, unable to finance their own treatment, are suffering needless pain and invalidism because of their refusal, the trustees, executives and staff of Spears Chiropractic Sanitarium and Hospital - most of whom are themselves veterans and owe their lives and good health to chiropractic - wish to make the following proposal:
>
> (1) That the Veterans Administration place a committee of three or five unprejudiced lay investigators in this institution for six months at our expense, to check on and observe the results of chiropractic treatment;
>
> (2) That if, at the end of said six months, the Veterans Administration wants additional proof of the efficiency of chiropractic, the saving it will bring to taxpayers, and the misery it will relieve if granted our veterans;
>
> (3) The Spears Chiropractic Sanitarium and Hospital will then accept, treat and share equally with the Veterans Administration the expense of hospitalizing and treating for necessary periods up to one year, one hundred veterans who (a) are totally disabled, (b) have multiple sclerosis, polio or heart trouble, and (c) have been declared incurable by

the Veterans Administration.

This proposal is made with the understanding that (1) the Veterans Administration will have its own staff of doctors constantly observe and check on the results of our treatment; (2) veterans organizations, newspapers, magazines and other publicity media shall have the right to observe and publish their opinions of the results of such treatment.[2]

Although the letter had been addressed to Administrator Gray, a curt reply came from Dr. Joel T. Boone, the VA's chief medical officer:

There was brought to my attention the letter you wrote to the Administrator on March 13, 1953, proposing that the Veterans Administration send lay investigators to your institution at your expense to evaluate the results of chiropractic treatment with certain stipulations which you specified.

For the Veterans Administration to engage in such a project was not favorably considered, and your offer is herewith declined.[3]

The VA's expected rejection triggered the next step of the plan. Spears then sent copies of his correspondence with the VA to all members of Congress, saying, in part:

The enclosed copies of our proposals to the Veterans Administration and two case histories typical of thousands of veterans who, at their own expense, have learned the value of chiropractic are self-explanatory.

You are probably not aware of the pitiable state of many thousands of veterans who have failed to find relief through the excellent, but limited, medical means now being provided them by the government. And it is doubtful that you hear the many heart-rending pleas of indigent veterans for obtaining government assistance in obtaining the treatment that offers greatest relief for their particular ailments. Since it is almost unbelievable that these pleas are being coldly rejected by the agency whose duty it is to look after the welfare of those who sacrificed their health and careers to defend the very liberties they are now denied, we beg leave to bring the facts to your attention.

It is indeed difficult for our veterans, or anyone else, to understand why the interests of a system of healing would be given preference over their health and welfare. They and their families, all of whom pay taxes, feel that no treatment that might relieve their miseries should be denied them. In the name of freedom and humanity, liberty and common justice, we ask that immediate steps be taken by the United States Congress to correct this heartless discrimination.

There is nothing in our present laws to prevent the Veterans Administration from providing chiropractic care for those veterans who want it. But its flat refusal makes it mandatory that a law be passed that will require it to humanize its medical policy. God grant that you will demand such a law at the earliest possible moment.

May our veterans depend on you? [4]

North Dakota Senator William Langer, who had a well-earned reputation both as a political maverick and defender of controversial causes, was one of the few who took Spears seriously. As chairman of the powerful U.S. Senate Judiciary Committee, the hearings he would convene on the Spears complaint would be pioneering although, as it turned out, not groundbreaking.

The historic investigation took place May 14-16 and June 19, 1953, in the Senate Office Building. Veterans Administration representatives were summoned from the highest echelons of the bureaucracy: Major General Gray; Medical Director Boone; Dr. Herman Kretschmar, chief of the inquiry division; Dr. Henry A. Davidson, chief of program analysis and planning; Dr. Harry Kessler, coordinator of paraplegia affairs; Dr. Charles F. Hill, chief of orthopedics; Dr. Tiffany Lawyer, chief of neurology; and Mr. Donald C. Knapp of the VA office of legislation.

Dr. Leo Spears, speaking both as a veteran and a chiropractor, set the tone for the proceedings with a long, somewhat preachy statement. (*See Appendix G.*)

The VA witnesses calmly conceded that only medically approved therapies were employed in the tax-built hospitals over which they held jurisdiction. They confessed frequent failures of medicine and surgery, weakness in diagnostic procedures, and their inability often to cope with paralytic conditions, but asserted their conviction that no relief for sufferers existed anywhere if patients were unresponsive to medicine and surgery. This attitude remained unshaken even after a dozen witnesses testified to their recovery or marked improvement under chiropractic treatment after the best resources of VA methods had been thoroughly and efficiently explored in VA hospitals, private hospitals, in nationally-famed clinics, and by individual specialists who were highly respected in their fields. "All had been declared 'incurable' or 'hopeless' cases by acknowledged authorities," Spears insisted, "but all attributed their recoveries entirely to chiropractic." Their disabilities were reportedly in such categories as cancer, multiple sclerosis, tuberculosis (pulmonary and bone).[5]

The VA witnesses "could not explain" the apparent improvement achieved by the disabled veterans who testified, but confessed, with some asperity, that they knew nothing whatever about chiropractic.

Chairman Langer pointed out that these witnesses were merely "samples of chiropractic accomplishment in the realm of the seemingly impossible;" that Dr. Spears "offered to bring a thousand ex-patients to Washington but I told him a dozen would be enough." Langer chided the VA representatives for their opposition to the Rogers bill which, if passed, would make the appointment of D.C.'s in the Veterans Administration mandatory. He reminded the VA authorities that their status is that of government employees, on the public payroll, and that their duty was to obey laws enacted by Congress, not to influence or formulate legislation to conform with their personal or professional bias.

Testimony revealed that the VA medical and surgical department scope covered such fields as chiropody, osteopathy, physical therapy and even veterinary services, in addition to conventional services, but excluded chiropractic for which, they admitted, there had been frequent demands by individual veterans and by major veterans' organizations.[6]

When an incredulous Langer asked, "Why can't these men have the right to choose the treatment they want and need?" the collective answer was: "Nothing else is needed."

Evidence was introduced by Dr. Spears to disclose the "intimate relationship between the American Medical Association and the Veterans Administration in their program to deprive veterans of chiropractic care." This took the form of an article in *Medical Economics*, January 1953, describing organized resistance to the American Legion's 1952 resolution demanding recognition of chiropractic for veterans: "... this chiropractic resolution would have been passed without question if it had not been for the hard and effective work of one man..." followed by a recommendation that the American Medical Association "give official praise to the doctor whose efforts defeated the will of convention delegates in behalf of their suffering buddies." This was designated as a "clear cut victory for the physicians." Reference was made in the same magazine to the Legion's 1950 national convention in California, where the resolution was passed and the Legion went on record as urging the VA to mandate chiropractic treatment. However, the article continued: "The mere passage of the resolution was a thumping victory for the chiropractors," and plans to defeat a repetition of the success in 1953 at St. Louis were outlined.[7]

Spears also quoted from the *New York State Journal of Medicine*: "In the State of New York, we are not talking about licensing chiropractors. In the State of New York, we are talking about the destruction of the chiropractors..." That was dated September 1, 1949.

Though the VA physicians denied they were governed by the American Medical Association, they acknowledged membership in that body, and freely conceded the VA's medical advisory committee consists of prominent AMA stalwarts.

In addition to the veterans who testified in person at the hearings were many letters from veterans appealing to the President, to Congresswoman Rogers, to the Veterans Administration, Senator Langer, to U.S. congressmen and senators, to the American Legion, to Disabled American Veterans, to Veterans of Foreign Wars, and to state and national service officers, "all pleading for, or demanding, chiropractic health care at government expense." This correspondence, which was entered in the hearing record, contained the same general message: "I am sick. I have been a patient in a Veterans hospital (or several VA facilities) without relief. I am now taking chiropractic treatment at my own expense but must discontinue because my money is gone. Am I to continue to suffer, or to die, because the Veterans Administration will not recognize chiropractic?"[8]

Clear from the testimony was that the employment of chiropractic in the VA was not permitted under present law. This point was emphasized in this exchange between Chairman Langer and Donald C. Knapp, the VA's legislative director:

Langer: "As I understand it... you gentlemen claim that under the law you cannot permit chiropractors in these (VA) institutions, is that right?"

Knapp: "That is the legal position."

Langer: "It is not a matter of your willingness or unwillingness, but you are simply obeying the law?"

Knapp: "That is correct."

Subsequent questioning disclosed that the VA opposed any amendment to Public Law 293, which would allow chiropractic services in VA hospitals or on an out-patient basis.

Langer: "I want to find out why a veteran who goes out to fight for his country who wants chiropractic treatment should not have it, and why you oppose it. What is the objection if a fellow wants a chiropractor to come in? Why should he not have the right?"

Knapp: "The authorized professional services are medical, dental and nursing, and the law limits the eligibility for appointment in the (VA) Medical Service to persons who hold the degree of doctor of medicine or doctor of osteopathy from schools approved by the Administrator, and who have completed an internship satisfactory to the Administrator, and who are licensed to practice medicine, surgery or osteopathy."

Langer: "Why does the Veterans Administration object to the chiropractors coming in? Why are they interested in keeping the word 'chiropractor' out of the law?"

Knapp: "It is their opinion... that the veteran needs the services of the professional man trained in medicine and surgery."

Referring to Congresswoman Edith Rogers' bill to authorize chiropractic in the Veterans Administration, Langer asked whether the VA's opposition is "so deep seated that in the event the House bill were passed by Congress that the VA would urge the President to veto the bill?"

Knapp demurred that he was "not in a position to speculate on that question." [9]

Later testimony by Dr. Herman Kretschmar, the VA's inquiry division director, reemphasized the VA's opposition to any legislation to recognize chiropractic: "After some discussion it was moved, seconded and unanimously passed that the Special Medical Advisory Board definitely is opposed to the inclusion of chiropractors for appointment in the Department of Medicine and Surgery."

It was Kretschmar who opened this aspect of testimony by saying, "If chiropractic treatment is indicated... it can be accomplished by physical therapy in the Department of Medicine and Surgery, under supervision of practitioners of the regular schools of medicine." [10]

Adm. Joel T. Boone, the VA's chief of medicine and surgery, was the last witness called. Although admitting he knew nothing about the profession, Boone said that he still disapproved of chiropractic as a treatment option for veterans, adding: "I do not think it would be becoming of me to discuss the merits of chiropractic. I have never been to a chiropractor, I have never associated with them, and I must say, I guess that Dr. Spears is the first one I have ever met." Boone committed himself only as subscribing to the VA's unfavorable report on H.R. 54 mandating chiropractic care for veterans.[11]

In summary, the May and June hearings forecast: H.R. 54 would receive more vigorous support; a new bill would be written (if H.R. 54 failed) spelling out the Veterans Administration's responsibility to furnish chiropractic care for veterans; impetus given to the several veterans' organizations in their demand for chiropractic at government expense.[12]

Concluding the hearings, Chairman Langer announced, "We are not adjourning this hearing... we are recessing it. The staff will go over this matter and consider what further testimony they want to take."

The Denver press noted that while several senators had been assigned to the subcommittee, Chairman Langer was the only one who attended the hearings in Washington. The eleven disabled veterans who testified had been transported from Denver by Spears Hospital.[13]

By midsummer, Langer called for the investigation to reopen, with the probe now moving to the Tenth U.S. Circuit Court, Denver.

On August 26, the subcommittee heard testimony from an unspecified number of veterans who had notified Senator Langer in advance of their willingness to appear, as well as other witnesses.[14]

Langer had already been at Spears Hospital for 10 days, reportedly as a patient. While he did not confirm this, he did admit that he had been taking evidence informally from 30 other veterans who were patients.[15]

But the biggest news from the renewed investigation was Langer's angry blast at what he called the conspiracy on the part of the press and the medical profession to discredit chiropractic. His charge came during testimony from Dr. Orin E. Madson, a Wayne University chemistry professor and chairman of the Michigan Basic Science Board. Reportedly near tears, Madson testified that in his view "the press and medics had combined to block veterans from receiving government-paid chiropractic treatments."[16] "The *Denver Post* and other newspapers complain that the veterans are getting too much," Langer charged, "yet (they) are willing to pass out billions all over the world."

Langer denounced the AMA for its stand against hospitalization for veterans with non-service connected disabilities, and also accused the nation's press of engaging in a "conspiracy of silence" for ignoring veterans' pleas for chiropractic care. "The press is supposed to be free," Langer thundered as he pointed to the alleged conspiracy, "but what can be done to give veterans a fair deal when the newspapers and the medical profession combine to make veterans look less worthy?" He also criticized the *Denver Post* of partiality when it gave page one play to a recent speech by Dr. Edward J. McCormick, president of the AMA, who called for cutbacks in VA services and not giving similar play to Dr. Madson's defense of free chiropractic care for veterans.[17]

During the afternoon, the hearing shifted to Spears Hospital, with Dr. Spears, Senator Langer, subcommittee attorney Wayne Smithey, and a court reporter sitting around a large table in the lobby to take testimony from six bedfast patients, one a World War I veteran. Afterward, the hearings were adjourned.

The first official government reactions to the Denver hearings were in a statement from VA deputy medical director Dr. R.A. Wolford reiterating that "it has no authority to employ chiropractors," and a letter from Budget Director Joseph M. Dodge to the House Veterans Subcommittee saying "the Eisenhower administration believes the government has gone about as far as it can go with the veterans medical program." Looking ahead to a probable retention of the draft, Dodge said, "The time will come when substantially all the adult male population will be veterans and the government will be confronted with a critical problem in attempting to provide them with hospital care."[18]

A skeptical *Post* editorial suggested that the Langer hearings might have been more publicity than substance:

> Denverites who are not acquainted with Senator William Langer (Rep.) of North Dakota and his occasional sponsorship of unorthodox ideas may be puzzled by the vehemence of his charge that newspapers and the medical profession have conspired to discredit chiropractic.
>
> These charges came as the senator opened a hearing in Denver which is intended to show that war veterans suffering from disease or injury should be allowed to have chiropractic care at government expense, rather than medical care, if they wish it.
>
> Some war veterans who have been patients at a local chiropractic hospital, some chiropractors and possibly some non-veteran enthusiasts for chiropractic are expected to testify. Senator Langer himself has been under the care of the local hospital.
>
> In his typical free-swinging style, the senator threw a lot of punches at the opening session. He insinuated that newspapers are not "free" if they object to treatment – at taxpayers' expense – of veterans whose illnesses or injuries are in no way connected with their military duty.
>
> The inference was that newspapers are controlled by the American Medical Association. The press has been accused of lots of things. Senator Langer is entitled to take his turn.
>
> We find from a quick look at the Congressional Record that the senator's interest in "cures" not endorsed by the medical profession is not entirely new. Back in May, 1951, after the National Cancer Institute had refused to study the cancer "cures" claimed by the Hoxsey Cancer clinic at Dallas, Texas, Senator Langer proposed that a senate committee make the investigation Mr. Hoxsey had requested.
>
> At that time the U.S. pure food and drug administration had already looked into "cancer" medicine Mr. Hoxsey was selling by mail and had sought an injunction to stop him.
>
> Since then, the fifth U.S. circuit court of appeals has decided there should be an

injunction and the U.S. supreme court has found no ground for interfering.

The federal district court in Dallas has issued an injunction which is unacceptable to the government, in that it merely requires Mr. Hoxsey to say on the labels attached to his medicine that there is a difference of opinion regarding its efficacy. Hence, the government is back in the circuit court seeking an injunction in different language at this time.

We find, likewise, that in March, 1952, Senator Langer placed in the Congressional Record a lengthy article by the director of public relations of the National Chiropractic Association.

Ostensibly, the purpose of the article was to commemorate "Correct Posture Week." But it also turned out to be a complete "plug" for the chiropractic profession. It pointed out that only four states did not license chiropractors. It mentions that G.I. schooling at public expense is given veterans who want to study chiropractic and it said various veterans organizations, including the American Legion, are behind the move to require "free" Veterans Administration chiropractic treatment for those ex-servicemen who ask for it.

If the senator wants to become the champion of cures and treatments not endorsed by medical men, we do not object. At the same time we reserve the right to object if we believe the VA "free" medical and hospital program includes veterans who are not entitled to it. We also would object if Senator Langer's hearings resulted in a serious attempt to add "free" VA chiropractic service to the expensive "free" medical service already being provided.[19]

At least one *Post* reader was suspicious of the newspaper's motives:

Let's be good natured and intelligent in the matter of Senator William Langer's espousal of "unorthodox" causes. Senator Langer believes veterans should have the benefit of chiropractic as a health service financed by the government, in the same manner that medical and surgical therapies are provided by the veterans administration. Unorthodox, no doubt, but what progress in all history was accomplished by adhering strictly to the orthodox line? A strictly orthodox policy would leave this nation still a liege of Great Britain. Complete subservience to orthodoxy would have narrowed religion to one church. Henry Ford departed from orthodox horse-and-buggy transportation when he created the "tin lizzie."

Why didn't you include Senator Langer's espousal of Sister Kenny's treatment of polio, after she tried vainly to give it to the medical profession? Without Langer's support, Sister Kenny would have been sunk without a trace, and polio victims now normal, healthy citizens, would either be in their graves or hopeless cripples.

It is The Post's privilege, and duty, to oppose overspending on veterans. However, your implication that chiropractic added to present VA health services would increase expense to taxpayers is down the wrong alley. The reverse is true: Chiropractic costs less to apply, and would eliminate from disability rolls many thousands of veterans whose afflictions now prevent them from supporting themselves and their families. A controlled test to prove this point has been offered and rejected by the veterans administration.[20]

Langer's interest in the Kenny polio treatment became part of the record during the Senate subcommittee's Washington hearings when he rebutted a VA witness who had expressed a dim view of any unapproved therapy:

A few years ago, a lady known as Sister Kenny came here. She went to every senator, or at least a lot of them. And no one would give her the courtesy of a real interview. She finally came to my office, and some of you doctors who have been here some time know that we got the (Washington) *Times Herald* interested... and we finally had her take some cases in front of 400 doctors here in the city of Washington. The State of Minnesota had provided funds for placement of a Kenny Clinic within the Mayo Clinic at Rochester. And yet, when the woman came here, practically every doctor opposed her. Some called her a quack. Are any of you familiar with that situation? [21]

Dr. Tiffany Lawyer, the witness Langer was admonishing, responded that the main objection to Sister Kenny were her theories regarding the disease, not her treatment as such. "Her contribution was a very definite one." [22] On this note, the hearings ended.

The "conspiracy" between organized medicine and the press which Langer had charged was the "Code of Cooperation" adopted in Denver April 16, 1948, and subsequently by the majority of country's print and television media. In December 1946, the Colorado Medical Society had hired a New York media firm to study problems of public relations in medicine. Langer, like Leo Spears and others, believed the "code" to be nothing less than a vehicle to censor and manipulate medical news. (*See Appendix H.*)

"Far from censoring the news, the plan was to take away as many gags as possible," said the *Rocky Mountain News.* "The whole trend and purpose is for fuller, freer flow of medical news and health reports." [23]

The results of the committee-of-one Langer hearings on "Medical Monopoly in the Military" – 550 pages of testimony – went the way of all Congressional rhetoric, into an obscure file to reside for the rest of time somewhere in the dusty bins of the National Archives.

As Republican Senator William Langer (he did not use a middle initial) was always quirky, unpredictable, even mischievous, a brief review of his rather remarkable political career is worthy. The following is from the *New York Times* on the occasion of Mr. Langer's death, Nov. 8, 1959:

William Langer, North Dakota's insurgent Republican Senator since 1941, died in his sleep today of a heart ailment. He was 73 years old.

The colorful Mr. Langer, who was anything but a party regular during his forty-five years of politicking, had phenomenal success in getting elected and re-elected – as Governor of his state and as U.S. Senator. He was noted for his many dissenting votes on great national decisions.

Last year, when Mr. Langer was denied endorsement of his state's Republican convention, he ran in the primary as an independent and carried every county in the state, defeating Lieut. Gov. Clyde Duffy, who was backed by the party. He then went on to win his fourth Senate term in the general election ...

The Senator's body was found by a daughter... who had been staying with him in recent weeks. Mr. Langer had not been well since the death of his wife, Lydia, on Aug. 4. He had returned home two weeks ago after three weeks' treatment at George Washington Univ. Hospital for pneumonia.

Visitors to the Senate could always spot Mr. Langer by the cigar he always chewed. It was never lit and always still in a cellophane wrapper. At home in North Dakota he was known as Big Bill and sometimes as Wild Bill.

His oratory was of the roaring, desk-pounding and arm-waving type, but since an illness in 1957 he had slowed down a bit. A clerk read most of his prepared speeches because of his failing eyesight. But he was his old self when he spoke extemporaneously.

Mr. Langer often delighted his colleagues with his boyish sense of humor. He once moved to an empty chair in front of an orating fellow Republican Senator and mischievously plucked cigars from the speaker's breast pocket until the orator sat down in befuddlement.

Mrs. Langer had been the Senator's political lieutenant. She was the former Lydia Cady of New York. They met when Mr. Langer was studying at Columbia University. He received a B.A. degree there in 1910, winning the Roelker Medal as the outstanding student. He was president of his class, valedictorian and voted "the biggest politician, nosiest student, most popular man and the one most likely to succeed."

Mr. Langer was born Sept. 30, 1886, on his parent's farm near Everest in what was then Dakota Territory. He was 3 years old when North Dakota was admitted to the union and not quite 4 when his father ... became a member of the first State Legislature.

Before attending Columbia, Mr. Langer had taken a law degree from the University of North Dakota and passed the bar examination at 18. He had to wait until he was 21 to practice in North Dakota. But in 1911 he hung out his shingle in Mandan, in Marion County across the Missouri from Bismark, the capital.

His political career was soon under way with his election as State's Attorney from Marion County in 1914. He became Attorney General in 1916, and was defeated for Governor as an independent in 1920.

Then came a lapse of twelve years in which Mr. Langer, who had moved his law business to Bismark, where it prospered, held no elective office. But in 1932 he was elected Governor the only Republican Governor elected in a state carried by Franklin D. Roosevelt, who was elected to his first term as President that year.

However, Mr. Langer was removed on July 17, 1934, by the Supreme Court of North Dakota because he had been convicted of soliciting political contributions from Federal employees. After his removal from office, his wife was nominated for the Governorship, but lost. Mr. Langer appealed his conviction, won and was elected for the 1937-39 term.

Senator Langer was long associated with the North Dakota Nonpartisan League, a farmer political organization. But he broke with it in 1956 when it chose to file its candidates as Democrats.

Mr. Langer first tried for the Senate in 1938 but was defeated. He was elected in 1940, but when he came to take his seat on Jan. 3, 1941, he was confronted with a petition by eight North Dakota voters that he not be seated. Although the Senate Privileges and Elections Committee voted (that he be barred), when the issue came to the floor early in 1942 the Senate voted... that he retain the seat he had been allowed provisionally.[24]

With respect to his removal as governor over illegal campaign contributions, Langer seemed to take pride in his dispute with the state, his biography in *Who's Who in America* stating: "Only person ever arrested in an English-speaking country for filing an affidavit of prejudice against a judge." [25]

9.

The Grand Jury

District Attorney Burt Keating announced on January 30, 1954, that he intended to conduct a probe of medical fraud and quackery in Denver and would strongly recommend that the county grand jury undertake a "sweeping" investigation with an eye toward returning indictments. He indicated that he could justify the probe from a "mountain of information" gathered about certain medical practices and frauds by the Denver Better Business Bureau and the *Denver Post* during a joint 14-month investigation, and said he would outline his case to the new grand jury when it convened February 2.[1]

Spokesmen for the various licensed health professions applauded the district attorney's announcement with the usual perfunctory statements. Dr. Lawrence Bertholf, president of the Rocky Mountain Chiropractic College and executive secretary of the state chiropractic association, went a bit further: "We know we have some fellows in our own profession who should not be allowed to practice. On investigation, we find that the state laws are so weak... it is virtually impossible for our Board of Examiners to clean them out." Bertholf said his association would soon meet "to draw up a profession-wide war against illegitimate chiropractic practitioners."

It was Tuesday morning, April 6, 1954. Federal agents arrived at Spears Hospital in mid-morning with seizure warrants for three electrical devices allegedly used to diagnose and treat cancer and other diseases. Stunned by the unexpected visit, Dr. Leo Spears protested that the devices, called neuromicrometers, were on loan to the hospital by the manufacturer and were used for research. Spears warned, "If you take these machines there's going to be trouble." U.S. Marshall D.T. Potter listened quietly, then said, "Well, now, I'll tell you something. I've got a court order here signed by Judge Lee Knous that tells me to take these machines. Now, I don't know how much trouble there's going to be, but I'm going to take these machines and I'm going to take them right now."[2]

The seizure orders filed by the U.S. attorney at the request of the Federal Food and Drug Administration (FDA) also described a booklet supplied by the manufacturer of the devices in which "false and misleading claims" were made. The government said the booklet, entitled "Manual of Research Findings," claimed that the neuromicrometer was "effective for diagnosing sickness, the level of cell life, one's health index, one's degree of reserve energy, internal toxicity, lung ailments, circulatory disorders, cancer, emotional undertones and resentments." [3]

Whatever resentment Spears felt at the surprise government action must have exacerbated on the spot. The spectacle was covered by the entire coterie of the local press, which had been tipped off beforehand.

The next day, much calmer, Spears called a news conference to talk about the government raid. "We don't use these machines for treatment," he repeated. "The newspapers will say they are quack equipment but that's not the case. They are used for legitimate purposes in a legitimate hospital. We use them in research. We can use anything in research." [4] Then, he made this astonishing announcement:

> Now take this down carefully. We have definitely found the causes of cancer. Note that I say causes and not cause. We have completed our research. We stand ready and willing to prove this statement to any unbiased committee or commission or group of newspaper people or any scientific mind capable of understanding these facts. Note that I said we are no longer looking for the cause of cancer. We have already found the causes of cancer. We will continue to do our scientific work here despite outrages such as this.
>
> I don't understand why this sudden attack unless it is for the purpose of smearing the good name of Spears Chiropractic Hospital in an effort to destroy this institution. If it is, it is only a continuation of a series of attacks heaped us during the past 30 years. Indeed, it may be one phase of a rumored pending attack calculated, we understand, to destroy us. We, however, have no fears, because we have never misrepresented, defrauded, lied, cheated, or done any other illegal or immoral thing. Our sole purpose in life has been and will continue to be to help suffering humanity.

The removal of the neuromicrometers from the hospital was not an isolated event; in fact, the same and similar devices were being confiscated by federal order elsewhere in Colorado and throughout the country.

Nothing had been made public about the extent of the grand jury probe until late March 1954, when the secret panel requested an extension of its normal three-months service. Then, on April 12, the *Denver Post* reported that the jury had subpoenaed the records of Spears Hospital.[5]

The subpoena had demanded practically every record and journal kept by the institution, each specifically listed: cash receipts, check registers, general ledgers, balance sheets, profit and loss statements, records of patient days, records of patient admissions and discharges, records of rates charged and paid by patients, accounts receivable, statements for professional and other fees paid by the hospital, accounts payable and purchase invoices. Also demanded were personal and corporate tax returns, minutes of corporate meetings and copies of all investments held by individuals and the institution. Subpoenas were also issued for Dr. Leo Spears, the hospital's bookkeeper and all trustees of the corporation.

As expected, the subpoenas were contested almost immediately. Charles Ginsberg filed a motion in District Court to quash the order, demanding that the court establish a valid purpose for such a "searching examination" before allowing the subpoenas to take effect.[6]

On April 14, in what was described as an "unprecedented judicial inquiry into grand jury proceedings," District Judge Edward C. Day said he would appear personally before the panel that very evening to determine if it had sufficient grounds to seize the books and records of the hospital.[7,8]

Day's decision came at the end of a contentious hearing on Spears' motion to quash. Sparks flew when Ginsberg denounced the Better Business Bureau (BBB) and the *Denver Post* as the "moving spirits" behind the subpoenas. He described the BBB as a "self-contained guardian of public morals" and said the *Post's* handling of recent news involving his client was a "reckless display of wanton disregard for personal rights unprecedented in the history of Colorado newspapering."[9]

"By virtue of recent news space devoted to Dr. Spears," Ginsberg said the hospital could be destroyed in the process. "What records have any bearing on any criminal offense?" he demanded to know. "The Spears institution is eager to lay before the public any and all pertinent facts. It has nothing to hide. But records cannot be delivered merely to satisfy the idle curiosity of jurors or the ulterior motives of the moving spirits."

Melvin Rossman, deputy district attorney representing the grand jury, denied the accusations: "The grand jury is not on a fishing expedition. These records are necessary and important to arrive at a decision as to whether crimes have or have not been committed. I can state categorically that the grand jury is not acting on the behalf or any newspaper or civil agency, but only in the interests of the people of the city and county of Denver."

After meeting with the grand jury, Judge Day upheld the subpoenas and appointed a local accounting firm to begin auditing the books in a special room at the hospital.[10-12]

An exasperated Leo Spears declared in a news release that he would be willing to let "anybody in the world" examine his books and records, even offering to place copies in the public library. "Everytime somebody jumps on us legally, they want to see our books. That raises the question in the public mind that something is wrong with our books. We want to end that idea forever. There's nothing wrong with our books."[13]

A new ingredient was added to the thickening stew when, on May 7, a top aide of Sen. Wlliam Langer arrived in Denver to investigate "possible reprisal action" against Dr. Spears. Sidney Davis told the press that the senator's concerns were discussed with both the U.S. and district attorneys and that more would be said in the near future.[14,15] But Leo Spears had much more to say:

(When I testified) in Washington, I named no names but it was obvious that I meant the medical fraternity has set up a monopoly in the VA hospitals. I don't know if (this) is a reprisal action because of my testimony or whether it is the same old conspiracy. Sen. Langer was here last week and talked to me. I gathered he receives the Denver newspapers in Washington and decided himself here must be some sort of reprisal action going on... It looks like my enemies are closing in for the kill.[16]

Ever since the grand jury revealed its intention to make a full-scale probe of medical quackery, a steady stream of witnesses had appeared before the panel. On May 13, more than three months into the hearings, its first report to the court was eagerly anticipated.

Perhaps surprisingly, indictments were returned against two naturopaths, one of whom had already left the state. Both were charged with practicing medicine and chiropractic without a license. The report went so far as recommending naturopathic medicine be outlawed in Colorado, although news accounts provided no explanation for the grand jury's opposition. Colorado laws dealing with the misdemeanor practice of medicine and chiropractic were oddly dissimilar: unlicensed medical practitioners could receive a maximum of 30 days in jail and a $500 fine, while the same violation of the chiropractic law called for a $200 fine and a year in jail.[17]

Also advocated by the grand jury were stricter laws to protect the public from interstate movement of misbranded foods, drugs, cosmetics and healing devices, and tighter restrictions on use of the title "doctor."

A week before the grand jury's interim report, the *Post* released information that the panel was looking into medical devices: "An indication of the panel's thinking was the revelation that the jury had called FDA director Ralph L. Horst to testify. He testified for over two hours, reportedly concerning fake electronic medical devices." It was a week after Horst's appearance when three devices were seized from Spears Hospital, and a week after that when the jury subpoenaed the hospital's records.

But the grand jury's most blistering criticism was leveled at "certain advertising practices" in the healing arts, especially testimonials claiming cures and touting "painless" treatment. It also recommended legislation to curb such advertising.

While the report made no direct mention of Dr. Spears, the *Denver Post* had these observations: "There was a terse 'no comment' from Chiropractor Leo L. Spears, Denver's biggest user of testimonial advertising. Spears himself has authored a book entitled *Spears Painless System*, while at the same time the chiropractic board is on record that advertising 'painless chiropractic treatment' is unethical." [18]

About advertising, the jury said: "Although advertising per se may be necessary in some instances, the profession has long ruled within its ranks against any form of advertising by physicians, but since there are branches of the healing arts outside the medical profession, it would seem that legislation is needed to protect the public."

The jury's recommendations were supported by the Colorado Chiropractic Association: "We want to make every effort to strengthen and advance our profession. We are against any advertised claims of individual superiority, the advertising of cures and the use of testimonials. Our profession will support any move to protect the public." [19]

"It is my God-given right," Leo Spears declared in his first public statement defending his use of testimonial advertising, and claimed any legislation outlawing it would be unconstitutional. "All testimonials," he said, "are strictly voluntary, spontaneous and unsolicited." "Advertising is the life blood of business, industry and the healing professions, including medical. It is the only way the public has of learning about the development or existence of worthwhile products. Since about the only free publicity the chiropractic profession receives is criticism and condemnation, chiropractors have to use paid advertising to acquaint the people with its healing virtues. Why should it be illegal for chiropractors to take their message to sick people?"

Spears restated his position on testimonial advertising in a long editorial published in the hospital's *Spears Sanigram.* (*See Appendix I.*)

On the same subject, the *Denver Post* reported that a U.S. Circuit Court of Appeals, in a Texas case, had ruled that patients may not testify competently regarding their own medical conditions or the success of treatment given them. [20]

Adding an unusual note to the investigations, Dr. Spears, in a letter to the grand jury, offered to testify about "conspiratorial activities to destroy his institution," which included the release of misleading information connecting his institution "with the deliberations of this grand jury." He added in a postscript to District Attorney Keating that he would be pleased to testify freely upon "any and all matters with which the grand jury may be concerned." [21]

The district attorney said Spears would appear before the jury because of his willingness to do so. Spears was invited to appear before the jury three times before it ended its probe. [22-27]

In its final report on July 1, the jury again blasted testimonial advertising and charged that "some healers use testimonials claiming cures of patients who are dead when the ads are circulated." [28]

Dr. Spears called the final report "a clean bill of health for us," despite the blast at advertising. "I never for a moment believed we would be indicted." *Spears Sanigram* characterized the proceedings as a "failure":

> The most recent, and probably the foulest, attempt to discredit Spears Chiropractic Santarium and Hospital - and, with it, the entire chiropractic profession - ended in failure June 30, 1954, when the Denver County Grand Jury, despite great pressure, failed to indict.
>
> This grand jury session was historic in more than one respect: (1) It was the longest ever conducted in Denver - nearly six months. (2) The members sternly resisted pressures to return true bills that might have done lasting damage to Chiropractic. They are

to be congratulated on their complete honesty and fairness in rejecting trumped-up charges on which a less resolute body might have acted. (3) Jurors invited Dr. Leo Spears to appear before them when it became apparent that they might not otherwise hear his testimony or that of the profession he represents. This unprecented action occupied three night sessions of the jury. After Dr. Spears' first entirely voluntary appearance he was twice requested to return when the jurors discovered in him an area of information that had been almost entirely closed to them.[29]

The report was critical of both the Board of Medical Examiners and Board of Chiropractic Examiners for what it called "a general attitude of reluctance" to proceed against shady healers and medics, to which State Senator Neal Bishop announced his intention to introduce legislation imposing curbs on testimonial advertising and the advertising practices of "some chiropractors." He said his bill was aimed at "tightly policing" abuses in business solicitation and had the support of the Colorado Chiropractic Association. When asked if the bill had Dr. Leo Spears in mind, he answered, "Yes - to curb and keep within bounds the advertising of Dr. Spears. I might say that I appeared three times before the grand jury, and I promised that jury that I would come forth with this kind of proposal if I ever sat in the Colorado legislature again." A longtime member of the legislature, Bishop was re-elected to his senate seat in November 1954 after a two-year absence during which time he ran an unsuccessful campaign for lieutenant governor.

The Bishop bill would empower the state to revoke the privileges of any licensed health practitioner who employed testimonial advertising and unearned specialty claims. "I'm not trying to put anybody out of business with this legislation," he cautioned. Citing phone directory advertising, he added, "I'm just trying to curb this kind of foolishness that misleads the public and damages the profession." [30]

Spears Hospital publicist Ed Hoover fired back that Bishop's bill was aimed at discrediting Dr. Leo Spears and would "rob the people of his skilled services." In an open letter to the state senate, Hoover said Spears' nationwide advertising was necessary because the "controlled press refuses to give its readership free access to this information which is so vital to the public." Calling Spears "a man with a message," Hoover charged that many chiropractors are not interested in "extending the benefits of their profession beyond their own selfish interests." "It is true... and this applies to you, Neal," the letter concluded.[31]

While the accomplishments of the 1954 grand jury were debatable--its find--ing objectionable the competitive advertising of eyeglasses and posting of fees in doctors' offices, among other things--for Leo Spears it was a prologue.

10.
Suing for Damages

The Maier Case

Charging "malice, fraud and deceipt," Dr. Leo Spears filed a suit for libel against Dr. Julian Maier on January 14, 1950. The charges grew out of the death in 1946 of Mrs. Susia A. Bowers, a former Spears patient, at St. Luke's Hospital, Denver, and notations on the death certificate by Maier, the attending physician, that the patient "died from criminal neglect at Spears Sanitarium." Spears was claiming libel because a copy of the death certificate with the notations was published December 3, 1949, in the *Rocky Mountain News* and was available for public inspection in the files of State Department of Health. He branded Maier's notations as "false and baseless" and asked $300,000 in damages.[1,2]

In preliminary motions before District Court Judge Edward C. Day, defense attorney Philip Van Cise asked for dismissal of the suit, arguing that a corporation cannot sue for libel under Colorado laws. Further, he argued that Maier's notation on the death certificate was a privileged communication and not libelous itself, and that if the clinic was libeled, the alleged libel needed explaining. Van Cise further argued that Dr. Maier was compelled by law to state what he believed caused the patient's death.[3]

Judge Day refused the motion to dismiss and held that a corporation can sue for libel in Colorado. He also ruled that Spears must show special damages. Agreeing that the notation on the death certificate can be considered privileged, he further held that its publication could present "a claim upon which relief might be granted." [4-6]

Spears' motion to require the State Health Department to produce the original death certificate was upheld. This motion brought up the possibility that the certificate may have been tampered with.[7-9]

Trial proceeded on September 7, 1951, before Judge William A. Black. Given Dr. Spears' long history of battle with the medical profession, this latest encounter seemed to especially fascinate the public.

Charles Ginsberg, representing the plaintiff, quizzed Dr. Maier closely concerning the sequence of events leading to Mrs. Bowers' arrival at St. Luke's

Hospital.[10]

"I agreed to see the patient at the request of Dr. Hamilton Barnard if she could be admitted to St. Luke's Hospital," Maier testified. "That evening I was advised by Dr. Hall (an intern) that she had arrived."

"What time and on what day?"

"June 3, 1946, about 9:30 or 10 p.m."

"Where were you?"

"At my home."

"How long would it take you to drive to the hospital?"

"About 15 or 20 minutes."

"Did Dr. Hall tell you she was an emergency case?"

"He told me she was quite ill."

"Yet you didn't go there to see her?"

"That is right."

"When did you first see Susia Bowers?"

"June 4 - close to 8:30 in the morning."

When asked what care was provided for the patient between the night of June 3 and the morning of June 4, Maier said he had telephoned orders for medication to ease the pain, and intravenous glucose and salt solutions to prepare the patient for possible surgery.

Dr. Maier testified that he turned the patient over to Dr. Robert Packard, who determined that the patient had a perforated duodenal ulcer and peritonitis and would not survive without surgery, but allowed that he had not attended the operation himself.[11]

After admitting that Mrs. Bowers died following surgery, Maier was asked if it was still his contention that the patient died as a result of "criminal neglect" at Spears Sanitarium? "She was desperately ill," was his response.[12]

Asked if he had talked to *Rocky Mountain News* reporter Ken Wayman, Maier said he had received a call from Dr. Roy Cleere, who informed him that a reporter was in his office investigating the Spears case. The reporter then got on the line.[13]

"You knew he was a reporter? And he inquired of you about your statement on the death certificate?"

"He asked me to identify and authenticate the death statement."

"And you did?"

"Yes."

"And when you were talking to Wayman, did you not seek to tell him you wanted to change anything in the document signed by you?"

"No."

When Philip Van Cise objected, Ginsberg shouted, "We are trying to show that a conspiracy of medical doctors, headed by Dr. Roy L. Cleere, is trying to drive Dr. Leo Spears to destruction. We want to show by a chain of actions that this is part of a conspiracy, and that these physicians consulted with a newspaper reporter for the very purpose of getting notoriety." With this, Ginsberg suddenly clutched his left side and exclaimed, "I can't go on." [14]

Judge Black immediately called a recess, then advised Ginsberg that he should seek medical assistance to determine if he could continue with the case. He was taken to a room next to the judge's chambers where Dr. Spears administered to him. After resting for ten minutes, Ginsberg told the court that he was ready to continue arguments. Spears explained that his attorney has worked very hard on this case and was exhausted. "Mr. Ginsberg would have been in very serious condition if he had not had immediate treatment." At this point, the trial was recessed for the day. [15]

When testimony resumed the next afternoon, Spears was cross-examined by Philip Van Cise. [16]

Denying that Mrs. Susia Bowers ever displayed symptoms of a perforated ulcer, Spears said, "She wouldn't have lived with a perforated ulcer. We would not hesitate referring her to a medical doctor or a surgeon if there were any reason for doing so."

Q. "She suddenly got worse while she was at your sanitarium, did she not?"
A. "Not systemically, I'd say."
Q. "She walked into your institution?"
A. "I didn't see her when she entered."
Q. "And she was dismissed per ambulance?"
A. "I didn't see her."

Dr. Spears then answered in detail describing the treatment given the patient.

Asked to describe the specific damages suffered through publication of an article in the *Rocky Mountain News* on December 3, 1949, Spears answered, "Loss of considerable money; reduction in the number of patients, particularly a great reduction in the number of new patients; loss of some $3 million the Chiropractic Research Foundation refuses to give us – a fund they promised us; inability to raise funds in a drive we had contemplated; loss of credit; refusal of publishers to give us 10 million papers we'd already ordered; loss of the effect of $118,500 worth of publicity already put out that should have doubled the business of our institution, and instead of that our business went down. Also the loss of funds with which we could have treated very many poor children. We value lives more than we do money." [17]

He was next asked to explain why he filed the suit only against Dr. Maier and not against Governor Lee Knous, Attorney General John Metzger and Dr. Roy Cleere, or against the *Rocky Mountain News*.

Charles Ginsberg objected to the line of questioning on the grounds that it was up to the the plaintiff to determine which parties he wished to sue. Ginsberg argued that the privilege of signing a death certificate belonged to the physician last in charge of the patient; that it was surgeon George Packard and not Dr. Maier who was last in charge. "Privileges do not extend to republication," Ginsberg further argued, referring to Maier's confirmation of the death certificate in a newspaper story.[18]

When Ginsberg argued that it was against a recent state Supreme Court decision to allow members of one branch of the healing arts to "pass judgment" on a competitive healing arts, he was overruled.[19-21]

Dr. Roy Cleere was called to the witness stand for cross-examination about his acquaintance with Dr. Maier. He testified that he met with Maier and Denver attorney Kenaz Huffman for lunch in 1946 and that the latter had invited him. Asked if Huffman explained the purpose of the meeting, Cleere answered: "He told me he was the attorney for the Bowers family and that he understood that there should be a death certificate filed with the state health department relating to Mrs. Bowers. He apparently wanted to be retained as an attorney by the Board of Health."

"Did he ask that specifically?"

"He stated that he'd had previous litigation involving Dr. Spears and thought that he might be of great benefit in a hearing before the Board of Health. I told Huffman that I had no authority to hire an attorney and suggested that he consult with John W. Metzger, who was then the attorney general."

Cleere also said that Huffman asked if he were familiar with several other cases involving the Spears institution, and admitted that he gave a photostatic copy of Mrs. Bowers' death certificate to the reporter on December 1, 1949.[22]

The long trial came to an end on Friday, September 20, after daylong closing arguments. The jury began deliberations at about 4:45 p.m. and returned its verdict at 11:32 p.m. They had ruled against Dr. Spears.[23]

It was a bitter case for everyone involved, and one of the most memorable in Colorado trial annals. (See Author's Introduction.)

Charles Ginsberg asked for a new trial and was granted 20 days to file a petition. "Naturally, I was shocked at the verdict," he said. "I cannot understand how the jury could possibly reach this verdict under the instructions given it by the court." He added that despite the unsuccessful prosecution of this libel suit, "we'll still follow the policy of not letting any abuse of this type go unchallenged."

Dr. Spears, who was not present for the verdict, was reached for comment the next day and told reporters the jury verdict had no effect on his plans for expanding the hospital. He said a $50 million chiropractic hospital of 12 buildings was still his goal: "We'd have it now if I hadn't been fought by the conspiracy of the medical profession. These lawsuits are defensive measures. That's the reason back of all of them."

In the bid for a new trial in District Court, Ginsberg asserted that defense attorney Van Cise had argued improperly to the jury the testimony of medical doctors about chiropractic treatment. Judge Black denied the petition on December 31, 1951, but gave Spears 30 days to prepare a record for appeal to the Supreme Court.[24]

The libel case finally ended on September 21, 1953, when the Supreme Court struck down the appeal, ruling that the statute of limitations had already expired when the original suit was filed. As to Spears' contention that the trial court had improperly allowed testimony from medical people on the competency of the witnesses representing a competing profession, the court held that witness competency was not the question, but "competency of the evidence sought to be introduced through them."[25] (*See Appendix J.*)

"Malicious Prosecution"

The 1943 arrest and trial of Drs. Leo and Dan Spears on a manslaughter indictment along with the forced closing of the sanitarium was, in their opinion, a "malicious" attempt to harm them professionally and to put the institution out of business. In June 1946, they filed suit against four public health officials and asked $500,000 in damages. But for reasons that are not clear, the case was never prosecuted in a timely manner (one year) and was stricken from the court docket under Rule 18, which provided for such action.

On March 11, 1950, District Court Judge Edward C. Day granted a petition allowing the case to be refiled.[26]

Named as defendants in the action were Dr. Roy Cleere, head of the State Health Department; Dr. R.L. Drinkwater and Mr. Joseph A. Myers, members of the Board of Health when the complaint was filed; and Dr. Carl Schwalb, former Manager of Public Health for the city of Denver. Schwalb had signed the criminal complaint after a coroner's jury ruled that the death of Marion Daugherty at Spears Sanitarium resulted from "gross culpable negligence."

The suit charged that these defendants and "other conspirators" had filed false information with the office of the Denver District Attorney leading to an indictment action.

The complaint also declared that Dr. Leo Spears was suffering mentally and physically from the stress of the long, unresolved prosecution and that his diabetic condition was aggravated by his arrest.

Pre-trial depositions proceeded only sporadically over the next five years, owing to numerous other legal entanglements in which Dr. Spears found himself involved.

Granting a defense motion, District Judge Robert W. Steele ordered Spears to undergo a complete physical examination, but a motion demanding psychiatric evaluation was denied.[27]

As the defense was contending "financial difficulties" had provoked the suit, Dr. Spears' personal income tax records as well as the hospital's income and expenditure ledgers and corporate minutes were ordered into evidence.

During pre-trial depositions in April 1953, before Judge Steele, the hospital's bookkepper testified Dr. Spears' average salary during the previous nine-year period was $7,750. His personal financial dealings, however, were quite complicated.[28]

Testimony revealed that over a period of time Dr. Spears had made several loans to the hospital, one from cash borrowed against securities jointly owned by himself and his then-wife Laura Ellen Spears. Mrs. Spears, who had co-signed demand payment notes, filed suit in January 1953 for $28,592 she maintained belonged to her but was denied by the hospital. The notes, she said, were an arrangement to protect her in the event of Dr. Leo's death.

Remarking on the extraordinary suit brought by Mrs. Spears, the *Denver Post* noted that "since 1943 Dr. Spears and his chiropractic institution have been involved in 39 different District Court actions in Denver."[29]

Dr. J.C. Mendenhall, an internist, reported that he examined Dr. Spears May 28, 1953, on court orders and confirmed a diabetic condition that could well be exacerbated by emotional stress. "This is a rather unusual thing for a diabetic and from his physical standpoint I am not able to find any definite reason why it should react this way." Mendenhall recommended a thorough neurological and psychiatric examination "to see if there is an underlying problem that could be hooked up to his diabetic condition."[30] Dr. Charles A. Rymer, psychiatrist, and Dr. William R. Lipscomb, neurologist, were then appointed by the court to make the recommended evaluations.[31,32]

Depositions in the case had already consumed eight years when, on April 9, 1954, Attorney General Duke Dunbar demanded that Leo Spears be cited for contempt and possibly jailed for refusing to undergo the court-ordered medical examinations and for withholding financial records the court had ordered him to make available for an audit. Dunbar warned that Spears could receive a year in jail for civil contempt and that his refusal to comply with court orders could result in dismissal of the suit.[33,34]

"I have not disobeyed a single order of the court," Spears insisted. "I have gone beyond what I believe to be the purpose of the court in ordering me to undergo an examination and submit our hospital books for inspection. The auditor spent the better part of five weeks checking our books." Spears also said he spent five afternoons with the psychiatrist appointed to examine him, and that his attorney, Charles Ginsberg, felt that was "more than ample time."[35]

A hearing was set for May 13, 1954, for Spears to show cause why he should not be held in contempt, but neither Dr. Spears nor his attorneys were present. Ginsberg succeeded in getting a continuance when he later explained in the judge's chambers that they had made an "honest mistake" in not realizing a hearing had been scheduled that day.[36]

The "time mixup" might have been understandable in view of the fact that Dr. Spears was simultaneously involved in 10 separate legal actions, either in progress or being filed.

Even though neither Spears nor his attorneys were present, the court ordered that the contempt hearing proceed without them.

Accountant Allan Redeker testified that Dr. Spears and his bookkeeper had made it difficult for him by refusing certain records and not providing sufficient workspace, this slowing down what he was allowed to do.

Dr. William Lipscomb said that blood tests showed Spears to be suffering from extreme diabetes which "could cause changes in nervous and brain tissue," but that he had refused a spinal fluid examination because he feared becoming paralyzed.

Psychiatrist Charles Rymer testified that Spears refused to come back after the fifth interview and, therefore, his examination was inconclusive.

After almost 10 years of pre-trial skirmishing, the malicious prosecution suit finally went to trial on Monday, January 16, 1956, before Judge Albert Frantz.[37]

Defense attorney James T. Burke hit hard at Leo Spears during his cross-examination.

"Why didn't you tell Mrs. Daugherty (mother of the deceased) the hospital was not licensed?"

"At the time, our attorney, Frank Seydel, was advising us on how to get a license," Spears answered. "He said the best way was to be charged with populating a hospital without a license. That would get us to court the fastest."

"Your purpose in failing to tell Mrs. Daugherty you were unlicensed was to provoke criminal prosecution?"

"Not criminal prosecution, but prosecution for a civil offense, operating a hospital without a license, a misdemeanor. That was his advice."

"But now you charge these defendants with malicious prosecution?"

"That's what my attorney advised. I didn't know what else to do."

"Did you do anything else to bring yourself into court?"

"I don't recall anything. Get the judge to give us a license in court."

"If a person admits to a crime," Burke argued, "he cannot later charge malicious prosecution."[38, 39]

Charles Ginsberg admitted, "I can't state that was good advice, but because Dr. Spears transgressed the licensing code, that did not warrant filing manslaughter charges. The manslaughter charge was just as ill-advised as the advice given this plaintiff by counsel."

Without any testimony from the defendants, Judge Frantz abruptly dismissed the charges on the basis of Spears' own admission to breaking the law by opening the hospital without a license. Frantz further held that it was District Attorney Davis Rosner, not the defendants, who caused the manslaughter indictment to be filed, and noted that Rosner was not named in the complaint and therefore could not be examined.[40]

A surprise postscript to the trial was Leo Spears' admission that it was a fair decision. "Anyone who heard the evidence could make no other decision." [41]

Restraint of Trade

Charging conspiracy to "restrain trade in the healing arts," Dr. Leo Spears had filed a $3 million damage suit in Federal District Court on December 10, 1949, against the Denver Medical Society and 30 present and former members of the society and the Colorado Board of Health. The damages sought were said to have been the largest within the memory of officials of the federal court. [42,43]

The complaint reviewed the stormy history surrounding the construction and operation of the hospital; attempts to block issuance of a hospital license; the manslaughter indictment; refusal of the Board of Health to allow the institution to be called a "hospital;" accumulated "specious" charges against the institution by the Board of Health "at the suggestion of the medical society;" and revocation of the sanitarium's temporary permit by the board in May 1946.

The complaint also charged that Dr. Roy L. Cleere "often" represented to insurance companies that the Spears Sanitarium was not a hospital under the law. The medical society was charged with "seeking to prevent patients from coming from other states through the channels of commerce" to the sanitarium.

Federal Judge Lee Knous ruled on July 13, 1951, that the court had no jurisdiction over the two-year-old complaint in that Spears was not engaged in interstate commerce, a necessary requirement to maintain the suit in federal court. [44]

On May 10, 1952, the U.S. Tenth Circuit Court of Appeals quashed Spears' claim for damages. "The practice of the healing arts in Colorado, including chiropractic, is wholly local in character," the opinion read in part. "There was no intent to injure, obstruct or restrain interstate or foreign commerce." [45] (*See Appendix K.*)

The Collier's and Winchell Cases

A 1951 article in *Collier's* seemed to insinuate that Spears Chiropractic Sanitarium and Hospital was engaging in "cancer quackery." Soon after publication, America's most popular radio gossip, Walter Winchell, talked about the article and urged his listeners to read it. Dr. Leo Spears, believing that he and his institution had been defamed, promptly filed for libel against the magazine, the American Broadcasting Co., Winchell, his sponsor and others, asking an astonishing $86 million in damages. It was one of the largest civil actions of its time, and dragged on for several years in a New York federal court amid much publicity and speculation.

The article titled "Cancer Quacks" was published in the May 26, 1951, issue of the magazine. An account of the activities of several alleged cancer healers in the U.S. and Canada, it devoted only two short paragraphs to Spears:

At Denver, Colorado, a chiropractor named Leo Spears advertises, "We have lately been successful in the relief, through natural methods, of certain types of cancer." Spears operates a pretentious sanitorium and health club estimated to be worth $8 million.

Spears' flamboyant advertising, distributed nationally in a 48-page tabloid, claims chiropractic "cures" in cases involving diabetes, epilepsy, goiter, undulant fever, nervousness, arthritis, eczema, asthma, multiple sclerosis, St. Vitus' dance, infantile paralysis, sleeping sickness, appendicitis, heart disease, kidney disease, spastic paralysis, constipation, liver trouble, stomach ulcers and crossed eyes. A report submitted in 1949 to the Attorney General of Colorado, John W. Metzger, revealed that a large number of deaths at the Spears Sanitarium were due to cancer.[46]

Walter Winchell was not exactly an impartial observer when he recommended the article to his radio listeners, being in fact an unpaid director of the Damon Runyon Memorial Fund for Cancer Research, which he founded in honor of his friend and fellow columnist who died of cancer in 1946. The *Collier's* article prominently displayed a sidebar captioned "Why Quacks Succeed," indicating the Damon Runyon Memorial Fund as its source. The Fund, according to the *New York Times*, by 1970 "had collected and disbursed $32 million, with no expenses for administration." [47]

In lodging the conjoined suits, Spears named as defendants the Crowell-Collier Publishing Co.; Bill Fay, a staff writer who bylined the article; Edward Anthony, *Collier's* publisher; Louis Ruppel, editor-in-chief; and Gordon Manning, managing editor. $24 million in damages were asked. Winchell and his sponsor, Warner-Hudnut, Inc., were sued for $25 million each, while the American Broadcasting Co. (ABC) was named for $12 million. The actions totaling $86 million were filed in Federal Court for southern district of New York.[48-51] This federal courthouse on New York's Foley Square was somewhat famous for a 1949 trial in which 11 top leaders of the American Communist Party were found guilty of conspiring to overthrow the government.

The *Collier's* case was the first to go to trial, on Monday, March 7, 1955, almost four years after the offending article was published.[52]

With Judge David Edelstein presiding, a jury of three women and nine men were selected. Both attorneys--Charles Ginsberg for Spears and Arthur Monyihan representing *Collier's*--having indicated that they would have lengthy opening statements, the trial was recessed until the next morning.[53] Testimony would take four days.

Just prior to opening, Spears withdrew one of the two counts for libel, paring total damages sought from $24 million to $12 million. The original complaint contained two causes of action for $12 million each, but since both counts stemmed from the same magazine article, the second count was dropped by mutual agreement.[54]

Dr. Spears occupied the witness chair for all of the first day and a good part of the second. On direct examination, he described at length the methods of treating cancer used at Spears Chiropractic Hospital and said he sincerely believed they were effective. He produced records of 56 former patients whom he said had been "successfully relieved" of cancer. Since most of them were treated after the *Collier's* article appeared, the court limited his testimony to seven cases whose treatment preceded publication of the article. He said under questioning by his attorney that outside of patients who came to the hospital after "being given up elsewhere," the death rate among cancer patients at Spears was "about three percent." [55]

Spears and Judge Edelstein clashed over the definition of "successful relief." "It means as nearly corrected as possible through our methods," Spears said. When Edelstein said he still didn't understand, Spears responded, "Well, it can range from relief of pain to arrestment of the condition." "That's a very broad definition," the judge retorted. When Spears tried to draw a comparison between "successful relief" and a "successful automobile driver," Edelstein stopped him: "I'm not interested in automobiles--I want to know what you mean by the words 'successful relief.'" Spears then pinned it down to "arresting" the condition; "no further symptoms."

The defense successfully objected when Ginsberg questioned Spears about the "Code of Cooperation" between Denver newspapers, the Colorado State Medical Society and the Colorado Hospital Association. Ginsberg argued that it is important to show that because of the code "ordinary avenues of publicity are denied Spears Hospital and chiropractic in general making it necessary to advertise."

Concluding the direct examination, Spears testified that one-third of patients admitted to the hospital are "charity cases" and that all statements made about patients in his advertising were true to the best of his knowledge.

Cross examination began as defense attorney Arthur Moynihan disclosed to the court that two patients widely advertised as being "cured" of cancer at Spears Hospital had actually died. When Spears admitted this was so, Moynihan introduced advertisements from Spears' nationally circulated tabloid "Chiropractic Proof," from which he read at length.

Charles Ginsberg objected strenuously when Moynihan attempted to question Spears' published statements that his hospital was a nonprofit institution. It was Moynihan's contention the hospital made "substantial profits" during the previous two years and produced audited statements to that effect. On this point, both attorneys retired to the judge's chambers to argue the meaning of "nonprofit."

Chief-of-Staff Dr. Dan Spears, called as a rebuttal witness, restated the claim that one-third of the hospital's work was charity, not 3.5 percent claimed by the defense. Ginsberg succeeded in getting before the jury the fact that an auditor's review of the hospital's business records did not include work done during free clinics at the Spears out-patient facilty.

Collier's officials testified next. Louis Ruppel, editor-in-chief, said he personally doubted that cures could be achieved in some of the diseases claimed by Spears, but added, "we did not say in the article that they could not be cured." Edward Anthony, publisher, while admitting that the material gathered against Spears was supplied by the American Medical Association, vehemently denied that the AMA had paid *Collier's* to publish the article. Staff writer Bill Fay admitted that he had not visited Spears Hospital in his research and had relied solely on materials provided by the AMA.[56]

The defense introduced two recognized cancer experts -- Dr. Charles Huggins of the University of Chicago and Dr. C.P. Rhodes of New York Memorial Hospital--to give their opinions on the causes and treatment of cancer. As expected, their opinions differed sharply with similar testimony given by Dr. Spears, and even with each other.[57]

After the defense rested shortly before noon on Friday, the last day of testimony, Spears produced as a rebuttal witness Dr. Sigismund Peller, a Vienna-born New York cancer specialist and author for the acclaimed book *Cancer in Man*. Not only did Peller not find anything wrong with Spears' approach to cancer treatment, he made headlines by asserting that "a final and definitive cure could very well come from an institution like his chiropractic hospital in Denver."[58]

In his closing, Moynihan defined "quack" as a person "who pretends to skills he does not possess." Speaking of the large number of witnesses from throughout the country who came to testify, including families of deceased ex-Spears patients, he said, "Nobody came here just because of *Collier's*. They came here for something more than that... because the American people should know the truth about this place."[59]

Charles Ginsberg denounced the defendants' claims that they had proved Spears was engaged in quackery and contended the *Collier's* article was a "malicious attack" on an institution which serves the public "legally and well." He sharply refuted Moynihan's charges of patient ill treatment, saying those who had died were actually under medical care at the time. He attacked the inferences in the article about diseases other than cancer, saying the magazine had not produced evidence about anything except cancer. And about writer Bill Fay, he charged that only a "haphazard" investigation was made. "He didn't even bother to go to the hospital and look at it." Ginsberg further claimed that, although Spears Hospital has treated several thousand cancer patients, the magazine's defense of "truth" was based on only a handful of cases. Finally, he told the jury that a "verdict for *Collier's* is in substance to convict the plaintiff."[60]

Judge Edelstein instructed the jury that they could find the defendants guilty inasmuch as inclusion of references to Spears in the article amounted to libel *per se* even though it did not call him a quack. The instruction meant that the plaintiff did not have to prove actual damages.

After only two hours and twenty minutes, the jury announced its verdict in favor of the defendants. According to the *Denver Post*, Spears appeared "visibly shaken." A poll showed seven jurors were for *Collier's* on the first ballot, with three undecided and two for Spears. The verdict came on the fourth ballot. Charles Ginsberg said a new trial would be asked.[61,62]

In *Spears Sanigram*, Dr. Dan Spears commented on trial testimony he felt had not been adequately covered in the rather sensational press accounts:

> The defendants in these legal actions had four years to build their defense before trial. During that time they had special investigators out seeking confirmatory evidence. Out of many hundreds of our testimonials and publications investigated, they presented case histories of only twelve cases as their defense. They claimed the statements made by these patients were untrue and our publication of same was fraudulent. This despite the fact that our publications made no claims of cure. Most of the patients had been given up after extended periods of treatment by medical specialists and they came to us for help only as a last resort. Three of the 12 are still living, working and apparently getting along well. Statements of or about nine patients who are now (deceased) were not published after they died. Some of these patients died of conditions other than cancer. Eight of the nine died, not under our care, but under medical care. The one and only case who died in Spears Hospital was of an 18-month-old boy whom we had relieved of leukemia and allowed to go home for a rest. While home, he contracted influenza. When he arrived back at Spears he was in a terminal state. We published no statements about this case.
>
> One of the 12 was a three-year-old lad who was brought to us for treatment after a specialist had recommended amputation of his leg (because of) sarcoma. After two and one-half months of treatment, the leg completely cleared up and the child returned home. We published pictures and a statement of our accomplishment. The specialist who had recommended amputation later re-examined this lad and testified "it appeared to be normal in every respect." He showed X-rays to verify his statement that the cancer of the thigh was cured and stated the child had two years of normal life, which was very gratifying and extremely unusual. He also testified that this type of cancer was fatal and that amputation of the leg could not possibly have resulted in more than life extension of a few weeks to a few months. Two years after correction of the leg at Spears Hospital, the child developed pneumonia which turned into pulmonary carcinoma and expired under medical care. No evidence of lung cancer was present when first examined at Spears, or seven months later by the specialist who had recommended amputation of the leg.
>
> Four medical doctors claming to be cancer specialists testified for Collier's. Their ideas as to the cause and correction of cancer varied greatly. Each admitted he knew nothing about chiropractic. One stated chiropractic was unscientific and not a science. Apparently he was less informed than was Dr. Ray Lyman Wilbur, MD, PhD, former president of Stanford University and the American Academy of Medicine, who, in speaking to the delegates to the fortieth annual Congress on Medical Education and Licensure, said: "New treatments make use of heat, cold, water, electricity and specific manipulations; they bring biological responses more potent than many of the drugs gathered through centuries by trial and error. Medicine based on pills and potions is becoming obsolete. The new philosophy, with the help of physics, has taught us many ways to deal with the human body that were dreamed of only a decade ago by us but comparatively successfully pursued by those of the 'irregular schools.' The medical profession will profit by

recognizing this new concept, and must insist that its schools promptly mold their instruction to conform with the new knowledge of body mechanics. They must also consider damage inflicted on the nervous system by fatigue, malnutrition and strain.

As a surprise rebuttal witness, we produced Sigismund Peller, MD, a New York cancer specialist who has researched cancer since 1921. He testified that in his opinion "the causes of cancer are still unknown and that present methods of treatment by surgery and X-rays are inadequate." He further stated: "You can never predict from where the cure for cancer may come. Louis Pasteur was not a medical doctor."

Dr. Peller studied medicine in Vienna and has researched in the United States for more than twenty years. He was once attached to Johns Hopkins Medical School in Baltimore, the New York University Medical School and other top institutions. He is author of "Cancer in Man," which is one of the finest books ever written on cancer.

In charging the jury, Judge Edelstein stated that although the Collier's article did not say in so many words that Spears was a quack, inclusion of references to him in the article amounted to libel per se.

Though the burden of proof rested with Collier's, they certainly presented no evidence to justify the libel. They were as surprised as we when the jury decided in their favor.[63]

On April 1, 1955, a new development caught almost all observers by surprise. The suit against Walter Winchell, his network and his sponsor, scheduled imminently, was negotiated out of court in Denver. While the amount of the settlement was not reported in the press by agreement, Leo Spears claimed it to be a major victory.[64] A spokesman for Winchell emphasized that all negotiations and payments were by the Massachusetts Bonding Co., insurer for all the defendants.[65] At the same time, Spears' motion to retry the Collier's suit was withdrawn.[66]

Walter Winchell was fired by ABC in a contract dispute in 1956. His contract with Hearst was terminated in 1967, his last column appearing in the New York Mirror on November 30.[67] Winchell died from prostate cancer February 20, 1972, in a Los Angeles hospital.[68] His death was so unlamented, biographer Neal Gabler observed: "In the end, few really remembered, few cared. His daughter Welda was the only mourner at his funeral, and a memorial service six weeks later on what would have been his 75th birthday attracted only 150 invited guests, many leaving before the eulogies were completed. Nothing he left seemed to endure."[69]

Collier's published its last issue on January 4, 1957, ending a nearly 69-year run as one of America's premier general interest periodicals.[70-72]

Aerial view of hospital in Denver and Colorado's snow-capped Rockies, 1956. The Pioneers Building is under construction at left.

(Left) Dr. Leo L. Spears, founder of Spears Chiropractic Hospital, with young patient, 1955.

A small group of the many of children being treated in Spears' Free Clinic for Poor Children in Denver, Colorado. Dr. Spears is shown holding two of the babies. Three hundred children were being treated in this clinic three nights a week during the 1930's depression years.

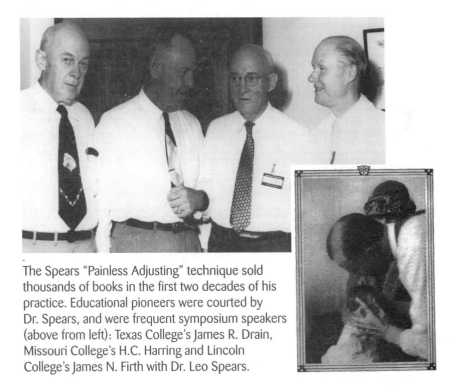

The Spears "Painless Adjusting" technique sold thousands of books in the first two decades of his practice. Educational pioneers were courted by Dr. Spears, and were frequent symposium speakers (above from left): Texas College's James R. Drain, Missouri College's H.C. Harring and Lincoln College's James N. Firth with Dr. Leo Spears.

CHIROPRACTOR

=== COMING TO ===

Evanston S.D.

Daily, Starting July 26, 1926, at 3 7 m.

WATCH THIS CARD FOR APPOINTED TIME OF DAY

Dr. Wilbur W. West, D. C. Ph. C., of Castle Rock, Colo. using the

SPEARS PAINLESS
SYSTEM OF ADJUSTING

Dr. West has several towns on his list to make each day; so it will be very easy for the people of each town and Community he makes, to get his services. The SPEARS PAINLESS SYSTEM is very mild in application and quick in obtaining results.

Why Suffer and Complain?

When just a few dollars will get you well through the SPEARS PAINLESS SYSTEM of adjusting your backbone. Now anyone knows that to feel bad means that his work is anything but a pleasure. When feeling good and your suffering is gone, your work is play and you enjoy it and actually want to do something worth while. A STITCH IN TIME SAVES NINE. Therefore you may be a sufferer of some ailment in the winter and not so much in the summer. Now is your time to actually build up and regain your health through NATURE'S NATURAL WAY.

95 per cent of all Diseases

And ailments of the human body can be taken care of through Chiropractic and a cure obtained. A few of the many diseases are listed below:

Tumors, Gastritis, Gallstones, Renal Stones, Enteritis, Laryngitis, Pancreatitis, Nervousness, Headache, Catarrh, Eye Strain, Constipation, Female Troubles, Diphtheria, Scarlet Fever, Typhoid Fever, Pneumonia, Influenza, Colds, Lumbago, Rheumatism, Goitre, Cancer, Hemorrhage, Dropsy, Hemorrhoids, Paralysis, Gout, Skin Disease, Measles, Mumps, Neuralgia, Pleurisy, Lung, Heart, Liver, Stomach, Bowel and Kidney Disorders.

In cases of long standing, "CHRONIC." it takes more time for Chiropractic and nature to get you back to normal. ACUTE cases respond more quickly to the adjustments as so much tissue has not undergone a change in structure.

Health is a Great Asset

When all else has failed to get RESULTS and with no more hopes of recovery, Chiropractic has stepped in and brought health to the patient. Two million people in the United States alone use Chiropractic adjustments for all their ills—people from all walks of life. CHIROPRACTIC IS THE GREATEST HEALTH SCIENCE IN THE WORLD TO DAY. It is applied to the old and young alike, on either chronic or acute ailments with gratifying results.

In cases of long standing, in which each time the pains or aches are a little worse, is a bad sign, as it indicates that there is more pressure going onto the nerves which supply that part. START NOW; THERE IS DANGER IN THE NEGLECT OF YOUR HEALTH.

I will be at this town at a set time each day for two weeks, at the end of that time, in case it does not pay, I will discontinue to stop here.

Entrepreneurism, typified by this broadside, was encouraged by Dr. Leo Spears. Before and after World War II, the Spears Clinic sponsored many itinerant excursions into rural areas.

No. 646   Revenue No. _____

LICENSE

ISSUED BY
Board of
Colorado State Department of Public Health

This is to Certify that Spears Free Clinic and Hospital For Poor Children, Inc.

of _____ Denver, Colorado _____

is hereby granted a license to conduct and maintain a

_____ Chiropractic Hospital _____

known as _____ Spears Chiropractic Sanitarium and Hospital _____

at _____ 927 Jersey Street _____

subject to the laws of the State of Colorado and the rules and regulations of the Colorado State Board of Health relating thereto.

Issued at Denver, Colorado, this ____27th____ day of ____September____ 19 43

COLORADO STATE DEPARTMENT OF PUBLIC HEALTH

State Board of

_____ President

_____ Secretary

The original Colorado State Board of Health license in 1943 and (below) the last authorization issued prior to its closure in 1984 — two pieces of paper that cost years of courtroom struggle, appeals and ultimately a State Supreme Court decision.

STATE OF COLORADO
DEPARTMENT OF HEALTH

SPEARS CHIROPRACTIC HOSPITAL
Denver, Colorado

Is authorized and licensed to engage in business as a
Chiropractic Hospital

In accordance with the provisions of the laws and regulations of the Department of Revenue and Department of Health.

600
Licensed Bed Capacity

131
License Number

March 9, 1984
Expiration Date

_____
President, State Board of Health

_____
Executive Director, Department of Health

TO BE FRAMED AND DISPLAYED CONSPICUOUSLY

The Spears Mobile Clinic, c. 1939–1940, also called the "Mercy Trailer," operated in rural eastern Colorado until the onset of World War II. The Denver Civic Center is the backdrop for this photo, which also pictures Leo Spears.

Spears Clinic, c. 1947. This Spanish-style residence at 13th Ave. and Gaylord St. was purchased by Dr. Spears during the Depression and served as the Spears Clinic from 1947 to 1956, when it relocated to the hospital. The "Gaylord House" was the clinic's third location since its founding, having earlier been housed in the Majestic Building and the Steele Building in downtown Denver.

SPEARS SANITARIUM
DENVER, COLORADO.
· WALTER H. SIMON, ARCHITECT ·
DENVER, COLORADO

Denver architect Walter H. Simon envisioned a huge hospital and school complex in the 15 acres that Spears had acquired in the eastern suburbs. Three of the units became a reality: the Willard Carver Building opened in 1943 (top), the D.D. Palmer Building in 1950 (facing page), and the Chiropractic Pioneers Building (center) was about half-completed when Spears died in 1956.

CHIROPRACTIC MEMORIAL NOW RISING

EARLY STAGES OF CONSTRUCTION work on the second unit of SPEARS SANITARIUM are shown in the picture below. The D. D. Palmer Building will overshadow it also the first unit, visible in background, with device the amount of bed space and double other existing facilities. Two wings will comprise the structure, thus keeping the architectural pattern complete. Many weeks were for the institution to expand to capacity acreage, all of which is owned by SPEARS SANITARIUM. With its advancement, facing east, was taken several weeks before SPEARS SANITARIUM NEWS went to press. The edifice is now approaching the fourth floor.

CHIROPRACTORS MAY HONOR D. D. PALMER BY FURNISHING ROOMS

Dr. Leo L. Spears, whose practical vision brings to reality the Sanitarium's expansion program.

There is honor enough to go around! Each room and each bed in the D. D. Palmer building will provide a means for chiropractors and laymen to render tribute to the founder of chiropractic.

Already one state association has voted $1,000 to endow a bed in the institution. Several individual chiropractors and laymen who owe their success and lives to the profession are asking for the privilege of participating in the 400-bed project.

To simplify this participation in such manner that each contributor will have a definite part in the enterprise, donations may be made on these terms:

Each person endowing or furnishing a room will be identified by a copper plate on the door of such room. A similar plate will be attached to the donated ward beds.

A one-bed room may be endowed for $1,000.

A one-bed room may be furnished for $300; a two-bed room for $500.

A ward bed may be furnished for $100.

A distinction is made between "endowment" and "furnishing." The former assumes a proportionate share of construction costs; the latter provides highly essential furnishings but does not absorb any of the structural expense. Furnishing a ward bed finances the purchase of a bed and bed-clothing without participating in the cost of other furniture in the ward.

(Note: Total cost of the D. D. Palmer building, without furniture or laboratory equipment, will be around $490,000. Fully equipped and furnished, it will cost about $800,000.

Practically chiropractors and grateful ex-patients point out that a wonderful tribute would be rendered the Old Master if every room and ward might be furnished or endowed by his followers in memory of Dr. Palmer, whose pioneering and discoveries created a new school of healing—an effective approach to age-old therapeutic problems which previously had been unsolved. As one enthusiastic chiropractor expressed it: "Every chiropractor would invent Dr. Palmer with a signal distinction never accorded any other man; and the memorial plates would be everlasting expressions of personal love and loyalty.

For those who wish to share in this opportunity but do not have the lump sum available, arrangements can be made for monthly or periodical payments.

The door to the "Hall of Fame" is wide open. All who wish to do so may enter. Chiropractors have the double opportunity of personally contributing and urging grateful patients to do the same.

A detail in this connection is important: All such contributions or donations are deductible from income taxes.

LOOKING WEST AT ENIPERIRO skyline over north wing of new Palmer Memorial, where workmen are bending every effort to complete the building in time to receive sick people during the summer of 1946. The camera man caught him scene shortly after construction operations began, in November, 1945.

The second unit of the hospital, the D.D. Palmer Memorial Building, was under construction in 1946. Spears predated the boom in chiropractic educational institutions and their new construction some two decades later.

The Dedication of D.D. Palmer Memorial Building (Unit 2) January 26, 1950.

This 1953 advertisement in the *Denver Post* demonstrated the side of Leo Spears that caused alienation in the chiropractic community and enraged the medical societies and boards. Spears was a disciple of B.J. Palmer in little but a flair for advertising, at a time when it was considered "unprofessional" to do so. The "cancer educational information" trailer that was to have traversed the Rocky Mountain states caused both eyebrows and tempers to raise.

North Dakota Senator William Langer, a populist who challenged the medical and veterans lobby, held hearings for his Subcommittee on Veteran's Affairs in the lobby of unit two to dramatize the denial of chiropractic benefits.

Spears Attorney Charles Ginsberg led the hospital's legal team in municipal and federal courts in over 20 years of litigation. Some landmark victories for nonmedical hospitals were won under his leadership.

Intern class, 1956. The author is standing, second row, left of center.
More than 500 chiropractors would complete an internship at the hospital
during the 40's and 50's.

(below, left) Pennsylvania industrialist Andrew J. Sordoni was a longtime trustee
of the hospital and sent many of his employees to the hospital for treatment.
(right) Dr. George Wilson coordinated the "cancer research" at Spears. The
Pioneers Building under construction is seen through the window behind him.

Nursing staff at Spears, c. 1950's. For a brief time in the previous decade, a School of Nursing was conducted at the hospital.

Leo Spears, his nephews and their wives (from left): Howard and Mae, Leo and Laura, Dan and Dorothy Spears, c. 1950.

HEART ATTACK KILLS SPEARS

Story In Column 1

The Voice of the
Rocky Mountain
Empire

THE DENVER POST

HOME
★
EDITION

VOL. 64, NO. 286 ⸺⸺⸺⸺⸺ DENVER, COLO.—**Climate Capital of the World** —WEDNESDAY, MAY 16, 1956   5 CENTS—55 PAGES

"Heart attack kills Spears" according to the *Denver Post* newspaper
of Wednesday, May 16, 1956.

Before the wrecking ball. An internist at Denver Jewish Hospital
alerted chiropractic educators and historians before the unannounced
demolition of the vacant Spears' hospital buildings in July, 1993.
From left are: the author Dr. William Rehm, Dr. Charles Kirkpatrick,
National College president James Winterstein, and Cleveland
College president Carl Cleveland.

"A Massive Conspiracy"

On May 20, 1954, before his offer to testify before the grand jury, Leo Spears filed a $10 million suit in district court against the Denver branch of the Better Business Bureau (BBB), charging that each of its 65 officers and its executive director, W. Dan Bell, had "willfully and wantonly conspired to destroy the hospital by devious methods," which included:

1-Distributing misleading information to the public, "the purpose of which was to give a bad reputation to the hospital;"

2-Encouraging patients and ex-patients to sue the hospital out of "malice;"

3-Advising people indebted to the hospital to refuse to pay their bills;

4-Appearing before the grand jury with information developed in a BBB-*Denver Post* probe of medical quackery in which it "became obvious and widely publicized that the principal target of the alleged disclosure was the Spears Free Clinic and Hospital for Poor Children, Inc." [1,2]

Nearly seven months of depositions would be necessary before the case was scheduled for trial, while the press followed the proceedings every step of the way.

When the depositions began on July 6, the *Denver Post* and medical reporter Robert Byers were added to the case as co-defendants. Spears alleged that the reporter illegally recorded the names of 104 cancer patients from confidential files and had turned them over to the BBB. "They are part and parcel of a massive conspiracy." [3,4] The court later allowed the two suits to be conjoined. [5]

"Vast oil and uranium holdings of the nationally advertised Spears chiropractic institution were bared," is how the *Denver Post* characterized the corporation's rather modest investment portfolio. The holdings were shown to be about $100,000, invested by Spears' trustees in Colorado and Wyoming oil ventures and a Colorado uranium speculation producing between $4,000 and $5,000 a month income to the corporation. [6]

A $100,000 bank loan was also disclosed, which Spears said was pooled with corporation savings to begin construction of the new building. Construction was halted in November 1954 because of bad weather and had not been resumed because "we haven't been financially able," he explained. This, he blamed on BBB's activities which "ruined our business."

Under questioning by defense attorney Philip Van Cise, Spears defended advertisements that said he receives no salary from the hospital: "It is the clinic, not the hospital, which pays me $800 a month."

Spears produced a copy of what he called the "half-rate" letter mailed out to 25,000 prospective patients after the grand jury began its investigation in February. He said he didn't know how many prospects took advantage of the offer which was to expire in 30 days. The half-rate offer was made to "keep patients in the hospital and help us maintain a skeleton crew." [7]

Asked if chiropractors who refer to the hospital get "kickbacks," Spears said 5 percent of what the patient pays is "credited" to the referring doctor. The credit, he explained, can be used to help defray the cost of indigent patients they may send or to purchase literature from the hospital. Fund raising practices were explored, Spears admitting that his advertising agent, publishing house and hospital suppliers made donations at various times. He testified that he once went to New York City and was paid $1,000 a day to treat a patient and, yes, this same patient also made a donation for construction of the new building. He also admitted that the patient died at the hospital before making good on his pledge.

Asked about his 1926 book *Spears Painless System*, he agreed that the first 1,000 copies sold for $100 each even though printing costs were only $1.65 each, and that a 1950 printing of 2,000 copies sold for $24 each to doctors and $12 to chiropractic students. But all profits went to the hospital, he emphasized.

When questioning turned to cancer treatment, he said that a burning salve called an "escharotic" was sometimes used to remove external cancerous growths, and that pain-killing drugs were used when needed, measures directed or prescribed by a licensed osteopathic physician. "But it is the chiropractic adjustment which relieves the cancer condition itself," he hastened to explain. Spears said that he never has claimed to "cure" cancer, only "relieve it... but we have a lot of patients who say we cured them." [8]

Spears renewed his charge that the *Denver Post* collaborated with the Colorado Medical Society to deny his institution "favorable publicity" through a "code of cooperation" he said exists between Denver newspapers and the medical profession. The taking of Spears' deposition, already underway for two weeks, took an unusual turn when Judge Robert S. Steele disqualified himself upon learning he once served as attorney for some BBB directors named in the case as co-defendants. He was replaced by Judge Robert McWilliams, Jr. when depositions resumed. [9]

The defense produced testimony from Spears that the hospital's income from patient fees in 1953 was $1,551,000, compared with expenses of $1,325,000 - a net profit of $183,000. [10]

It was next revealed that Dr. Spears had launched a nationwide business selling a "vitamin product" by direct mail. He said he formed the Booster Products Co. a few months earlier and that, although he owned the company, "all profits go to the hospital." In return for profits, the hospital allowed the company to use its mailing permit for advertising while bearing the cost of printing Booster literature. Spears emphasized that the product was a "body conditioner" comprised principally of herbs and other natural ingredients.

As deposition turned to the defendants, Judge McWilliams ruled that the Better Business Bureau must turn over to Spears all consumer complaints made to the BBB against firms owned by its various directors. The ruling came over the strong objections by Philip Van Cise that such files "can in no way contribute to the plaintiff's conspiracy complaint." [11]

Charles Ginsberg charged the BBB is "nothing but a racket" wherein a few privileged businessmen can "blackmail" their competitors and that the files would show this. He described the BBB as a "self-constituted guardian of business morals and ethics... without regard for the duly elected law enforcement agencies of the city." He compared the BBB to the Ku Klux Klan and the communist party, and also characterized the defendants as "gansters, thugs and character assassins."

When he asked BBB Executive Director W. Dan Bell what information he gave to the recent grand jury, the judge instructed Bell not to answer and said he would have to rule on the matter later. Ginsberg did win from Bell the names of 44 Denver area healing art practitioners subpoenaed by the grand jury, although his demand for the files was rejected.[12,13]

Denying Spears the opportunity to inspect files adverse to the BBB, the judge instructed Bell to tell the court orally how many complaints had been made against directors' firms and how these complaints were handled. Ginsberg declared that, unless the files were made available, he would immediately terminate a court-ordered audit of the hospital's books.[14]

In another ruling, McWilliams denied Spears' motion for an injunction against the defendants to prevent them from "continuing the conspiracy" by contacting former patients.

Bell testified that his office began inquiring into Spears Hospital only a few days after the BBB opened its Denver office in November 1951, because of inquiries already coming in when the office opening was announced. He said further, the BBB later undertook an investigation of health practitioners and that the probe was joined in December 1953 by a similar investigation being conducted by the *Post*. In connection with the joint probe, Bell said, one meeting was held with *Post* publisher Palmer Hoyt, and that there were several meetings with the paper's managing editor and reporter Robert Byers. "It was from these meetings it was decided to make known to District Attorney Bert M. Keating the information developed." [15]

Asked about 120 letters which the BBB had sent by registered mail to patients advertised in the Spears tabloid publication *Chiropractic Proof*, Bell answered the letters were only "inquiries about their impressions of Denver and did not specifically mention Spears." They were sent by registered mail to determine who was still living, he said. Bell admitted having discussions with attorneys for defendants in another suit brought by Spears, with the State Board of Medical Examiners, Assistant District Attorney Melvin Rossman, and with lawyers for *Collier's* magazine.[16]

Van Cise asked for an explanation of notations in Spears' books of "sizable donations" from two mortuary establishments from 1950 through 1953. Spears vigorously denied any connection between donations and business: "It is a dastardly trick for you to make such terrible insinuations."[17]

Ginsberg protested that no matter what depositions from mortuary owners would show, it would not be relevant to the suit:

> Here are people who have assumed to themselves without any legal basis the role of enforcement of the law in this community. Now, under the law, they are permitted to prod into every record and every deed of this institution and further their conspiracy. Are they to be allowed to destroy this institution - an institution which has been upheld by the Supreme Court of this state - by the means of this action just because they don't agree with the hospital's advertising? The rehashing of antiquated facts, true as they may be, is libel to which truth is not a defense. And truth is not a defense in a conspiracy suit.[18]

Van Cise, contending that chiropractors do not enjoy a confidential, privileged relationship with their patients similar to that enjoyed by physicians, argued that under Colorado law Spears cannot be granted immunity from questions about his patients. He went further, stating Spears had waived such presumed rights by publishing patient testimonials.[19]

Ginsberg charged that defense efforts to obtain case records of widely advertised cancer patients was part of a "continuing conspiracy," adding that the defendants had given testimony to the grand jury of alleged untruthful advertising: "They are seeking to justify what they have already done."

Van Cise said he wanted the patient records to check on Spears' claims regarding successful treatment of such diseases as cancer, polio, multiple sclerosis, cerebral palsy and others.

In an impassioned plea to the court, Ginsberg denounced the *Denver Post* as a "vicious" and "notorious" newspaper wherein views "changed with the days and the weather": "The *Post* has distorted the truth, belied it. If it were not for the power of the *Post*, these defendants would be in jail for criminal conspiracy."

Linwood L. Downs, D.O., testified that he was frequently called to Spears Hospital to prescribe medications or perform procedures outside the scope of the hospital's license. He emphasized that he was not employed by Spears but was retained by the individual patient, who is charged for his services. Downs confirmed that he authorized the escharotics used to remove external cancer growths from some Spears patients but said the paste was compounded by a pharmacist.[20]

A Denver pharmacist acknowledged that Downs' prescriptions are filled at his pharmacy and that, on occasion and under Downs' direction, Dr. Dan Spears also phones in prescriptions.[21,22]

Depositions in the conspiracy suit were recessed on December 21, 1954, after several rulings from the bench:

■ Grand jury witnesses would not be bound by secrecy: "Such law is up to the legislature, not the courts."

■ The defense would be denied the right to question mortuaries about donations to Spears in return to the hospital "funneling" business to them.

■ The defendants were denied a more definite complaint from Spears, the matter in which Charles Ginsberg had threatened to block a court-ordered audit of Spears' books.[23]

Throughout the long and tedious deposition process, lawyers on both sides fequently became antagonistic. At one point, Ginsberg accused Van Cise of "wearing an asinine, stupid grin" and of "conduct unbecoming an attorney." Calling Ginsberg "a disgrace to the bar," Van Cise suggested his insulting remarks were subject to contempt of court action. Judge McWilliams ordered both counsels to "restrain your emotions... even though it may be difficult."[24]

In its formal response on January 26 to the various charges alleged in the suit, the defendants asked the court to dismiss the suit and assess all costs for the action against Spears.[25]

Three of the defendants – the *Denver Post*, its business manager Charles Buxton, and medical reporter Robert Byers – alleged that Spears brought the investigation on himself by repeatedly urging the newspaper to investigate his claims of cures, and were "justified and acting in the public interest" to subject the hospital to investigation. A letter to publisher Palmer Hoyt was exhibited in which Dr. Spears appeals for such an investigation:

> Many people throughout the country are suffering untold misery because we have no means other than publicity of informing them of the great work we are doing. Almost every day someone reaching us in a terminal stage says: "If I had only known about this place before - why don't you let people know what you are doing?"
>
> Time does not mean so much to people who are healthy and happy; but it is precious to those who are flirting with eternity.
>
> We sincerely hope you will not overlook our work because we are a local institution. If, however, The Post does decide against the use of our stories, we hope you will notify us immediately so we can release them to someone else. We are most anxious that The Post use them first but, with so many cancer victims at the crossroads between life and death, time is an important factor.[26]

The *Denver Post* said it relied on Spears' invitation when it assigned medical reporter Robert Byers to do an investigation "but without accepting the offer therein to pay 'both salary and the expense resulting from such investigations.'"

Denying any responsibility, the Better Business Bureau stated that the Spears corporation "illegally" amended its articles of incorporation of 1937 by changing the corporate purpose. The affidavit made these points:

■ Spears Hospital is supposed to be for the free treatment of poor children, but the majority of persons admitted are paying adults.
■ The Spears corporation employs chiropractors and therefore is engaged in the corporate practice of medicine but holds no license to so practice.
■ The Spears hospital advertises--an advertising budget in 1953 alone of $371,426--by means of testimonials from ex-patients and that such "advertisements were false and misleading, and many such patients died from the diseases claimed to have been cured." [27]

Spears reemphasized that caustic paste was used for cosmetic purposes and had "nothing to do with eliminating the cause of cancer or its cure." He admitted that advertisements about two patients "relieved of cancer" did not mention that the paste had been used on them. Elsewhere in his concluding deposition, Spears admitted that he could not back up with statistical records certain claims made in his advertising, that only 3 percent of all acute and chronic patients die at Spears Hospital, and that 90 percent of all hospital patients are given up as "hopeless" before arriving at the hospital. "The proof is in the individual records," he said.[28]

Seven months of depositions finally concluded on February 3, with final testimony from W. Dan Bell about his grand jury testimony.

Bell told the court that in December 1953, a BBB investigator checked out 96 testimonials that appeared in Spears' publication *More Proof.* Of these, he said five had died, 47 were known to be alive, 32 could not be located, five were apparently employed at Spears, and that seven questioned the content of testimonials attributed to them.[29] Along with this, Bell said he told the grand jury that *Post* reporter Byers had information "of another nature." [30]

Presiding District Court Judge Albert T. Frantz set September 12, 1955, for trial to begin. Judge Robert H. McWilliams would hear the case expected to last six weeks.[31]

Palmer Hoyt, called as the first witness, testified that the *Post* in 1951 did not print a series of articles written by one of its reporters about claims of cancer cures by Spears "because we didn't consider the stories up to our journalistic standards." Asked why, Hoyt answered, "The claims lacked proof and verification." Asked what public interest was served by his grand jury testimony, Hoyt replied, "We would consider it of the highest import if a cure for cancer had been discovered or was about to be discovered. We also feel it would be in the public interest that false hopes not be aroused... We believe it would be in the public interest to assure that advertising be truthful and factual." [32]

When asked what the *Post* meant in one of its news stories during the grand jury hearings about a "mountain of evidence against quackery," Hoyt said it was material developed by Byers and the BBB. When Ginsberg asked him to produce the evidence, Van Cise interrupted and said that Byers carried most of the material in his head, to which Ginsberg sarcastically commented, "We now know the mountain of evidence has been stored away in the monumental head of Mr. Byers."

Questioned about his relations with the BBB, and asked when the *Post* "decided to join forces in a drive against Spears Hospital," Hoyt objected to the characterization: "We merely exchanged information on a joint investigation."

When Ginsberg asked about the *Post's* policy on accepting advertising from Spears, Hoyt said,"We didn't permit some of his advertising, because we just didn't believe it was true." There followed this exchange:

"Should the healing arts attempt to relieve cancer?"

"I don't know. It depends somewhat on equipment. Certainly for a trained doctor it is part of his job."

"Is Spears a trained doctor?"

"In my opinion, no."

Returning for a second day of testimony, Hoyt said he holds "no personal bias against chiropractors or any of the healing arts," but admitted that he was "not fully cognizant of everything chiropractors can do" with their treatment. "I have been treated by medical doctors, osteopaths and chiropractors. I think chiropractors have a very sound theory and at times I have felt very critical of standard doctors for not using more osteopathic and chiropractic methods." [33]

Ginsberg returned to the *Post's* advertising policy, introducing exhibits attempting to show that his paper took Spears' advertising while investigating the hospital. Hoyt said that when he took over management of the *Denver Post* in February 1946, the paper carried a number of "cure ads," but three months later put orders into effect to eliminate them. "As a general thing, they are not wanted in our paper."

Hoyt, when asked by Van Cise to discuss his personal views on the cure of cancer, replied, "I have long been interested in cancer and other so-called incurable diseases. To my knowledge there is now no accepted cure for cancer. We wouldn't run ads from anyone – from a standard medical institution or doctor, or anyone else – unless we were satisfied such a cure existed. We shall continue to carry stories on efforts to find a cure. Perhaps Dr. Spears or some other of the healing arts can find a cure. That's why we devoted lots of time and space in our investigations."

Before he left the witness stand, Hoyt was asked by Charles Ginsberg if he ever had discussions in his office with New York lawyer Sidney Davis.

"I remember he told us about a hearing Senator Langer was about to call to investigate charges of monopoly by some of the healing arts."

"Did you discuss with him the Spears institution and Dr. Spears?"

"I don't remember."

"Do you remember telling Davis the *Post* was going to close Spears Hospital and 'before this is over, we'll have Dr. Spears in jail' ?"

"No, I don't recall that."

"Did you say that to anyone?"

"Not that I'm aware of." [34]

Robert M. Byers, *Denver Post* medical reporter, took the witness chair on Wednesday afternoon and remained there for the balance of the week.

He began his long testimony saying his superiors, principally Palmer Hoyt, told him that "osteopathy and chiropractic too long had been excluded from the public press and that he was to get news stories from these hospitals also." His sole purpose in starting an investigation of Spears Hospital was, he said, "to determine whether Dr. Spears had developed a cure for cancer, as he claimed." He said the hospital made available to him the names of 149 patients who were treated... "Of this number, 104 were treated for cancer and the rest for various other diseases."

He testified he gave the names of these patients to Dan Bell, executive director of the BBB, and asked him to send registered letters to the 104 cancer patients. In answer to a question, he explained he wasn't adequately staffed to do the mailing himself.

Byers said he subsequently appeared before the grand jury three times. He said he told the jury that he went to Spears Hospital between November 30 and December 6, 1953, at the invitation of Dr. Spears. [35]

Asked by Ginsberg if he had written about other Denver hospitals, Byers said that he had many times. Here, at Ginsberg's demand, Judge McWilliams ordered Byers to produce in court stories that were critical of other hospitals.

To further questioning, Byers said he told the grand jury that he found "some irregularities in the conduct of the hospital," explaining that the hospital was practicing chiropractic and osteopathy as an institution, and that under state law, such a license cannot be issued to an institution. When Ginsberg asked if he had ever stated to anyone that he would "put Spears in jail" as a result of his investigation, Byers replied, "Not that I recall, but if I had, it was just in rollicking good fun."

Answering another question about Palmer Hoyt's attitude toward Spears, Byers said the publisher told him to investigate the cancer claims because, "if true, it would be the most important news story of the century."

Byers said he told the grand jury that in November 1953 he received a telephone call from Spears about a "surefire" cancer screening test he had discovered; that Spears told him it was 90 percent accurate in more than 7,000 instances and asked him to publicize the discovery. "It is not my intention to give publicity without validity of the test proven beyond a shadow of a doubt," he said he told Spears at the time. To determine the truthfulness of Spears' claim, Byers said he sought the aid of Colorado General Hospital and the American Cancer Society, which refused. At that point, he said he sought to check the validity of the claims by himself.[36] Asked if he had worked himself into Dr. Spears' confidence, he replied, "No, sir." [37]

Ginsberg asked Byers how he concluded there were "irregularities" in procedures at the hospital. He responded that there were instances of chiropractors prescribing medication and lack of follow-up examinations.

Asked if he had told the grand jury, Byers answered, "I had no recommendations to make to the grand jury. I told (them) I shouldn't be asked to make recommendations. I told them it was my thinking that something ought to be done in Colorado... (since) apparently you can get away with anything in this state. I told them then that I did not think the material I had presented to them, as such, constituted sufficient grounds for indictment."

"You advised the grand jury as to what the law was?"

"I reviewed for them a similar situation now in the courts in Iowa" (pertaining to alleged illegal corporate practice).

"How did you determine what the law was?"

"I read the law."

"What cases did you read?"

"None."

"You passed on validity of Dr. Spears' cancer screening test?"

"I passed on the statistical analysis of the test."

"You are willing to be an advisor to the grand jury as an expert on science, on medicine, on chiropractic, and on the law?"

"I did not advise the grand jury."

Byers described his study of the cancer cases as "the first time that I know of that a sincere and honest effort was made to discover the post-hospital conditions of former patients at Spears Hospital." [38]

Ginsberg next began questioning a parade of directors of the BBB about their relations with the organization. All testified that at no time prior to the lawsuits did the matter of an investigation of Spears' advertising come before the board of directors.[39]

When Ginsberg sought permission to call to the witness stand 200 to 300 former patients to testify to the efficacy of their treatment, he was bitterly opposed by Edwin Van Cise. Judge McWilliams ruled that, at least for the time being, he would not allow these witnesses to testify, but said that a later decision would be based on whether the defendants attempted to produce the testimonial-type of evidence. Ginsberg estimated the testimony would have taken three or four days.[40]

At the request of Charles Ginsberg, W. Dan Bell, BBB executive director, produced as evidence numerous reports and publications of the bureau, including materials sent out to persons inquiring about the Spears institution. Bell said the bureau sends each person inquiring a mimeographed report and a copy of the BBB's publication,"The Fact Finder," reporting on the suit.[41]

On Wednesday, September 22, the long-anticipated testimony of Dr. Leo Spears began with questions from Charles Ginsberg:

"What has been the effect of the publicity on the hospital's business?"

"It has caused a terrific loss of business and has damaged the prestige and good name of the institution."

"What had been the institution's rate of progress and growth?"

"It had been considerable every year."

Ginsberg asked for a precise statement of business loss.

"I couldn't give a percentage except during the past five or six months to a year after the publicity we were doing 25 to 50 percent of our normal business."

"Are you in the process of building a new building?"

"That's right."

"Is it a large unit?"

"It will have 2,150 beds."

"Did your needs call for this additional space?"

"Yes, they certainly did."

"Did you stop the building program?"

"Yes, sir, that's right."

"Did the city building and zoning departments require you to resume work whether you needed to or not?"

Spears said construction was resumed in May when the city ordered that work must resume. "If work were not started, the city would order the unfinished building torn down."

Ginsberg asked if the decline in patients was continuing.

"Oh yes."

Concerning a series of stories former *Post* reporter Tom Swearington had written, Ginsberg asked if Palmer Hoyt told him they would not publish the report.

"No, sir."

"Did anyone at the *Post* tell you the Swearington report would be published?"

Spears said Ed Dooley, managing editor, told him several times the stories would be published.

Asked how many patients had been treated at the hospital since it opened in 1943, Spears said about 19,000.

Ginsberg asked how many had died at the institution and Spears answered 473, or about 2.50 percent.

"Out of 19,000 patients, how many were cancer patients?"

"About 3,000."

"What percentage of those died?"

"About 5.56 percent."

Spears denied that either the *Post* or the BBB had contacted him during the investigation of the institution's advertising.

"Is your advertising truthful?"

"If I know the definition of the word truthful, I can say that our advertising is truthful."

"And you know the meaning of truthful?"

"I do." [42]

Beginning its cross-examination, the defense introduced many exhibits, primarily newspaper stories and advertisements.

Edwin Van Cise asked Spears about an advertisement which stated that over 600 insurance companies recognized chiropractic, which was later advertised as 400.

"Because I wanted to be ultraconservative in the advertising," he answered.

Van Cise introduced a number of news stories reporting on the grand jury investigation of racketeering and quackery and asked Spears if the name of his institution appeared in any of them. "Only by innuendo," he answered. "The public knew Mr. Byers was investigating this institution." [43]

At Ginsberg's request, Spears gave a lengthy description of his institution's approach to the treatment of cancer, and the theory behind the causes of cancer. "It is the final step in a deterioration of diseased nerve and body tissue," he told the court. The only way to get rid of the disease, he said, is to restore the proper function of nerve and cell flow. "We don't cure. We don't ever claim to cure disease, and I never have so claimed. Only nature, God, the Infinite Intelligence that builds life from two tiny cells can cure."

"There is no mystery about it," he said. "We simply reverse the process of deterioration or uncontrolled growth. This is our way of getting rid of the causes of disease. We know that the body is self-regulating, self-eliminating and self-healing." [44]

Spears listed eight causes of cancer:

1- Interference to nerve supply to the area affected.

2- Body wastes (poisons) resulting from poor elimination from one or more of the eliminative organs.

3- Wrong foods and food combinations which cause **vitamin imbalances** and over-stimulation of the growth of **cancer cells**.

4- Trauma of tissue cells.

5- Hormonal imbalances resulting from some hormone-forming glands manufacturing too much and others too little of their natural secretions.

6- Enzyme imbalances, resulting from chemical alterations in digestive juices and body metabolism,

7- Imbalance of vital combinations between hormones, enzymes and vitamins, resulting from chemical alterations in these substances.

8- Pathogens and malignans – poisonous excretions thrown into the blood stream from the diseases progressing into cancer – and the first and succeeding lesions of cancer itself.

Asked on cross-examination if he claimed that diabetes could be cured by chiropractic, Spears replied, "We've had a good many cases in which the person so treated didn't have to take insulin."

After admitting that he too was a diabetic, Spears added, "I wouldn't be alive today if it had not been for chiropractic treatment."

"You wouldn't be alive without insulin either, would you?"

"Probably not. I'm not at all ashamed of that. I'm pround of what the medical doctors are doing. I have no criticism at all." [45]

Defense attorneys introduced as evidence testimonials accompanied by death certificates to show that persons who gave the testimonials were dead. Charles Ginsberg objected that the statements made in the testimonials were true and that the subsequent death of certain individuals had no bearing on the validity of the testimonials. No warranty goes with patients treated at Spears that they will never die," Ginsberg said. "If that were true, there would not be enough room at Spears to accommodate all the people in the world." [46,47]

The second week of witness testimony wrapped up with Dr. Dan Spears, hospital chief of staff, who was questioned on the impact of the alleged conspiracy on the institution's business. A "great loss" of income resulted from the publicity, he said; so much so that staff employees took a wage cut in 1954, which continued in effect. "It was the employees' contribution to save the institution." [48]

Defense motions for judgment and for dismissal were introduced on September 26. Judge McWilliams dismissed a general motion for dismissal but granted motions to dismiss the 26 corporations named in the suit as well as the state medical society. [49-52]

McWilliams took the case under advisement Tuesday, October 4, the second day of the fourth week of trial. He informed attorneys that he would hand down a written opinion within 10 days. [53-55]

The decision came down on October 14, when Judge Robert McWilliams cleared all defendants of the conspiracy charge. At the same time, McWilliams ruled that the Spears corporation had no legal status to bring an action in court. [56]

Assessing costs of the defendants against Spears, the judge granted motions to file for a new trial.

Attorney General Burt Keating said he would study the court decision "with a view toward prosecution" as soon as a motion for a new trial is disposed of.[57] The *Denver Post* took note of the legal conundrum:

> A District Court ruling Thursday holding that chiropractors working for a salary at Spears Chiropractic Hospital place the corporation in a position of practicing medicine and chiropractic without a license could draw attention from medical-legal circles throughout the nation.
>
> A major feud has been underway for several years between hospitals and the medical profession over hospital employment of doctors on salary. The employed doctors are specialists in pathology and radiology and head hospital laboratories and X-ray departments.
>
> The medical profession has long contended that hospital employment of these specialists places the hospital corporations in the position of practicing medicine without a license.
>
> In Colorado, the question became a major issue in 1954 and although the State Board of Medical Examiners emerged the apparent victor, the president of the board was virtually fired from his position by Governor Johnson.
>
> The board, whose president was then Dr. George R. Buck of Denver, obtained a ruling from Attorney General Duke W. Dunbar holding that hospitals employing radiologists and pathologists were practicing medicine through those employees but without a license. Dunbar also held that the individual doctors, in working for corporations, even though they only head labs and X-ray departments, were themselves in violation of the medical practice act.
>
> Thus armed, the Board of Medical Examiners held in 1954 all radiologists and pathologists employed by hospitals to enter into special contracts with those hospital corporations under which the doctors would be independent agents leasing working space for their specialties from the hospital.
>
> The hospitals opposed the board vigorously, but all radiologists and pathologists complied.
>
> In June of this year, however, after all hospitals were complying with the law by contract, Governor Johnson refused to reappoint Dr. Buck to the board and cited Buck's activities in the corporate practice of medicine as his reason.
>
> In Iowa, hospitals and the medical profession have already reached the courts with their battle over hospital employment of doctors.[58]

"Spears Hospital is operating and will continue to do so. It is enroute now to the Colorado Supreme Court seeking reversal of the District Court decision," Leo Spears said in his first comment on the verdict.[59,60] (*See Appendix L.*)

12.
Transition

During the early hours of Wednesday, May 16, 1956, Dr. Leo L. Spears suffered a fatal heart attack at his residence. According to house guests, he was reading in bed when the massive seizure struck at about 1:30 a.m. As would be expected, his death was major news, not only in Colorado but nationwide.[1,2]

Locally, the *Denver Post* announced the news with a banner headline and front page coverage, while the *Rocky Mountain News* chose to place the story on page 24.[3,4]

While Leo Spears did not hold to any religious belief in the traditional sense,[5] he was not irreverent. His might have been described as a kind of cosmic consciousness. In an eerily prescient way, this was evident on his last day when he addressed the hospital staff meeting. Usually at such meetings he would comment on matters of immediate import to the hospital. That morning, however, he spoke at some length of the journey of the "spirit" after death. "They are all around us," he is remembered saying.[6]

Funeral services were held May 21 at the Calvary (Baptist) Temple on West Colfax Ave., with interment at Fairmount Cemetery. His longtime friend Rev. Charles E. Blair officiated. A policeman directing traffic, commenting on the size of the cortege, was heard to say that it was the largest he had ever seen.[7]

Literally thousands of expressions of sympathy were received at the hospital from friends, colleagues and former patients.[8]

On August 7, during the weeklong annual Spears Seminar, longtime friend and attorney Charles Ginsberg delivered a stirring eulogy (*See Appendix M.*) The ceremony concluded by unveiling of the bust of Dr. Leo which adorned the hospital lobby for many years. It was sculpted by Victor Personette, a grateful former patient.[9] Another familiar Personette creation was a cherub on the hospital's front lawn.

Reorganization of the hospital's executive tier was accomplished swiftly and almost unnoticed. Dr. Dan Spears took his uncle's position as secretary-treasurer of the board of trustees, while Dr. Howard Spears was named president of the board. Both would share the day -to-day responsibilities as hospital co-directors. Dr. Paul Grant became chief-of-staff of the clinic, a post formerly occupied by Dr. Howard.[10]

Dan Spears told the press that his uncle's death would not interrupt the multimillion dollar hospital expansion plans.[11] Mr. Ginsberg said it would have no effect on status of an appeal of the $11 million suit for alleged conspiracy against the *Denver Post*, the Denver Better Business Bureau and more than 80 businessmen who were BBB officers, a suit lost in District Court a year earlier and appealed to the Colorado Supreme Court.[12] The appeal was decided on June 10, 1957, when the Supreme Court ruled that the defendants did not conspire to put Spears Hospital out of business. But the high court declined to rule on the trial court's further finding that the hospital was operating in an illegal manner.[13] (*See Appendix N.*) No further action in the case is indicated in the public records.[14]

Dr. Leo Spears would prove as controversial in death as he was in life. Only three days after his funeral, the press reported the existence of four separate wills filed in the Orphan's Court, only one of which had actually been witnessed. Mr. Ginsberg said he believed all four were probably invalid but that a judge would make a determination. As to Spears' supposed "enormous wealth," Ginsberg estimated the estate's value at less than $30,000.[15]

When Dr. Leo found himself in domestic relations court in November 1954, the chief issue of dispute with his ex-wife were two notes originally totaling $28,592 endorsed to Mrs. Spears in 1948, but who now testified that she had no independent source of income. The judge denied Dr. Spears' contention that the notes were community property and held that they were "freely endorsed" and "belong exclusively to Mrs. Spears." Deducting personal loans made on the notes to his wife, he was ordered to pay the balance now due -- $16,781.[16] The court also ruled that the hospital return to Dr. Leo the residence and clinic at 2209 - 13th Ave., which he bought in 1937 and sold to the corporation. The property was then to be sold with Mrs. Spears receiving 45 percent of the net proceeds.[17] (Spears Clinic relocated to the hospital shortly after Dr. Leo's death.)

The property settlement hearing in the judge's words was "entirely free from selfishness, vindictiveness and hostility." Spears had suggested to the court that his ex-wife be given a monthly sum rather than a lump payment "because she might lose it and I'm interested in seeing she is taken care the rest of her life." He had also offered his former wife a job at the hospital, "if she wishes." "I haven't spent any money for years," he also told the court. "I have very little idea where my money goes. I have very little time for that."[18] The first will was dated July 22, 1937, and carried the signatures of two witnesses — Clara Ehrlich and F.R. Margetts (presumably Dr. Frank R. Margetts, another local chiropractor of some note). In it was an intriguing notation, and indication that he had received a promise from Denver Mayor Ben Stapleton to give a wing in the county hospital for continuing his clinic for poor children. "If he does not keep his promise, I hope the people of Denver will demand that he do so and that all tax-supported hospitals be forced to provide chiropractic... to all the poor and the people who support them," the will said. "Were it not for the fact that I have many brothers, sisters, nephews and nieces who are very poor and whose chances in life have been very few and who desperately need my help, I would leave my entire estate to the perpetuation of my free clinic for poor children." [19]

Other wills were dated June 6, 1952, March 29, 1954, and March 5, 1955, and carried no witness' signature.

The 1952 will left 50 percent of his estate to his then-wife Laura, with the remainder to be distributed to his and his wife's immediate family. A codicil dated September 29 of that year noted that his wife left him on September 11 and expressed her desire to file for divorce. He directed that all bequests to her be rescinded and given to his family.

In the 1954 will, written in pen and ink on the stationery of the Mayflower Hotel, Washington, D.C., he bequeathed "my worldly goods," to his mother, a sister and two of her children and other family members "according to their immediate needs." Any funds left over, he directed that they should be used as a student loan fund for "poor but worthy young men and women who want to become chiropractors."

The most recent will left his estate for the benefit of his relatives and directed that his former wife, Laura Lyle Spears Ohlson, who had divorced him in 1954, should receive help should she need it. Distribution would be determined by the administrators--nephews Dan and Howard Spears and Perry McClellan, and a sister, Mrs. Daisy Ivey. "To suffering humanity and especially little children, I leave the Spears Chiropractic Sanitarium and Hospital to be directed by the board of directors in perpetuity."

After direction of the hospital passed into the hands of Drs. Dan and Howard Spears, the institution continued to flourish albeit with a new tone and in a different direction. Gone were the flamboyant testimonials and claims that so characterized Dr. Leo's approach and often dismayed even his most loyal supporters.

Doubtless, most staffers found the calm diplomacy of Dan and Howard a welcome change from the impatience and bayonet directness of Dr. Leo. Well remembered by those who were there was his display of unbridled rage just before Christmas 1955. In this instance, the Ford Foundation had snubbed Spears while gifting each of Colorado's private hospitals.[20,21] Dr. Leo's shoot-from-the-hip response would have seen one staff member's new Ford Fairlane torched before rolling TV cameras at 16th and Broadway. Fortunately, cooler heads prevailed.[22]

Two national media productions, one released at the very time of Dr. Leo's death and the other in late summer, emphasized the divergency of views that were possible in presenting any story about Dr. Leo Spears.

In May, a startup scandal magazine out of New York, in its first edition, featured Spears as "The Nation's Most Notorious Quack Healer." The author, one Herbert Wiener, rehashed the usual controversies while unabashedly injecting his own bias. Of the landmark 1950 Supreme Court verdict, Wiener wrote that Spears "wheedled a unanimous decision in his favor." (Nine justices sit on the Colorado Supreme bench.) Neither could Wiener see much good in chiropractic, or any drugless treatment. Certainly his knowledge of chiropractic has to be questioned when a photo caption with the article reads: "Palmer Memorial Building, just one unit of Spears' Denver hospital, was named after the founder of chiropractic, D.D. Palmer, who taught Spears all he knows."[23]

The other was a film – "The Spears Hospital Story",– completed during the summer and shown September 9, 1956, on ABC-TV's "Cavalcade of Progress." The weekly program was hosted by well-known radio-TV personality Norman Brokenshire.[24]

During the summer of 1958, Spears Hospital was being touted as the logical site for a proposed new chiropractic college, created out of the possible merger of up to three existing schools.[25-27] But Dr. Dan Spears sought to end such speculation:

> At the present time we are in no position to enter the school business as it is not our desire to injure the other schools. So for now, I guess we will just have to let the schools forge for themselves and we will continue to accept interns from all of the recognized colleges.[28]

Denver's own University of the Natural of the Healing Arts (UNHA) did, in fact, briefly occupy space in the hospital's Unit 1, according to then-president Dr. Louis O. Gearhart:

> In 1959, the UNHA board of trustees and the Colorado Chiropractic Association decided to develop the (school) property and close the college. UNHA needed a place to finish the schooling of the last class of students. Dr. Dan offered space in the empty Willard Carver building so UNHA and the CCA could continue to function.
>
> Our last class did its final work there and graduated in 1961. There was no affiliation with Spears Hospital. They were kind enough to assist UNHA and the CCA through a difficult transition.[29]

The shell of the burdensome Pioneers Building was sold in 1966 to developers and completed for a planned senior citizen residence and nursing home, but the venture fell into bankruptcy.[30-31] Another operator later met the same fate. That the building was perhaps just too large and its interior design too unwieldy to be operated profitably can be appreciated from the fact that it remained vacant many more years, in the hands of its bank receiver. Boarded up and vandalized, it seemed doomed to a clientless limbo. A change of fortune, however, revived the structure in the mid 1990s. Today, as The Towers at Eighth Avenue, the building appears to have found prosperity as a moderately priced apartment block.

Remaining in the shadows for years as a stalwart friend and advisor of Dr. Leo, seldom seen but a presence nonetheless, was one Andrew J. Sordoni. A self-made multimillionaire, he was president of Sordoni Enterprises of Wilkes-Barre, Pennsylvania, a real estate and construction behemoth that included a telephone company, a chain of hotels and employed 5,000 people. Sordoni had been a Pennsylvania state senator and the secretary of commerce.

It was Sordoni's clinical interest in the construction of Unit 3 that give rise to persistent rumors that he was Spears' "angel," something both parties vehemently denied.[32-33]

What made Andrew Sordoni unique to the chiropractic profession was his willingness to explore the value of its services in industry, testified to by the fact that he employed five full-time D.C's to serve his employees,- productivity and efficiency being paramount to his way of doing business.[34-37] Mr. Sordoni died in 1963.[38]

Dr. Roy L. Cleere, implacable Colorado health commissioner who may have been Leo Spears' bitterest foe, resigned from his post in August 1973, during a pro-forma cabinet reorganization of incoming Governor John Vanderhoof. He died from cancer September 27, 1983, at the age of 77.[39-40]

Bert M. Keating, bombastic Denver district attorney who had vowed to see Spears Hospital put out of business, died from cancer July 5, 1967. He was 63.[41]

Charles Ginsberg, attorney and passionately loyal friend of Dr. Leo, died at age 81 on May 7, 1975, of complications from surgery following an automobile accident.[42-43]

Dr. Neal Bishop, Colorado legislator for more than 20 years, died May 20, 1980, at the age of 79. Although not always appearing to be on the friendliest of terms with Leo Spears, he maintained that he was fair and impartial as a state lawmaker and colleague.[44]

Dr. George A. Wilson, the hospital's former director of research, died in Salt Lake City, November 26, 1969.[45]

Dr. Dan Spears died unexpectedly December 13, 1988 of a heart attack,[46] while his brother, Dr. Howard Spears, lives in retirement in suburban Denver.

Dan's sons--Raymond, Richard and Charles--followed their father into chiropractic and still operate the clinic founded by the great-uncle in 1921. The Spears Clinic is located in Englewood, Colorado.

B.J. Palmer and Leo Spears, although they occasionally appeared together at professional functions, maintained at best an arm's length relationship. Leo had made a genuine attempt to repair the rift in their friendship with an offer to name Unit 1 in his honor, but B.J. would have none of it.[47] For Palmer to be in any way associated with a "quasi-medical" institution was anathema.[48] In fact, B.J., in his book *Fight to Climb*, was openly hostile in characterizing Leo's hospital and its protocols on patient care.[49]

With B.J.'s wife Mabel, Leo had always enjoyed a cordial friendship. But in 1947, when Mabel Palmer became ill and Leo invited her to the hospital for treatment, she declined. According to Dr. Dan Spears, she declined only because of B.J.[50] Mabel Heath Palmer died in Arizona in 1949.[51] B.J. died at his Sarasota, Florida, residence in 1961.[52]

Dan Spears described a social call that he and Howard made on B.J. not long after their uncle's death. "He was a very gracious host and I am sure many of the ill feelings that he may have had prior to that time were erased as a result of our visit." [53]

Charges occasionally hurled that Spears Free Clinic and Hospital for Poor Children, Inc. was not a nonprofit institution, including those in the infamous Herbert Wiener article, were, of course, ridiculous. At the very least, such charges belied knowledge of the law. As with any corporation, even a non-profit must show an operating profit or cease to exist. The Spears corporation's announced charitable purpose was never violated nor did its officers ever share in distribution of the corporation's legal profits, the very definition of 501(c)(3) nonprofit, tax-exempt status. Financial reports required annually by state and federal government indicate that through the years $10 million in charitable services had been rendered.[54] More than 150,000 patients, many from foreign countries, had received care from the Spears Clinic over the years,[55] but how many had also been patients at the hospital is unknown.

Like an uninvited guest, Medicare would cast a cloud of uncertainty on the future of the hospital. The 1972 amendment to the federal program allowed limited in-office benefits for chiropractic services but stopped short of recognizing hospitalization. As other insurers began to imitate Medicare limitations, Spears found itself cut off from its most important source of revenue and no longer able to compete.

The hospital closed in March 1983. Ironically, while many trumpeted Medicare inclusion as an advance for the profession, more than any single factor it was responsible for the demise of one of chiropractic's most visible symbols of strength. The 50-year-old landmark was sold by the family in January 1993 and by summer had fallen under the wrecker's ball. Upscale townhomes were built on the 10-acre tract. The five remaining acres, where once a chiropractic college, nursing school, hotel and mid-rise housing units were envisioned, became a city park. Except for the apartment tower once intended to be the Pioneers Building, there are no reminders of the past. It seems an ignoble ending for the once thriving institution that had overcome so much adversity just to open its doors and keep them open.

Afterword

I first heard of Spears Hospital when about 15 and my father was practicing in a small town in western New York. Testimonials in the hospital's mass-mailed tabloids would be a topic of dinner conversations and it was then that I was told that Leo Spears was a member of my father's graduating class at the Palmer School of Chiropractic in 1921.

Yes, it was true that Leo wore his World War I Marine uniform to class - though not every day. And yes, he did build a hospital that was the largest in the profession and one of the largest in Colorado. Some years later, in 1980, I visited it for the first time when Bill Rehm convened the organizational meeting of the Association for the History of Chiropractic in the D.D. Palmer Memorial Building.

Reading Bill's text evoked those memories, but it also placed Spears into the larger context of his times, recalling the forces of adversity and organized opposition which he seemingly thrived upon in his 35 years of practice. Spears was, after all, a flawed and complicated person--as are most men and women of achievement. Is not history but a chronicle of such flawed yet exceptional human beings?

Spears had a "central casting" birth and childhood – born poor in a log cabin, thirsting for knowledge, practicing the work ethic and seeking to explore the outside world through the talents and education he would acquire on the way. Two years in the Marine Corps and the clinical experience of chiropractic as a patient completed his profile before he embarked to Davenport.

If that was Horatio Alger then his chiropractic career would embody all of the attributions which the century would employ in classifying those who would make their mark in the turmoil and turbulence between and after the Great Wars. Spears was, in every sense of their definitions, an entrepreneur, a radical, a maverick, a progressive and a humanitarian.

And on the flawed and complicated side, Leo Spears was also excessively litigious, flamboyant and "unprofessional," not to say his hallmark, controversial. An objective overview of Leo Spears might also conclude that his public announcements in the areas of cancer and cancer research, multiple sclerosis and "skull molding" were borderline if not outright quackery.

Yet despite all this, Spears remains a tower of influence and significance in the turmoil of chiropractic in its first century. He would not accept a second-class role for his hospital or for the profession. He was willing to go to court in every instance, despite the fact that the media, many in the business community and the forces of the hospital and medical lobbies were arrayed against him. That he antagonized many of his fellow chiropractors was to be expected. Like B.J. Palmer, you either loved him or hated him, but you knew that he was making a difference.

Leo Spears anticipated the "practice builders" by decades, and his personal and institutional success was reaped by his professional peers. Dr. Bill Rehm patiently and meticulously takes us through the turmoil and even torment that was his path. He is shown to be generous, not only to countless children in Depression-era Denver, but also to his fellow chiropractors. Spears' energy was constant, despite his hospital becoming a firewall for defamation and calumny against his profession.

Consider that Leo Spears was the head of his hospital for only 13 of its 40 years and that expansion stopped with his death. The seemingly impossible dream envisioned by his architect friend Walter Simon in the multiple campus in east Denver could have become a reality--the Pioneers Building was well on its way to completion when Spears died. His whole life suggests that rusty hinge on the doors of history --"what if?"

What if Spears had won one of the libel and defamation suits, and it had been upheld? What if the medical and political establishment had accommodated to his presence? What if chiropractic leaders had endorsed an educational and clinical marriage on his campus, with internship as a prerequisite? Any of those could have happened, and together would have changed the course of chiropractic history. Yet the largest "what if" would have been necessary for implementation of any and all of these--what if Leo Spears had lived for another 10 or 20 years?

The possibilities are intriguing, as is the story of Spears and his hospital--a fascinating account of perseverance and determination in difficult times for his profession.

Russell W. Gibbons
Editor Emeritus
Chiropractic History

End Notes

Author's Introduction

1. James Truslow Adams: The Epic of America (Garden City Books, Garden City, N.Y., 1933), p. 190.
2. Leo L. Spears (Guest editorial): Stop manufacture and sale of pistols. Denver Post, Dec. 8, 1948.
3. Leo L. Spears (Guest editorial): Pistol elimination would reduce crime. Denver Post, Jan. 1, 1949.
4. Related to author anonymously.
5. Inside City Hall (Column). Denver Post, Sept. 23, 1951.
6. Why do I publish my picture? Rocky Mountain News, Feb. 22, 1925.

Prologue

1. Dan C. Spears: Tape-recorded interview by Brian Greer, 1983.
2. In world in 9 years: handicapped by lack of education, man wins his way. Rocky Mountain News, Sept. 16, 1921.
3. Ibid.
4. Dan Spears, op cit.
5. Op cit.
6. Op cit.
7. General matriculation data, Palmer College of Chiropractic Archives.
8. Large framed photograph on display in the library of Life Chiropractic College West, Hayward, Calif.
9. Dan Spears, op cit.
10. Commencement Program, Palmer School of Chiropractic.
11. The date of April 4, 1921, is indicated in the Palmer College Archives, suggesting that commencement exercises preceded completion of course work.
12. Erna Rex: *The Lengthening Shadow* (Golden Bell Press, Denver, 1962), p. 56.
13. Arts and Humanities Department, Denver Public Library.
14. The revised Colorado Medical Practice Act of 1917 provided for licensing of chiropractors by the Board of Medical Examiners. The Board of Chiropractic Examiners was authorized by statute in 1933 (Editorial, *Colochirogram*, Sept. 1938). Leo L. Spears was issued license #300 by the medical board in 1921 and license #54 by the chiropractic board in 1933 (Colorado Department of Regulatory Agencies, standard demographic data).
15. Dan Spears, op cit.
16. Op cit.
17. Leo L. Spears: Testimony in disciplinary hearing before State Board of Medical Examiners, April 11, 1924.

Early Controversies

1. Kenneth W. Maxcy: *Rosenau's Preventive Medicine and Hygiene* (Appleton-Century-Crofts, New York, 1951), p. 2.
2. Maxcy, 16-17.
3. Ibid. 4. Five more die of smallpox. *Denver Times*, Nov. 25, 1922.
5. Throngs seek vaccination. *Denver Times*, Nov. 22, 1922.
6. Vaccination of all persons in Denver ordered. *Denver Post*, Nov. 21, 1922.
7. 3,000 children are vaccinated. *Denver Times*, Nov. 24, 1922.
8. Rex, p. 5.
9. Advertisement. *Denver Times*, Nov. 23, 1922.
10. Advertisement. *Denver Post*, Nov. 22, 1922.
11. Smallpox fatal to five. *Denver Post*, Nov. 27, 1922.
12. Federal surgeon to take charge in epidemic. *Denver Post*, Nov. 28, 1922.
13. Osteopaths urge vaccination to check smallpox. *Denver Post*, Nov. 29, 1922.

END NOTES

14. U.S. surgeon sent to war on smallpox. *Denver Times*, Nov. 28, 1922.

15. Full vaccination to end smallpox within ten days. *Denver Post*, Dec. 2, 1922.

16. Vaccines not required by law. *Denver Post*, Jan. 18, 1967.

17. Letter from Leo L. Spears to Board of Medical Examiners, April 4, 1927, to wit: "I have refused to run any ads favoring the present anti-compulsory vaccination bill now in the legislature despite the accusations of my friends that I have turned coward."

18. Advertisement. *Denver Post*, Feb. 24, 1924.

19. Letter from Benjamin I. Hall to the *Rocky Mountain News*, Feb. 26, 1924.

20. Letter from G.B. West to the *Rocky Mountain News*, Feb. 26, 1924.

21. Notice and notorized complaint, Board of Medical Examiners to Leo L. Spears, Feb. 28, 1924.

22. Telegram from U.S. Surgeon General to Board of Medical Examiners, March 16, 1924.

23. List of subpoenas (Colorado State Archives).

24. Request to Yuma County, Colo., Clerk & Recorder for certified copy of marriage certificate, March 20, 1924.

25. Certified copy of marriage certificate, March 25, 1924.

26. Letters between Whitehead, Vogl & Miles, attorneys at law, and Board of Medical Examiners et al. (Colorado State Archives).

27. Testimony in hearing before Board of Medical Examiners, April 1, 1924.

28. Op cit.

29. Recorder's minutes, April 11, 1924.

30. Testimony, April 11, 1924.

31. Op cit.

32. Op cit.

33. Resolution of Board of Medical Examiners, April 16, 1924.

34. License revocation order, April 17, 1924.

35. Letter from Board of Medical Examiners to Clerk & Recorder of the County of Denver April 17, 1924.

36. That's That (Column), unattributed & undated (Colorado State Archives).

37. Advertisement. Community Herald, April 19, 1924.

38. Opinion of Judge Charles C. Butler, District Court, Division 3, in Spears v. State Board of Medical Examiners, Case #95765, Sept. 25, 1924.

39. Letter from H.T. Young to Board of Medical Examiners, July 28, 1925.

40. Spears v. Board of Medical Examiners, 79 Colo. 588, July 6, 1926.

41. Chiropractor loses fight for license. *Denver Post*, June 6, 1926.

42. High court upholds revoking of license of Dr. Leo Spears. *Rocky Mountain News*, June 8, 1926.

43. Spears v. Board of Medical Examiners, 275 U.S. 508, Dec. 12, 1927.

44. Letter from Samuel W. Crosby to Board of Medical Examiners, Jan. 16, 1928.

45. Opinion from the bench in Federal District Court, Spears v. State Board of Medical Examiners et al., Jan. 23, 1928.

46. Letter from Samuel W. Crosby to Board of Medical Examiners, Jan. 27, 1928.

47. Transcript of Federal Court opinion in Spears v. State Board of Medical Examiners et al., March 27, 1928.

48. Leo Spears to Board of Medical Examiners, March 31, 1928.

49. Joint resolution of Colorado Chiropractic Association and Denver Chiropractic Association, March 31, 1928.

50. File correspondence (Colorado State Archives).

51. Memorandum of agreement between Colorado State Board of Medical Examiners and Leo L. Spears, April 2, 1928.

52. Agreement on ethical standards signed by Leo L. Spears, D.C., C.E. Johnson, D.C., and Leo E. Wunsch, D.C., April 2, 1929.

53. Letter from Board of Medical Examiners to D.H. Burwell, April 18, 1927.

54. File correspondence (Colorado State Archives).

55. Letter from Charles W. Burgess to Leo L. Spears, Jan. 17, 1927.

56. Letter from Charles W. Burgess to David A. Strickler, Jan. 18, 1927.

57. Letter from Frank R. Spencer to Alphonse Ardourel, Colorado, Sept. 9, 1929.

58. Marked-up copy of A Pleasant Way to Health (booklet) by Leo L. Spears & Associates. (Colorado State Archives.)

59. Resolution of State Board of Medical Examiners, Jan. 5, 1932.

60. Statement of Leo L. Spears to disciplinary hearing before Board of Medical Examiners, April 5, 1932.

61. File correspondence (Colorado State Archives).

62. Letter from W. Whitridge Williams to Board of Medical Examiners, July 11, 1932.

63. Letter from W. Whitridge Williams to Leo L. Spears, Aug. 19, 1932.

64. Ibid.

An "Astounding" Practice

1. Dan C. Spears, interview, 1983.

2. Rex, *The Lengthening Shadow*, p. 94.

3. Leo L. Spears: Children's Clinics. *The Chiropractic Journal*, Sept. 1935.

4. Ibid.

4. Leo Spears: Children's Clinics. *The Chiropractic Journal*, Nov. 1935.

5. Ibid.

6. Leo Spears: Children's Clinics. *The Chiropractic Journal*, Oct. 1936.

7. Leo Spears: Children's Clinics. *The Chiropractic Journal*, Aug. 1936.

8. Property settlement awarded to Mrs. Leo Spears. *Rocky Mountain News,* Nov. 23, 1954.

9. Esmond Wright (ed.): *An Illustrated History of the Modern World* (Barnes & Noble, New York, 1993), p. 367.

10. Kenneth C. Davis: *Don't Know Much About History?* (Avon, New York, 1990), p. 273.

11. Stephan J. Leonard: Trials and Triumphs: *A Colorado Portrait of the Great Depression* (University Press, Boulder, 1993).

12. Rex, ibid.

13. Dan Spears, op cit.

14. Leo Spears: Children's Clinics. *The Chiropractic Journal*, June 1936.

15. Dan Spears, op cit..

16. Op cit.

17. Op cit.

18. Leo L. Spears and Associates: The Pleasant Way to Health (booklet).

19. Leo L. Spears: *Spears Painless System of Chiropractic* (Great America Press, Denver, 1926).

20. Chester C. Stowell: Lincoln college and the "big four": a chiropractic protest." *Chiropractic History*, 3:1, 1983.

21. See note #8.

22. L.M. Rogers (Editorial): The brew boiled over. *National Chiropractic Association Journal*, 2:2, 1932.

23. Dzaman, Fern L., et al. (eds.): *Who's Who in Chiropractic International* (WWIC Publishing Co., Littleton, Colo., 1980), p. 225.

24. Dzaman, et al., p. 226.

25. Dzaman, et al., p. 165.

26. Tribute to Dr. J. Paul Grant. *Florida Chiropractic Association Journal*, Spring 1999.

27. Related to author by Loren Trotter. (Author's diary, 1955-1956.)

28. Jeff Miller: *Stapleton International Airport: The First Fifty Years* (Pruell Press, Boulder, 1983).

29. Op cit.

30. Leonard. 31. Rex, p. 88.

32. Rex, p. 112.
33. See note #8.
34. Dan Spears, op cit..
35. Op cit.
36. Op cit.
37. Op cit.
38. Op cit.
39. Op cit.
40. Op cit.
41. Dzaman, et al., p. 225.
42. Dzaman, et al., p. 226.

The Hospital: Unit 1
1. Facts ... *Spears Sanitarium News*, (3) 1947.
2. Dan C. Spears, interview, 1983.
3. Op cit.
4. Compiled from various sources.
5. *Who's Who in America*, 1951-1952 (A.N. Marquis, Chicago, 1952).
6. Dan C. Spears in conversation with author, June 5, 1988.
7. Minutes of the Colorado State Board of Health, Feb. 1, 1943.
8. Minutes, June 4, 1943.
9. Dan Spears, op cit..
10. Op cit.
11. Rex, *The Lengthening Shadow*, p. 10
12. Dan Spears, op cit..
13. Rex, ibid.
14. Minutes, May 4, 1943.
15. License is denied new Spears clinic. *Rocky Mountain News*, May 6, 1943.
16. State board explains denial of license to Spears. *Rocky Mountain News*, May 7, 1943.
17. Spears hospital sues in attempt to obtain license. *Denver Post*, May 22, 1943.
18. Spears sues city and state to obtain license. *Rocky Mountain News*, May 22, 1943.
19. Minutes, June 4, 1943.
20. Suit to obtain license for Spears clinic fails. *Rocky Mountain News*, June 11, 1943.
21. Minutes, June 4, 1943.
22. Op cit.
23. Letter from Charles Ginsberg to Gov. John C. Vivian, June 17, 1943.
24. Letter from Gov. Vivian to Roy L. Cleere, June 19, 1943.
25. Manslaughter is charged to chiropractors. *Denver Post,* June 14, 1943.
26. Dr. Spears arrested; accused of manslaughter. Rocky Mountain News, June 15, 1943.
27. Handwritten notes on file (Colorado State Archives).
28. Patients moved as court closes new Spears hospital. *Rocky Mountain News*, June 16, 1943.
29. Dan Spears, op cit.
30. Op cit.
31. Op cit.
32. Op cit.
33. Disbarment charges filed. *Denver Post*, Dec. 17, 1929.
34. See note #27.
35. Charles Ginsberg barred as lawyer for one year. *Rocky Mountain News*, Feb. 18, 1930.
36. Veteran Denver lawyer fined for contempt of court. *Rocky Mountain News*, Nov. 13, 1958.
37. Keating to file $1 million libel suit against Ginsberg. *Rocky Mountain News*, July 8, 1962.
38. Keating files $1 million suit for slander. *Rocky Mountain News*, July 11, 1962.
39. Well-known attorney ordered to pay $17,300 fine. *Denver Post*, March 22, 1971.
40. Minutes, Sept. 9, 1943.

41. Minutes, Oct. 5, 1943.

42. Op cit.

43. Minutes, April 4, 1944

44. License application, July 31, 1943.

45. Various reports on file. (Colorado State Archives.)

46. Minutes, Dec. 3, 1945.

47. Minutes, May 7, 1946.

48. Minutes, June 4, 1946.

49. The relevant minutes of the Board of Health in the Colorado State Archives end at this point with the notation: "The complete transcript of the hearing in the Spears case are now in the hands of the Supreme Court. 1-18-50."

50. Sanitarium license dispute is spirited. *Rocky Mountain News*, July 10, 1946.

51. Hearing on sanitarium license becomes series of verbal bouts. *Rocky Mountain News*, July 11, 1946.

52. Spears case is recessed. *Denver Post*, July 11, 1946.

53. Drinkwater to appear at prejudice hearing. *Rocky Mountain News*, July 21, 1946.

54. Drinkwater must take testimony. *Denver Post*, July 21, 1946.

55. Dr. R.L. Drinkwater upheld in hot prejudice hearing. *Rocky Mountain News*, Aug. 7, 1946.

56. Health board order dooms Spears clinic. *Rocky Mountain News*, Nov. 23, 1946.

57. Court to review Spears hearing. *Rocky Mountain News*, Jan. 14, 1947.

58. Spears bid for license refused. *Denver Post*, Dec. 17, 1948.

59. High court gets Leo Spears case. *Denver Post*, May 22, 1950.

60. Supreme court hears Spears sanitarium suit. *Rocky Mountain News*, May 23, 1950.

The Hospital: Unit 2

1. Work is started on second unit of Spears hospital. *Denver Post*, Sept. 2, 1945. 2. Dan C. Spears, interview, 1983.

3. D.D. Palmer building nearing completion. *Spears Sanitarium News*, 2, 1946.

4. $500,000 addition to sanitarium. *Rocky Mountain News*, Sept. 2, 1945.

5. Four hundred patients will be accommodated. *Denver Post*, Sept. 2, 1945.

6. Spears sanitarium growing. *Spears Sanitarium News*, 1, 1946.

7. Will cost $250,000 to furnish new building. *Spears Sanitarium News*, 3, 1949.

8. Profession has taken over Denver school. *Spears Sanitarium News*, 2, 1946.

9. Letter from Louis O. Gearhart to author, May 9, 1998.

10. See note #1.

11. See note #7.

12. Palmer building now open. *Spears Sanitarium News*, 6, 1949.

13. Ibid.

14. New sanitarium opens Sunday. *Denver Post*, Jan. 9, 1949.

15. Spears sanitarium opens new 600-bed addition. *Denver Post*, Jan. 12, 1949.

16. Spears opens building. *Rocky Mountain News*, Jan. 13, 1949.

17. Application blanks now available for postgraduate work and internship. *Spears Sanitarium News*, 3, 1948.

18. Ibid.

19. P.G. work will start first week of May - FREE! *Spears Sanitarium News*, 6, 1949.

20. Spears to operate nursing school. *Spears Sanitarium News*, 2, 1946.

21. Texas grad first interne [sic] at Spears sanitarium. *Spears Sanitarium News*, 6, 1949.

22. Letter from Arnold M. Goldschmidt to author, Feb. 12, 1994.

23. Spears Chiropractic Sanitarium & Hospital pictorial, undated.

24. City council okays Spears hospital bill. *Denver Post*, March 30, 1948.

25. Editorial: Spears-Stafford vs. the people. *Rocky Mountain News*, April 7, 1948.

26. Montclair assoc. asks mayor to veto Spears rezoning ordinance. *Rocky Mountain News*, April 1, 1948.

27. Mayor gives reasons for Spears plan veto. *Rocky Mountain News*, April 3, 1948.
28. Spears bill loses in council. *Denver Post*, May 4, 1954.
29. 2 Stafford rezoning measures given approval by city council. *Rocky Mountain News*, May 11, 1948.
30. Facts ... *Spears Sanitarium News*, 3, 1948.
31. Council kills measure to rezone 6-block area near Spears clinic. *Rocky Mountain News*, July 13, 1948.
32. City council okays Spears zoning bill. *Rocky Mountain News*, July 27, 1948.
33. A new chiropractic "babe" is born. *Spears Sanitarium News*, 9 (Oct.) 1949.
34. Ibid.

The Hospital: Unit 3
1. Huge underground shelter planned for Spears hospital. *Denver Post*, Feb. 25, 1951.
2. Ibid.
3. Spears sued by city for machinery taxes. *Denver Post*, March 20, 1951.
4. Spears' Free Clinic and Hospital for Poor Children v. Wilson. Supreme Court of Colorado, 103 Colo. 182, Oct. 24, 1938.
5. Spears discloses plan for cancer center. *Denver Post*, Jan. 7, 1952.
6. Ibid.
7. Dr. Leo Spears and labor have reached agreement on future building plans. *Spears Sanitarium News*, 7, 1949.
8. Dan C. Spears, interview, 1983.
9. Spears starts construction of 2150-bed cancer center. *Spears Sanigram*, 18 (Jan.) 1953.
10. Spears starts construction on $21,500.00 cancer unit. *Denver Post*, Dec. 21, 1952.
11. New Spears unit to contain chiropractic hall of fame. *Spears Sanigram*, 17 (Aug.) 1952.
12. City sues Spears clinic for $7500 taxes. *Rocky Mountain News*, Feb. 5, 1953.
13. Spears wins round in zoning battle. *Denver Post*, Dec. 22, 1953.
14. The pioneers building. *Spears Sanigram*, 32 (Sept.) 1957.
15. Spears hospital sues Denver. *Denver Post*, Feb. 16, 1959.
16. City and County of Denver v. Spears Free Clinic and Hospital for Poor Children. Supreme Court of Colorado, 350 P.2d 1057, April 11, 1960.
17. Court rules city cannot tax hospital. *Rocky Mountain News*, April 12, 1960.
18. Spears ground offered offered to C.U. *Denver Post*, Oct. 3, 1958.

War With the State
1. During the month of December, 1949, the *Denver Post* and *Rocky Mountain News* reported on developments with no fewer than eight banner headlines, 60 news stories (frequently redundant), two editorials, and eight letters to the editor favorable to Spears.
2. State health department renews probe of Spears Sanitarium. *Rocky Mountain News*, Dec. 2, 1949.
3. Clinic hit by outbreak of disease, *Denver Post*. Dec. 2, 1949.
4. Here are major charges hurled at Spears clinic. *Denver Post*, Dec. 3, 1949.
5. Ibid.
6. KNOUS ACTS TO CLOSE SPEARS SANITARIUM. "Negligent death" charged in report of Metzger-Cleere. *Rocky Mountain News*, Dec. 3, 1949.
6. New probes intensify fight over Spears sanitarium. *Rocky Mountain News*, Dec. 4, 1949.
7. SPEARS HELD 'PUBLIC NUISANCE.' Move to close sanitarium gets governor's okay. *Denver Post*, Dec. 3, 1949.
8. Quick court vedict hope of governor. *Denver Post*, Dec. 3, 1949.
9. Let profession handle Spears, Bishop urges. *Denver Post*, Dec. 4, 1949.
10. Clinic target of jealosy, prejudice. *Denver Post*, Dec. 3, 1949.
11. Spears charges critics employ unfair tactics. *Denver Post*, Dec. 6, 1949.
12. Sanitarium attack "ambush," Spears says. *Rocky Mountain News*, Dec. 6, 1949.

END NOTES

13. Spears case heads for highest court. *Denver Post*, Dec. 6, 1949.
14. Sanitarium control by health board asked. *Rocky Mountain News*, Dec. 8, 1949.
15. Letter from Leo Spears to Roy L. Cleere. Dec. 4, 1949.
16. Letter from William F. McClone to R.L. Cleere. Dec. 14, 1949.
17. Letter from R.L. Cleere to Osgoode Philpott, Dec. 15, 1949.
18. Howard M. Spears: Ambushed again. *Spears Sanitarium News*, Jan. 1950.
19. Brief hits move to close Spears hospital. *Denver Post*, Jan. 5, 1950.
20. Health unit denied rule over Spears. *Denver Post*, Jan. 5, 1950.
21. Ibid.
22. Spears wins license suit. *Denver Post*, July 1, 1950.
23. Editorial: Chiropractic wins one. *Denver Post*, July 1, 1950.
24. Bruce Gustin: That's That (Column). *Denver Post*, July 1, 1950.
25. Meaning of the Spears decision. *Spears Sanigram,* 12 (Jan.) 1951.
26. SPEARS WINS GREAT VICTORY. *Spears Sanigram,* 12 (Jan.) 1951.
27. Spears' license renewed. *Denver Post*, Oct. 14, 1950.
28. 6 out of 10 Denverites see good in chiropractic program. *Denver Post*, Jan. 21,
29. Read this amazing poll. *Spears Sanigram*, 11 (May) 1950.
30. Dr. Spears sponsors referendum. *Denver Post*, July 8, 1950.
31. Spears petition asks choice in health aid. *Spears Sanigram,* 12 (Jan.) 1951.
32. Blue Cross holds ban proper in Spears case. *Denver Post*, Nov. 19, 1951.
33. Blue Cross rejects bid by Spears. *Denver Post*, Nov. 19, 1951.
34. Spears scores Blue Cross policy as "discriminatory." *Denver Post*, Nov. 21, 1951.
35. Spears sanitarium declared to be hospital by district court. *Rocky Mountain News*, Nov. 30,
1949.

Research: Promise and Hyperbole

1. Chiropractic center changes planned. *Denver Post*, Aug. 6, 1947.
2. Chiropractors plan $25,000,000 plant here. *Rocky Mountain News*, Aug. 7, 1947.
3. Walter I. Wardwell: Chiropractic: History and Evolution of a New Profession
(Mosby-Yearbook, St. Louis, 1992), p. 192.
4. Dan C. Spears in letter to Russell W. Gibbons, July 1, 1983.
5. Frank O. Logic: A statement about Spears sanitarium. *National Chiropractic Journal*, Oct.
1948.
6. Letter from Leo L. Spears to Roy L. Cleere, July 9, 1953.
7. Death certificate may not be signed by chiropractors. *Denver Post*, Dec. 17, 1941.
8. Colorado Chiropractic Association v. State, 171 Colo. 395 467 P.2d 795 (1970).
9. Letter from Lloyd Florio, manager, Denver Department of Health and Hospitals, to Dr. Leo
Spears, Oct. 23, 1953.
10. Letter from Duke Dunbar to Roy L. Cleere, Oct. 28, 1953.
11. Spears claims blood test for cancer. *Denver Post*, Nov. 22, 1953.
12. Spears to demonstrate new cancer test claim. *Denver Post*, Nov. 24, 1953.
13. Spears "cancer test" unveiled. *Denver Post*, Nov. 26, 1953.
14. Reader's Forum: Spears cancer test. *Denver Post*, Nov. 27, 1953.
15. Spears keeps cancer test validity charts. *Denver Post*, Nov. 27, 1953.
16. Cancer expert labels Spears cancer test unreliable. *Denver Post*, Nov. 29, 1953.
17. Ibid.
18. Cancer screening test evidence destroyed, says Spears. *Denver Post*, Nov. 30,
19. George A. Wilson: *Things You Should Know About Cancer.* (Self-published, Salt Lake
City, 1956), pp. 42-44.
20. Ibid.
21. Ibib.
22. George A. Wilson: Report on first 211 cancer cases at Spears. *Spears Sanigram,*15 (Feb.)
1952.

END NOTES

23. Ed H. Hoover: Cancer report shows chiropractic progress through research at Spears hospital. *Spears Sanigram,* 14 (Oct.) 1951.

24. Wilson report, ibid.

25. Nation's press reports Spears cancer work. *Spears Sanigram,* 14 (Oct.) 1951.

26. Wilson report, ibid.

27. Dr.George Wilson heads research at Spears; brings 34 years experience. *Spears Sanigram,* 12 (Jan.) 1951.

28. Necrology. *Who's Who in Chiropractic International* (WWIC Publishing Co., Littleton, Colo. 1980), p. 301.

29. Spears cancer trailer to tour Western states. *Aurora (Colo.) Bulletin Free Press*, Dec. 19, 1953.

30. Chiropractors order test of Spears cancer claims. *Denver Post*, Nov. 30, 1953.

31. U.S. denies Spears aid – he'll go to Congress. *Denver Post*, Nov. 28, 1953.

32 Advertisement. *Spears Sanigram* undated special edition.

33. No real gang problems here, Senate probers told. *Denver Post*, Dec. 15, 1953.

34. Ibid.

36. Theory said "primitive." *Denver Post*, Dec. 15, 1953.

34. Secret of long life probed by peppy chiropractor, 60. *Omaha World-Hearld*, Sept. 13, 1954.

37. Spears sanitarium seeks 25 oldest centenarians. *Wichita Beacon*, Oct. 11, 1954.

38. Spears longevity project finds favor overseas and at home. *Spears Sanigram*, (June) 1955.

39. 167-year-old man found in Turkey. *Spears Sanigram,* 24 (Sept.) 1955.

40. Centenarians arrive at Spears. *Spears Sanigram,* 21 (Jan.) 1955.

41. Ibid.

42. Jesse James died in 1950, says old friend. *Denver Post*, Nov. 18, 1954.

43. Fruit picker, 113 years old, here for longevity study. *Denver Monitor*, July 21, 1955

44. Centenarian makes bus trip up Pikes Peak. *Pikes Peak Journal*, Aug. 12, 1955.

45. Robert Ripley: Believe it or Not (syndicated news feature). Sept. 25, 1955.

46. Elsie Hix: Strange as it Seems (syndicated news feature). March 4, 1956.

47. Lin Root and Agnes Ash: The first 124 years are the hardest. *Saturday Evening Post*, June 17, 1967.

48. See note #41.

49. Charlie Smith – an American legend. *Spears Hospital News*, Nov.-Dec. 1977.

50. Ibid.

51. Author's recollection.

52. Newsmakers. *Newsweek*, Feb. 9, 1976.

53. Author's recollection.

54. Charlie Smith, ex-slave, is dead; believed oldest American at 137. *New York Times*, Oct. 7, 1979.

55. De Aragon starts hospital in Peurto Rico. *Spears Sanigram,* 24 (Sept.) 1955.

The Langer Hearings

1. Advt.: Ex-servicemen denied freedom of choice. *Rocky Mountain News*, Sept. 10, 1921.

2. VA vetoes offer of Spears to treat 100 "ailing" vets under eye of press. *Spears Sanigram*, 19 (Aug.) 1953.

3. Ibid.

4. Public law No. 293 bans chiropractic for vets, say VA officials. *Spears Sanigram*, 19 (Aug.) 1953.

5. HR 54, sponsored by Congresswoman Rogers, would provide chiropractic as VA service. *Spears Sanigram*, 19 (Aug.) 1953.

6. Ibid.

7. See Note # 4.

8. Ibid.

9. VA medical chief, though admittedly ignorant of chiropractic, still opposed science for vets. *Spears Sanigram*, 19 (Aug.) 1953.

10. Ibid.

11. Historic meeting proves growing demand of veterans for healing choice. *Spears Sanigram*, 19 (Aug.) 1953.

12. Veterans testify to relief through chiropractic after VA facilities fail. *Spears Sanigram*, 19 (Aug.) 1953.

13. Plot charged on chiropractic. *Denver Post*, Aug. 27, 1953.

14. Hearings to open Wednesday on "freedom of medical choice." *Denver Post*, Aug. 25, 1953.

15. Senator Langer patient at Spears during hearings on care for vets. *Denver Post*, Aug. 24, 1953.

16. Langer charges press, medics conspire against chiropractic. *Denver Post*, Aug. 26, 1953.

17. VA stands fast despite senator's medical probe. *Rocky Mountain News*, Aug. 27,

18. Ibid.

19. Editorial: Riding a hobby. *Denver Post*, Aug. 27, 1953.

20. Reader's Forum: Chiropractic for vets. *Denver Post*, Sept. 5, 1953.

21. Senator Langer reveals he helped Sister Kenny. *Spears Sanigram,* 19 (Aug.)

22. Ibid.

23. Medical-press code does its job. *Rocky Mountain News*, Feb. 13, 1954.

24. Senator Langer, 73, G.O.P. rebel, dead. *New York Times*, Nov. 9, 1959.

25 *Who's Who in America* (A.N. Marquis, Chicago, Vol. 27, 1952-1953).

The Grand Jury

1. MEDICS HAIL PROBE OF QUACKS. State society president backs Keating's move. *Denver Post*, Jan. 30, 1954.

2. SPEARS 'HEALTH' GADGETS ORDERED SEIZED BY U.S. *Denver Post*, April 6, 1954.

3. U.S. seizes devices at Spears hospital. *Rocky Mounain News*, April 7, 1954.

4. Court move plot to ruin hospital, Spears claims. *Denver Post*, April 7, 1954.

5. ALL SPEARS' HOSPITAL RECORDS SUBPENAED [*sic*]. Grand jury to inspect accounts. *Denver Post*, April 12, 1954.

6. Spears granted delay on papers pending hearing. *Denver Post*, April 13, 1954.

7. Judge to decide fate of records. *Rocky Mountain News*, April 15, 1954.

8. JUDGE TO QUIZ JURY ON SPEARS RECORDS. Subpena [*sic*] okay to depend on aim of probers. *Denver Post*, April 14, 1954.

9. Attorney blasts *Denver Post*, BBB. *Denver Post*, April 14, 1954.

10. DELIVER ALL DATA, JUDGE TELLS SPEARS. Day okays quack quiz jury order. *Denver Post*, April 15, 1954.

11. Accountants named to eye Spears books. *Denver Post*, April 16, 1954.

12. Spears' attorney promises aid in study of books. *Denver Post*, April 26, 1954.

13. Spears offers clinic's books to world view. *Denver Post*, April 30, 1954.

14. LANGER CHECKS POSSIBLE 'REPRISAL ACTION' AGAINST DOCTOR. Senator's aide probes Spears case. *Rocky Mountain News*, May 7, 1954.

15. Langer studies charge Spears under "reprisal." *Denver Post*, May 7, 1954.

16. Senator's aide probes Spears case. *Rocky Mountain News*, May 8, 1954.

17. Grand jurors to report Wednesday in quack quiz. *Denver Post*, May 8, 1954.

18. Spears defends testimonial use in advertising. *Denver Post*, May 14, 1954.

19. JURY ASKS HEALING AD CURB. 2 indicted, new drug law urged. *Denver Post*, May 13, 1954.

20. Ibid.

21. Spears offers to testify before gand jury. *Denver Post*, June 1, 1954.

22. Spears, nephew to go before jury probers. *Denver Post*, June 1, 1954.

23. Dr. Spears to testify before grand jury. *Rocky Mountain News*, June 8, 1954.

24. Grand jury to hear Spears in night quiz. *Denver Post*, June 13, 1954.

25. Spears gets second call before jury. *Denver Post*, June 15, 1954.

26. Dr. Spears tells his side of story to grand jury. *Denver Post*, June 16, 1954.

27. Spears ends 3d session before grand jury. *Rocky Mountain News*, June 17, 1954.

28. TESTIMONIALS BY DEAD CITED. Jury indicts one here on fraud. *Denver Post*, July 1954.

29. Ibid.

30. State board raps chiropractic claim. *Denver Post*, July 15, 1954.

31. Ed Hoover: A call to arms (editorial). *Spears Sanigram*, 22 (May) 1955.

Suing For Damages

1. $300,000 libel suit filed by Spears clinic. *Denver Post*, Jan. 14, 1950.

2. Spears files $300,000 libel suit against doctor. *Rocky Mountain News*, Jan. 15,

3. Doctor sued by Spears hits court order. *Rocky Mountain News*, Jan. 26, 1950.

4. Judge modifies order for doctor to submit records in Spears suit. *Rocky Mountain News*, Jan. 27, 1950.

5. Spears suit forces deposition by Maier. *Denver Post*, Jan. 27, 1950.

6. Spears suit dismissal weighed. *Rocky Mountain News*, Feb. 14, 1950.

7. Libel suit dismissal rejected. *Denver Post*, Feb. 19, 1950.

8. Filing of suit by Spears is upheld by court. *Rocky Mountain News*, Feb. 19, 1950.

9. Libel suit dismissal requested. *Denver Post*, Aug. 17, 1950.

10. Highlights of Spears' libel suit testimony. *Denver Post*, Sept. 9, 1951.

11. Maier cool in quiz by Ginsberg. *Denver Post*, Sept. 7, 1951.

12. Patient "desperately ill," Spears suit M.D. testifies. *Denver Post*, Sept. 7, 1951.

13. See note #10.

14. SPEARS' LAWYER COLLAPSES IN COURT. Recess ordered for Ginsberg to get medical aid. *Denver Post*, Sept. 10, 1951.

15. Lawyer charges medical conspiracy in Spears suit. *Denver Post*, Sept. 11, 1951.

16. PATIENT WAS WITHOUT DIAGNOSIS: SPEARS. Spears testifies patient lacked ulcer symptoms. *Denver Post*, Sept. 12, 1951.

17. Spears claims article caused loss to clinic. *Denver Post*, Sept. 13, 1951.

18. Attorney asks Spears why he limited suit. *Denver Post*, Sept. 13, 1951.

19. Judge rules out testimony in Spears action. *Denver Post*, Sept. 17, 1951.

20. Legal questions stir arguments in Spears action. *Denver Post*, Sept. 14, 1951.

21. Defense motion to dismiss Spears suit denied. *Denver Post*, Sept. 14, 1951.

22. $300,000 libel claim of Spears rejected by jury. *Denver Post*, Sept. 20, 1951.

23. Spears clinic denied retrial of libel suit. *Rocky Mountain News*, Jan. 1, 1952.

24. Ibid.

25. Spears loses $300,000 suit against medic. *Denver Post*, Sept. 9, 1953.

26. Spears refiles $500,000 suit against 4 health board officers. *Rocky Mountain News*, March 12, 1950.

27. M.D. CHECKUP ORDERED FOR SPEARS IN SUIT. *Denver Post*, April 27,

28. Spears income up $2,275 in 9 years, bookkeeper says. *Denver Post*, April 27,

29. Ibid.

30. Physician reports on Spears. *Denver Post*, Oct. 1, 1953.

31. Psychiatrist named to examine Spears. *Rocky Mountain News*, Oct. 15, 1953.

32. Dr. Spears to undergo exam by two medics. *Denver Post*, Oct. 15, 1953.

33. Spears refuses submission to medical check. *Denver Post*, March 8, 1954.

34. SPEARS FACES CONTEMPT COUNT. Rejection of order charged. *Denver Post*, April 9, 1954.

35. Followed court order, Spears declares. *Denver Post*, April 10, 1954.

36. Spears granted 2d chance to avoid contempt. *Denver Post*, May 13, 1954.

37. Spears suit trial set Monday. *Denver Post*, Jan. 15, 1956.

38. Dr. Spears takes stand in his $500,000 suit. *Denver Post*, Jan. 17, 1956.

39. Advised to seek city suit over license. *Denver Post*, Jan. 18, 1956.

END NOTES

40. Spears suit against ex-officials dismissed. *Rocky Mountain News*, Jan. 18, 1956.
41. "Fair decision": Spears. *Denver Post*, Jan. 18,1956.
42. SPEARS SEEKS $3 MILLION IN SUIT AGAINST MEDICS. Trade curbs held as basis for legal row. *Denver Post*, Dec. 10, 1949.
43. Officials listed as defendants in Spears suit. *Denver Post*, Dec. 10, 1949.
44. Spears hospital loses $3 million suit for damages. *Denver Post*, July 13, 1951.
45. Appeals court dismisses Spears suit. *Rocky Mountain News*, May 11, 1952.
46. Bill Fay: Cancer quacks. *Collier's*, May 26, 1951.
47. Walter Winchell is dead on coast at 74. *New York Times*, Feb. 21, 1972.
48. Collier's magazine named. *Denver Post*, May 24, 1951.
49. Spears damage suit claim 3$^1/_2$ times hospital's worth. *Denver Post*, May 24, 1951.
50. Spears files vs. ABC and Richard Hudnut, Inc. *Denver Post*, July 14, 1951.
51. Spears sues ABC for $24 million. *Denver Post*, July 14, 1951.
52. $24 million libel suit to open Monday in N.Y. *Denver Post*, March 5, 1955.
53. Spears-Collier's libel case jurors selected. *Denver Post*, March 7, 1955.
54. Damage suit cut in half: Spears withdraws one of 2 libel counts. *Denver Post*, March 7, 1955.
55. Spears on stand admits 2 advertised as cured later died. *Denver Post*, March 9, 1955.
56. Collier's bares source of data in Spears suit. *Rocky Mountain News*, June 22, 1955.
57. Trial nears end in Spears suit for $12 million. *Denver Post*, March 12, 1955.
58. Chiropractor could find cure for cancer, medic says. *Denver Post*, March 12, 1955.
59. Spears case nears jury. *Denver Post*, March 14, 1955.
60. Attorneys sum up. Spears libel case near end. *Denver Post*, March 14, 1955.
61. Jury rules Collier's did not libel Spears. *Rocky Mountain News*, March 15, 1955.
62. COLLIER'S MAGAZINE CLEARED. Leo Spears loses $12 million libel suit in *Denver Post*, March 15, 1955.
63. Dan C. Spears: Editorial. *Spears Sanigram,* 22 (May) 1955.
64. Spears $62 million suit settled. *Denver Post*, April 1, 1955.
65. Spears settles Winchell suit. *Rocky Mountain News*, April 2, 1955.
66. Ibid.
67. Walter Shapiro: Ex-hoffer columnist gets big biog. *Time*, Oct. 10, 1995.
68. Walter Winchell, 74, dies on coast. *New York Times*, Feb. 20, 1972.
69. Neal Gabler: *Winchell: Gossip, Power and the Culture of Celebrity.* (Knopf, New York, 1994).
70. End at Collier's. *Newsweek*, Dec. 24, 1956.
71. Who killed Collier's? *Nation*, Jan. 5, 1957.
72. In its final issue (Vol. 139:1), *Collier's* offered no comment about its demise.

"A Massive Conspiracy"

1. SPEARS SUES FOR $10 MILLION. BBB faces claim on jury quiz. *Denver Post*, May 20, 1954.
2. Spears clinic sues BBB for $10 million. *Rocky Mountain News*, May 21, 1954.
3. Spears to name *Denver Post* in $10 million suit. *Denver Post*, July 6, 1954.
4. Spears sues Post reporter, 33 firms and 53 businessmen. *Denver Post*, July 15, 1954.
5. Consolidation approved of Spears' damage suits. *Denver Post*, Sept. 17, 1955.
6. Spears bares big oil, A-ore holdings. *Denver Post*, July 7, 1954.
7. Spears gives "credit" kickback to referring chiropractors. *Denver Post*, July 8, 1954.
8. Burning salve used on cancer, Spears testifies. *Denver Post*, July 20, 1954.
9. Judge withdraws from Spears case. *Denver Post*, July 20, 1954.
10. "Vitamin products" sold by Spears through mail. *Denver Post*, Aug. 17, 1954.
11. BBB ordered to give Spears complaint file. *Denver Post*, Aug. 19, 1954.
12. Ibid.
13. Spears lawyer takes slap at BBB board. *Denver Post*, Sept. 7, 1954.

14. Spears denied files on BBB directors. *Denver Post*, Sept. 8, 1954.

15. BBB Spears probe began in 1951: Bell. *Denver Post*, Sept. 9, 1954.

16. Spears seeking look at grand jury's records. *Denver Post*, Sept. 11, 1954.

17. Gifts by two mortuaries to Spears hospital told. *Denver Post*, Nov. 17, 1954.

18. Mortuary "gifts" to Spears cited. *Denver Post*, Nov. 17, 1954.

19. Spears cancer claims cited in court battle. *Denver Post*, Nov. 18, 1954.

20. Paste used for cancer at Spears, medic says. *Denver Post*, Nov. 19, 1954.

21. Druggist heard in Spears suit. *Denver Post*, Nov. 20, 1954.

22. Deposition in Spears suit taken. *Denver Post*, Nov. 20, 1954.

23. Attorney won't fight court rule. *Denver Post*, Dec. 21, 1954.

24. Grand jury secrecy hit by Spears' attorney. *Denver Post*, Nov. 16, 1954.

25. Spears' advertising called misleading. *Denver Post*, Jan. 26, 1955.

26. Ibid.

27. Ibid.

28. Spears says his clinic used caustic paste as cosmetic. *Denver Post*, Feb. 1, 1955.

29. Depositions in Spears suit closed. *Denver Post*, Feb. 3, 1955.

30. Spears case unfolds: writers of testimonials later died, Bell says. *Denver Post*, Feb. 4, 1955.

31. Spears conspiracy suit set for trial Sept. 12. *Denver Post*, Feb. 4, 1955.

32. Editor of Post testifies Spears cases doubted. *Denver Post*, Sept. 13, 1955.

33. Editor again testifies in Spears damage suit. *Rocky Mountain News*, Sept. 14, 1955.

34. Hoyt denies prejudice against chiropractic, cites Post policy. *Denver Post*, Sept. 14, 1955.

35. Reporter ordered to produce hospital stories. *Rocky Mountain News*, Sept. 15, 1955.

36. Reporter reviews probe of Spears cancer claims. *Denver Post*, Sept. 15, 1955.

37. Reporter tells his testimony to grand jury. *Rocky Mountain News*, Sept. 16, 1955.

38. Post writer tells case histories of Spears cancer patients. *Denver Post*, Sept. 16, 1955.

39. 10 businessmen questioned by Spears attorney. *Denver Post*, Sept. 19, 1955.

40. Patients barred. *Denver Post*, Sept. 19, 1955.

41. Bell tells of queries on Spears. *Denver Post*, Sept. 21, 1955.

42. Spears blames Post, BBB in building cuts. *Denver Post*, Sept. 22, 1955.

43. Spears takes stand. *Denver Post*, Sept. 21, 1955.

44. Spears tells system. Nerve goading used to treat cancers. *Denver Post*, Sept. 22, 1955.

45. Spears testifies he takes insulin for diabetes. *Denver Post*, Sept. 22, 1955.

46. Spears' testimonials introduced at trial. *Rocky Mountain News*, Sept. 23, 1955.

47. Spears' ads linked to testimonials of dead persons. *Denver Post*, Sept. 23, 1955.

48. Staff took wage cut at Spears. *Denver Post*, Sept. 24, 1955.

49. Spears libel trial ready for 3d week. *Denver Post*, Sept. 26, 1955.

50. Judge denies 5 of 7 defense bids in Spears suit. *Denver Post*, Sept. 28, 1955.

51. Judge to rule in Spears suit. *Rocky Mountain News*, Sept. 28, 1955.

52. Defense nears windup phase of Spears trial. *Denver Post*, Sept. 30, 1955.

53. Defense rests in suit by chiropractor. *Denver Post*, Oct. 2, 1955.

54. Plaintiff's arguments heard in $11 million suit. *Denver Post*, Oct. 3, 1955.

55. Denver judge ponders verdict as Spears trial ends. *Denver Post,* Oct. 4, 1955.

56. Spears case ends in Denver court. *Rocky Mountain News*, Oct. 5, 1955.

57. SPEARS LOSES $11 MILLION SUIT. JUDGE RULES HOSPITAL ILLEGAL. Evidence fails to back claim of conspiracy. *Denver Post*, Oct. 13, 1955.

58. DA's office to study ruling in Spears' suit. *Denver Post*, Oct. 13, 1955 59. Spears to appeal court decision. *Rocky Mountain News*, Oct. 23, 1955.

60. Spears maps appeal in conspiracy suit. *Denver Post*, Oct. 23, 1955.

Transition

1. Dr. Leo Spears, 62, dies. Controversial chiropractor set up hospital in Denver. *New York Times*, May 16, 1956.

END NOTES

2. Milestones. *Time*, May 28, 1956.

3. HEART ATTACK KILLS SPEARS. Hospital founder dies at 62. *Denver Post*, May 16, 1956.

4. Denver chiropractor - Leo Spears - dies. *Rocky Mountain News*, May 17, 1956.

5. Rex, pp. 71-72. 6. Author's diary, 1955-1956.

7. Op cit.

8. Thousands express grief over loss of chiropractic leader. *Spears Sanigram*, 27 (July) 1956.

9. Bust of Dr. Leo unveiled. *Spears Sanigram*, 28 (Sept.) 1956.

10. Personnel adjustment swiftly completed. *Spears Sanigram*, 27 (July) 1956.

11. Spears unit to continue operations. *Denver Post*, May 16, 1956.

12. Ibid.

13. Ruling upheld in Spears case. *Denver Post*, June 10, 1957.

14. Letter from Colorado Supreme Court Library to author, March 10, 2000.

15. 4 Spears wills seen as invalid. *Denver Post*, May 24, 1956.

16. $35,000 property settlement awarded ... *Denver Post*, Nov. 23, 1954.

17. Spears' ex-wife awarded settlement. *Rocky Mountain News*, Nov. 23, 1954.

18. Spears says salary only $800 a month. *Denver Post*, Nov. 23, 1954.

19. See note #15.

20. Public resents Ford Foundation's failure to recognize Spears hospital. *Spears Sanigram*, 26 (April) 1956.

21. Letter from Ford Foundation to author (then an intern), Jan. 27, 1956, to wit: "In order to be considered for a grant under the program, the organization must be an operating, voluntary (non-government) hospital accepted for listing as a nonprofit hospital by the American Hospital Association."

22. See note #6.

23. The nation's most notorious quack healer. *Rackets*, 1:1 (June) 1956.

24. Spears featured on television program. *Spears Sanigram*, 28 (Sept.) 1956.

25. Letter from Clyde M. Keeler to Arthur G. Hendricks, June 28, 1958.

26. Letter from Hendricks to Keeler, July 3, 1958.

27. Letter from Keeler to Dan C. Spears, July 11, 1958.

28. Dan C. Spears in letter to C. M. Keeler, July 15, 1958.

29. Louis Gearhart in letter to author, April 17, 1998.

30. Life center hospital bond drive opened. *Denver Post*, July 24, 1966.

31. Nursing center work resumes. *Denver Post*, Sept. 17, 1969.

32. Sordoni consults on building cancer center. *Spears Sanigram*, 15 (Feb.) 1952.

33. Rumor Spears backed by "angel" is false. *Spears Sanigram*, 21 (Jan.) 1955.

34. Sen. Sordoni lectures to Lincoln alumni and NCA. *Spears Sanitarium News*, 9, 1949.

35. Penn. sec'y of commerce asserts chiros save industry thousands of man-hours. *Spears Sanigram*, 15 (Feb.) 1952.

36. Chiropractic keeps Sordoni employees on toes, increases man-hour productivity. *Spears Sanigram*, 17 (Aug.) 1952.

37. Sordoni employs chiropractic "human maintenance" system. *Spears Sanigram*, 18 (Jan.) 1953.

38. Information provided by Dr. Ronald P. Beideman.

39. Dr. Cleere says resignation wasn't voluntary. *Rocky Mountain News*, Aug. 30, 1973.

40. Former health director buried. *Rocky Mountain News*, Oct. 1, 1983.

41. Denver DA dies after battle with cancer. *Rocky Mountain News*, July 5, 1967.

42. Charles Ginsberg, noted lawyer, dies. *Rocky Mountain News*, May 8, 1975.

43. Obituary: Charles Ginsberg. *Denver Post*, May 8, 1975.

44. Former Colorado legislator Neal Bishop dies at age 79. *Rocky Mountain News*, May 21, 1980.

45. Necrology. *Who's Who in Chiropractic International* (WWIC Publishing Co., Littleton, Colo., 1980), 301.

END NOTES

46. Information provided by Dr. Louis O. Gearhart.

47. For whom shall we name Unit 1? *Spears Sanitarium News*, 6, 1949.

48. Dan C. Spears in letter to Russell W. Gibbons, July 1, 1983.

49. B.J. Palmer: *Fight to Climb* (Palmer School of Chiropractic, Davenport, 1950), pp. 415-444.

50. See note #48.

51. Necrology, p. 276.

52 Necrology, pp. 275-276.

53. See note #48.

54. Ibid.

55. Dan Spears, interview, 1983.

Appendix A.

State Board of Medical Examiners
v.
Spears

[79 Colo. 588]

Supreme Court of Colorado. June 7, 1926
Rehearing denied July 6, 1926

1. Certiorari 15

As to reviewing action of inferior courts and tribunals, certiorari raises questions of jurisdiction and abuse of discretion only.

2. Physicians and Surgeons 11(2)

Advertisement of chiropractor falsely attacking hospital and Veterans' Bureau in order to increase his business held dishonorable conduct justifying revocation of license by medical examiners, under C.L. §§ 4526-4570.

3. Certiorari 68

On certiorari, reviewing court may not enter on merits and has not power to correct mistake of fact or erroneous conclusion from facts.

4. Physicians and Surgeons 11(2)

Libelous matter attacking hospital and Veterans' Bureau may be sufficient ground for revoking license of physician publishing libel.

Error to District Court, City and County of Denver; Charles C. Butler, Judge.

Proceeding before the State Board of Medical Examiners for revocation of the license of Leo L. Spears to practice chiropractic. An order of the Board revoking the license was annulled by the district court on certiorari, and the Board brings error. Reversed, with instructions.

$--o--$

Wm. L. Boatright, Atty. Gen., and Charles H. Haines, of Denver, for plaintiff in error.

Carle Whitehead, Albert L. Vogl, and Floyd F. Miles, all of Denver, for defendant in error.

CAMPBELL, J. This writ is to review a judgment in a certiorari proceeding wherein the district court annulled an order of the state board of medical examiners revoking the license of Leo Spears by which the board previously

135

had authorized him to practice chiropractic in this state. Our practice of medicine act passed by the General Assembly in 1915, and approved by the people on referendum in 1917, creates a board of medical examiners and gives it comprehensive enumerated powers relative to the protection of the public health and the control and regulation of the practice of medicine and chiropractic. Included in the enumeration are the power to grant licenses to those desiring to engage in such practice, and the power to revoke same upon the grounds and for the reasons specified in the statute. The procedure to be observed in revoking licenses is the same as to both classes of practitioners. It was followed in this case and affords due process of law.

Spears, respondent in this proceeding, held a license to practice chiropractic only. A verified complaint was filed with the state board charging him with immoral, unprofessional, and dishonorable conduct, in that he caused to be printed and published in a newspaper certain false statements concerning the medical case of one Charles Culbertson, a patient of the government Fitzsimons Hospital, which were made recklessly without reasonable and adequate investigation to ascertain if they were true, and for the purpose of unjustly discrediting the officers and authorities of the hospital and the Veterans' Bureau, and for the further purpose of increasing his practice and income as a chiropractor. The advertisement in large type is headed:
"Another Disabled Veteran Sacrificed Upon the Altar of Medical Greed."
Then follows in smaller type:
"Intolerance of Medical Profession to Chiropractic Forces War Hero Out of Fitzsimons Hospital to Slow Death."
As part of the advertisement is a copy of a petition said to have been numerously signed and addressed to the President and Congress of the United States, requesting these authorities "to provide and pay for (what is now prohibited in the hospital) the one method at least that will most quickly and permanently restore us to normal - Chiropractic." This advertisement is signed Spears & Mathis, Chiropractors. Mathis was at one time a partner of Spears, but is no longer associated with him, but Spears uses the firm name in his advertising and his own picture as a trademark. Included in the advertisement is a picture of Dr. Spears, and a cut of Culbertson as he appeared upon his arrival in Denver "under a sealed sentence," and of Culbertson's mouth and teeth showing their decayed condition. This brief description is perhaps unnecessary, but it is sufficient to disclose the general character of the charges, and it throws light upon one of the defenses of Spears, which is that the advertisement was inserted in the newspaper for the purpose of aiding a campaign which he was then conducting, in the interest of the veterans, to have Congress provide for treatment by chiropractors in their hospitals. In a prolonged hearing, Spears being represented by counsel, much evidence was taken. The board sustained

the charges and revoked his license. Thereupon Spears sued out a writ of certiorari in the district court and the district court upon the record certified by the medical board annulled and held for naught the order of the board of examiners revoking his license, and remanded the cause to that board for further proceedings, in conformity with the views of the district court, as might be necessary to carry out its judgment. The board has brought the case here for review of the judgment of the district court.

[1] The board, in hearing evidence, permitted the respondent great latitude and the result is this record is burdened with much evidence far beyond and foreign to the real and only issues of fact involved. The board in its findings and judgment adverted to this, but evidently deemed it advisable to receive whatever the respondent chose to offer. The argument of respondent's counsel is largely addressed to issues of fact and propositions of law that are entirely foreign to a proceeding in certiorari. This and all other courts have so often defined the purpose of this proceeding that we content ourselves by reference to some of our own pertinent cases. One of the most exhaustive discussions in our reports of the function of this writ is in an opinion by Judge Gunter in City Council of the City of Cripple Creek v. Hanley, 19 Colo. App. 390, wherein the learned judge said that district courts have jurisdiction to review the action of inferior courts and tribunals upon writ of certiorari only as to the question of their jurisdiction. Such was the nature of the common-law writ and such is the nature of our Dode writ, to which is added, what really was included in the common-law writ, that if the court abused its jurisdiction, or failed regularly to pursue its authority, which has the same meaning, the reviewing court might examine the evidence bearing on jurisdiction or abuse of discretion, but not with the view to determine facts or draw conclusions therefrom respecting guilt. As specially applicable to proceedings of the state board of examiners we cite several pertinent cases: Thompson v. State Board of Medical Examiners, 59 Colo. 549, is a review of an order of the medical board revoking a license. It is said there that on certiorari the district court is restricted to a determination of jurisdiction only, and will not go beyond this and inquire as to the sufficiency of the evidence or whether the state board reached a correct conclusion therefrom. In State Board v. Noble, 65 Colo. 410, this court, in an opinion by Mr. Justice Teller, cited with approval the Thompson case, and said only questions of jurisdiction and abuse of discretion may be passed upon; whether a decision on the merits is right or wrong is not within the issue. In State Board v. Boulls, 69 Colo. 361, the same doctrine is again announced. In the original opinion in Dilliard v. State Board, 69 Colo. 575, by Mr. Justice Denison and in his opinion on rehearing, it was said that no act of any tribunal, within its jurisdiction and not greatly abusive of its discretion, however erroneous it may be, can be reversed upon certiorari, and courts can consider the

evidence for no purpose, except to see whether the tribunal exceeded its jurisdiction or abused its discretion. In that case it was also held that the medical board has jurisdiction to determine what constitutes unprofessional and dishonorable conduct and to revoke a license on account of such conduct. In White v. Andrew, 70 Colo. 50, the limit of the district court in such proceedings is again announced in consonance with the former rulings of the court. In State Board v. Brown, 70 Colo. 116, the phrase "abuse of discretion" is said to be synonymous with "a failure by the lower tribunal regularly to pursue its authority"; and the court adds: "This does not include the commission of errors of law, or mistakes in the findings of fact." The court cites with approval City Council v. Hanley, supra, that under no circumstances can the review be extended to the merits of the case. Our latest expression is Doran v. State Board, 70 Colo. 153, to the same effect as the foregoing.

[2,3] The reprehensible conduct charged against the respondent is that he caused to be printed and published an advertisement, including his own picture, containing false statements about the hospital and the Veterans' Bureau; that these statements were made recklessly without any adequate investigation of their truth, in which he charged that the authorities of the Veterans' Bureau and Fitzsimons Hospital had practically caused the death of Culbertson by their barbarous and inhuman treatment. The state board in elaborate written findings found that these statements were false and scandalous and known to be such at the time respondent caused the advertisement to be inserted in the newspaper, and that they were made for the purpose of unjustly discrediting the officers of the two institutions, and for the purpose of increasing his practice and income as a chiropractor, and as a conclusion from the findings the board held that such conduct was immoral, unprofessional and dishonorable, and thereupon revoked his license.

The district court filed a written opinion in which the judge, in reviewing the grounds generally on which a physician or attorney's license may be revoked, states:

"After a long and tedious hearing the board found Spears guilty of dishonorable conduct. With the finding of fact the court has no power to interfere; and in the light of the evidence the court, even if it had the power to do so, would not feel justified in making a finding to the contrary. His misconduct, however, does not belong in that class of dishonorable conduct that justifies the revocation of his license."

Elsewhere in the opinion is the following:

"There is not that intimate relation between Spears' offense and the public health, safety, morals, or welfare that would warrant the revocation of his license. It is my opinion, therefore, that in revoking Spears' license the board did not regularly pursue its authority, and that it exceeded its jurisdiction."

It is apparent that the district court, while it concurred with the board - and even if it had not concurred it would have been obliged to accept as true its findings of facts - that Spears had been guilty of dishonorable conduct, but as such conduct did not pertain to the intimate relation between Spears' offense and the public health, safety, and morals, his license could not be revoked because the board did not regularly pursue its authority. The opinion of the trial court taken in its entirety satisfies us that the trial judge annulled the action of the board because he reached the conclusion that the unprofessional and dishonorable conduct of the respondent was not in connection with some patient, or did not take place in any of the dealings of a physician with his patient.

We say first that the court was mistaken in its conclusion. Taking as true, as we must, the finding of the board that publication was made by respondent for the purpose in part of increasing his business and his income and not in aid of his alleged campaign, his object necessarily was to induce patients to come to him from whom fees would be received. This was a method, according to the finding of the board, that the respondent adopted as a means of securing additional patients and additional income; a method which was promoted through, and attended by, untruthful and scandalous conduct, in which charges against government officers and government institutions were made of which they were innocent. Such is certainly dishonorable conduct, and it was conduct that manifested itself in an attempt to secure patients and increase professional income. But, if the relation was not strictly that of a physician and patient, the conclusion of the district does not follow. In the White case, 70 Colo. 50, we said that the medical board properly revoked the license of a physician who was convicted of a crime involving moral turpitude, which consisted of the sale of morphine by a physician for other than medicinal purposes and to a habitual user thereof who was not his patient. A licentiate, by that opinion, is not acting in the course of practicing medicine, whether it be medicine or chiropractic, when he sells narcotic drugs to a habitual user for the latter's fancied solace or enjoyment and not as an aid to a cure. Suppose that an attorney, a leader in his profession, had published such an advertisement of his professional business such as this. The court would not hesitate to revoke his license.

The district court was manifestly wrong in concluding that the board did not regularly pursue its authority and therein exceeded its jurisdiction, because the dishonorable conduct of Spears in making these false charges did not have that intimate relation between Spears' offense and the public health, safety, morals, or welfare that would justify a revocation. Such findings, by a medical tribunal, even if erroneous, that respondent's conduct was unprofessional and dishonorable, does not constitute a failure upon its part regularly to pursue its authority, nor was it an abuse of discretion. In no event was it, or could it be, other than a mistake in its finding of facts or an erroneous conclusion from these facts, and we cannot even say it was a mistake in either. But of all our cases on certiorari, the reviewing court may not enter upon the merits and has not the power to correct a mistake of fact or an erroneous conclusion from the facts made by the inferior tribunal.

Thus far we have not mentioned the specific points made by the respondent's counsel in their brief, which may be summarized into one general statement that the acts complained of do not constitute a violation of the medical practice act. In reviewing the board's decision as to what constitutes dishonorable and unprofessional conduct, the courts, as we have said, will not substitute their findings for the board's findings of facts or interfere with the board's legitimate conclusion from such facts. The Dilliard case, supra, is relied upon as overruling all other cases on this subject; it does not even purport to do so. But if the case is what respondent's counsel say it is, and if it is for the courts, as well as for the medical board, to determine whether the conduct charged is unprofessional or dishonorable, or whether it is an abuse of discretion, we might paraphrase the observation of the district court and say that we would not be able to disagree with the inferior medical tribunal.

[4] That the principles of the police power are applicable to and govern such controversies is not disputed. That the exercise of the police power by any tribunal or body may be tested by the courts is also admitted. Counsel further say that Spears was justified in making these charges, even though they were false and untrue, if he did so as a part of his campaign to obtain from Congress, for the Fitzsimons Hospital, chiropractic treatment, and he is liable only for damages by those whom he has libeled, if he has libeled them, in a civil action, or to a criminal prosecution from criminal libel in the courts, where in either case he is entitled to a jury trial. It is enough to say that neither of these contentions by counsel is meritorious.

It is true that one who is indicted from criminal libel, or is sued for damages by the one libeled, is entitled to a jury trial. This, however, is not a criminal prosecution or an action for damages. Libelous matter may be also sufficient ground for revoking the license of a physician who publishes a libel. We are of the opinion that it was not an abuse of discretion of the medical board to hold that the respondent's conduct was unprofessional and dishonorable. We must accept the finding of the medical board, and the trial court should have accepted it as a verity, that the defendant's conduct bore such an intimate relation to the public health and public morals as to justify the finding that the respondent's conduct was unprofessional and dishonorable. The inferior tribunal unquestionably had jurisdiction. It did not abuse its discretion or fail regularly to pursue its authority. Neither the district court nor this court may enter upon an investigation of its merits, or inquire if the board made a mistake in its findings of fact, or erred in its conclusions upon the facts.

The judgment of the district court is therefore reversed, and the cause remanded, with instructions to set aside its judgment and in lieu thereof to enter a judgment dismissing the writ of certiorari at the costs of the respondent.

Reversed, with instructions. En Banc. All justices concurring.

APPENDIX B.

Articles of Incorporation
of
Spears Free Clinic and Hospital for Poor Children

KNOW ALL MEN BY THESE PRESENTS, That we, Dr. Leo L. Spears, Frank Seydel and A.A. French, citizens of the United States, have associated together as a Corporation for the purpose of becoming a body corporate and politic, not for pecuniary profit, under and by virtue of the Laws of the State of Colorado, and we do hereby make, execute and acknowledge this certificate in writing of our intentions so to become a body corporate, under and by virtue of said Laws.

1.
The name of this corporation shall be Spears Free Clinic and Hospital for Poor Children.

2.
The term of existence of this corporation shall be perpetual from and after the date of filing these Articles.

3.
The objects for which this corporation is formed are to treat, relieve and cure sick, crippled or diseased poor children, to help the needy without compensation by means of Chiropractic and other methods of treatment, to acquire or dispose of by gift, sale, devise or purchase, personal and real property, and to conduct any business and to dispose of the same for the aforesaid objects as well as to do all things necessary, proper or incidental to said purposes.

4.
The affairs and management of said corporation will be under the control of a board of trustees, consisting of three members. Dr. Leo L. Spears, Frank Seydel, and Dr. A.A. French are hereby selected to act as said board of trustees and to manage the affairs and concerns of said corporation for the first year of its existence and until their successors are elected and qualified.

5.
The principal business of said corporation shall be carried on in the City and County of Denver, State of Colorado, and the principal office of said corporation shall be located in the City and County of Denver, State of Colorado.

6.

The board of trustees shall have power to make such prudential by-laws as they may deem proper for the management of the affairs of this corporation, according to the statutes in such case made and provided.

IN TESTIMONY WHEREOF, We have hereunto set our hands and seal this 22nd day of November, 1933, A.D.

STATE OF COLORADO   /ss/ Dr. Leo L. Spears
CITY AND COUNTY   /ss/ Frank L. Seydel
OF DENVER   /ss/ Dr. A.A. French

Before me, the undersigned authorities, on this date, personally appeared Dr. Leo L. Spears, Frank Seydel, and Dr. A.A. French, and acknowledged to me that they are the identical parties named as incorporators in the Articles of Incorporation of the Spears Free Clinic and Hospital for Poor Children, and they acknowledged the signing of the same for the purposes and considerations therein expressed.

Given under my hand and seal this 22nd day of November, 1933, A.D.
My commission expires September 20th, 1937.

/s/
Maitland Milliken
Notary Public

Filed with the Secretary of State, Nov. 22, 1933.

[*Colorado State Archives*]

Appendix C.

Spears Clinic and Hospital for Poor Children
v.
Colorado Board of Health et al.

[220 P.2d 872]

Supreme Court of Colorado. July 1, 1950

Spears Free Clinic and Hospital for Poor Children, Inc., brought an action in the nature of certiorari against the State Board of Health of Colorado and its members for review of the action of the Board in revoking plaintiff's license to operate a chiropractic sanitarium. The District Court, City and County of Denver, William H. Luby, J., entered judgment dismissing the action, and plaintiff brought error. The Supreme Court, Stone, J., held that the attempted revocation of the license by the Board was void, that the license so sought to be revoked was void, and that in its stead at the time of its issuance the Board should have issued a license in accordance with the laws under which it acted.

Judgment reversed.

1. Municipal corporations 64
Under provisions of corporation and its home rule charter, city acquired exclusive control of local and municipal affairs; but it remained as much amenable to state control in all matters public, as distinguished from matters of local character, as were other municipalities. Const. art. 20.

2. Hospitals 1, 3
Municipal corporations 597
Under its police power state retains right to regulate such matters affecting public health as are of general concern, including right to regulate and license hospitals wherever situated, but at the same time, congested living conditions within cities may produce health problems justifying further regulations than those deemed necessary by legislature, and as to such matters cities may possess police power of further regulations within their limits.

3. Hospitals 1
State Board of Health had jurisdiction to issue and revoke license to operate chiropractic sanitarium, notwithstanding that such sanitarium was located within home rule city and that said city had legislated the field of licensing hospitals and sanitariums by ordinance covering same field as state statute and subsequent thereto. '35 C.S.A. c.78,§§ 133-138.

4. Hospitals 3
Authority to issue and revoke license for practice of chiropractic which is delegated to board of chiropractic examiners, did not overlap authority to regu-

late hospital premises for treatment of sick in interest of general health, since no method of treatment legally employed will be unduly impinged by reasonable requirements for protection of public health in institutions where such treatment is to be performed. '35 C.S.A. c.78, §§ 133-138.

5. Administrative law and procedure 751
Hospitals 1

On certiorari, review of Board of Health's action in revoking license to operate chiropractic sanitarium would be limited to inquiry as to whether jurisdiction had been exceeded, discretion abused, or authority regularly pursued. Rules of Civil Procedure, rule 106(a)(4).

6. Administrative law and procedure 387

Authority to regulate does not include authority to legislate but is strictly limited by law under which it is pursued.

7. Physicians and surgeons 1

Practice of chiropractic is lawful occupation and may not be arbitrarily limited or discriminated against, and its advocates may lawfully erect and operate buildings and facilities for treatment, according to its tenets, of patients seeking its aid, subject only to limitations set out in law and to reasonable regulations under police power, which regulations must bear relation to public health or welfare and must apply to all persons alike.

8. Hospitals 1

Where temporary provisional permit to operate chiropractic sanitarium pending consideration of application for permanent license was not signed by president of Board of Health or attested by secretary of Board, and was not conditioned upon compliance with provisions of Act regulating and licensing hospitals but was conditioned upon five stated prohibitions bearing no relation to sanitary conditions or adequacy of equipment or to training, competence, or qualifications of its personnel, such attempted license was void. '35 C.S.A. c.78, §§ 133-138.

9. Hospitals 1

Rule that where license contains invalid provisions it constitutes valid when purged of such conditions could not be applied to temporary permit to operate chiropractic sanitarium when after such purging nothing would remain except place and date. '35 C.S.A. c.78, §§ 133-138.

10. Hospitals 1

Even though temporary provisional permit to operate sanitarium which was issued by Board of Health was void, fact that Board issued authority for opening and operation of sanitarium constituted finding by Board of proper application for license and satisfactory evidence of fitness to conduct and maintain sanitarium, and upon such finding Board was legally obligated to issue proper license in place of one actually issued. '35 C.S.A. c.78, §§ 133-138.

11. Evidence 83(1)
Hospitals 1

In action to revoke to operate chiropractic sanitarium based upon alleged violation of conditions imposed by temporary permit issue to licensee, where it appeared that temporary permit and conditions contained therein were void but that Board of Health had found licensee entitled to license, assuming that as done which should have been done, to wit, actual issuance of proper license, violation of void conditions stated in temporary permit would not justify revocation. '35 C.S.A. c. 78, §§ 133-138.

12. Administrative law and procedure 472
Hospitals 1

Only matters which Board of Health could consider at hearing on action to revoke license to operate a chiropractic sanitarium were those included in notice upon which action was based. '35 C.S.A. c.78, §§ 133-138.

13. Appeal and error 1176(1)

On review of trial court's dismissal of action in nature of certiorari to review action of Board of Health revoking license to operate chiropractic sanitarium, where it appeared that attempted revocation of license by Board was void, that license so sought to be revoked was void, and that in its stead at time of its issuance Board should have issued license in accordance with law under which it acted, judgment of dismissal would be reversed with instruction to trial court to enter decree for issuance of proper license as of date of issuance of void license. Rules of Civil Procedure, rules 54, 106(a)(4); '35 C.S.A. c. 78, §§ 133-138.

$$- - o - -$$

Charles Ginsberg, Dickerson, Morrissey & Zarlengo and Creamer & Creamer, all of Denver, for plaintiff in error.

John W. Metzger, Allen Moore, Frank A. Wachob and James D. Geissinger, all of Denver, for defendants in error.

STONE, Justice.

September 27, 1943, the state board of health issued a "temporary provisional license" to plaintiff in error to operate a chiropractic sanitarium. November 19, 1946, upon notice and after a hearing, said board ordered and adjudged that the license so issued be revoked. January 7, 1947, action in the nature of certiorari was instituted by plaintiff in error for review of the action of said board, under Rule 106(a)(4), R.C.P. Colo., and review is here sought of judgment of dismissal entered in such action by the trial court December 18,

1948. The record was filed in this court March 14, 1949, but as a result of numerous extensions of time stipulated or consented to by the parties, final briefs were not submitted until May 3, 1950. The matter was then set for oral argument and heard by us May 22, 1950. The record of the evidence before the state board of health covers 1623 folios and the briefs total 432 pages.

It is first urged that the state board of health was without jurisdiction to issue or revoke a license to plaintiff in error in that its sanitarium is located within the City and County of Denver, which is a home-rule city; that said city has legislated in the field of licensing hospitals and sanitariums by ordinance covering the same field as the state statute and subsequent thereto and that its ordinance supersedes the statute within its territorial limits.

[1-3] Under the provision of Article XX of the Constitution and of its Charter, the city acquired exclusive control of local and municipal affairs, but it remained "as much amenable to state control in all matters of a public, as distinguished from matters of a local, character, as are other municipalities." People ex rel. v. McNichols, 91 Colo. 141, 13 p. (2d) 266. Health is a matter which may be either of general or of municipal concern. Infectious diseases in particular recognize no city lines, and under its police power the state retains the right to regulate such matters affecting public health as are of general concern, including the right to license and regulate hospitals wherever situated. At the same time, congested living conditions within cities may produce health problems justifying further regulation than those deemed necessary by the legislature, and as to such matters cities may possess the police power of further regulation within their limits. We are not here confronted with any conflicting mandate of statute or ordinance or with a challenge to any particular statutory command, but only with challenge to the broad right of the legislature to provide for the licensing of hospitals within the limits of home-rule cities, in the interest of the general health. That challenge cannot be sustained.

[4] It is next urged that the action of the state board of health is void for the reason that by subsequent statute, jurisdiction over the practice of chiropractic has been taken away from the state board of health and transferred to the board of chiropractic examiners. Jurisdiction concerning the practice of chiropractic is but a small segment of the broader field of jurisdiction over matters concerning the general health, and authority to issue and revoke licenses for the practice of chiropractic, which was delegated to the board of chiropractic examiners, does not overlap the authority to regulate hospital premises for treatment of the sick in the interest of public health. No method of treatment legally employed will be unduly impinged by reasonable requirements for the protection of the public health in institutions where such treatment is to be performed.

APPENDIX C.

Many other questions are raised and argued in the briefs as to the procedure adopted, the admissibility of evidence received, the alleged prejudice of board members, their absence from sessions and voting without hearing all the evidence submitted and other matters appearing in the records but we do not find it necessary to consider these questions because of a more fundamental and precedent defect in the proceedings of the board.

[5] Consistent with the contention of the attorney general, we shall assume that the scope of our review here "is limited to the inquiry as to whether jurisdiction has been exceeded, discretion abused or authority regularly pursued," as stated in Utilities Commission v. Erie, 92 Colo. 151, 18 p.2d 906, 907.

[6,7] In considering the question of the regular pursuit of authority, it is fundamental that authority to regulate does not include authority to legislate, but is strictly limited by the law under which it is pursued. The practice of chiropractic is recognized and authorized by law. We must accept such practice as a lawful occupation and as in the public interest. It may not be arbitrarily limited or discriminated against and its advocates may lawfully erect and operate buildings and facilities for the treatment, according to its tenets, of patients seeking its aid, subject only to the limitations set out in the law and to reasonable regulations under the police power. Such regulations must bear relation to the public health or welfare and must apply to all persons alike.

The sole authority of the Board in the issuance and revocation of licenses is chapter 172, S.L. 1909, being now subdivision 1, article 5, chapter 78, '35 C.S.A., constituting sections 133 to 138 inclusive of said chapter. This statute provides, insofar as we are concerned, that it shall be unlawful to open or maintain any hospital or other institution for the treatment or care of the sick or injured without first having obtained a license therefor from the state board of health; that an application for such license shall be made as therein provided; that the board "shall issue licenses to such applicants furnishing satisfactory evidence of fitness to conduct and maintain such institution in accordance with the provisions of this act and the rules and regulations adopted by such Board; and such licenses shall be signed by the President and attested by the Secretary of said Board and have the seal thereof affixed thereto, "and that licenses may be refused to applicants not complying or meeting with the requirements of this act and of the rules and regulations of the Board," and that licenses may be revoked for like reasons. This statute, on which the Board must rely for its authority, provides only for the issuance of permanent licenses which shall continue until revoked; that they be signed by the president of the board, and attested by the secretary, and bear the seal thereof affixed thereto; that they issue upon showing of fitness to conduct the institution "in accordance with the provisions of this act and the rules and regulations adopted by such Board," and that they be refused or revoked solely by reason of not complying with the requirements of the act and rules and regulations of the board.

[8] As disclosed by the record, the form of the so-called license issued to plaintiff in error and by it attempted to be revoked reads as follows:

"STATE OF COLORADO
DIVISION OF PUBLIC HEALTH
DENVER, COLORADO

Spears Free Clinic and Hospital for Poor Children, Inc. of Denver, Colorado, Is Hereby Granted a Temporary Provisional License To Operate a Chiropractic Sanitarium Pending Consideration of an Application for a Permanent License by the State Board of Health and subject to the following conditions:

1-That maternity cases shall not be received.

2-That surgery will not be performed.

3-That drugs or medicine shall not be administered.

4-That no contagious or infectious cases will be admitted or treated.

5-That the name "hospital" shall not be used in describing or designating the institution.

6-That this temporary provisional license shall not become effective until the applicant has confirmed his understanding of these conditions by letter delivered to the Secretary of the Colorado Board of Health.

In the Event of the Denial or a Permanent License to the Applicant by the Board, this Temporary Provisional License Shall Become Null and Void, Upon Written Notice Thereof to the Applicant.

Dated at Denver, Colorado, This 27th Day of September, 1943.

....
Hospital Inspector, Division of
Maternal and Child Health.

Approved:

....
Secretary and Executive Officer,
Colorado State Board of Health."

Assuming that this instrument was in fact signed by an inspector and approved by Dr. Cleere as secretary and executive officer of the board, which does not appear from the record, it is at once apparent that the instrument issued to plaintiff in error was in no respect a compliance with the statute under which the board must act. By its very terms it was not a license as authorized by the statute, but an unauthorized temporary provisional permit issued "pending consideration of an application for a permanent license;" it was not signed by the president of the board nor even issued under its apparent authority; it was not attested to by the secretary of the board; it did not bear its seal; most important of all, it was not conditioned upon a compliance with "the provisions of this act and the rules and regulations adopted by such Board," rather, it was conditioned on five stated prohibitions, not one of which was either a provision of the statute or properly, or in fact, a rule or regulation of the board. These prohibitions bear no relation to the sanitary conditions or the adequacy of equipment of the sanitarium; no relations to the training, competence or qualification of its personnel, or those in attendance of its patients, and no relation to the public health, morals, welfare or security. They are not set up as rules or standards for chiropractic sanitariums generally, but are arbitrary and discriminatory restrictions against applicant alone.

[9] There is not one sentence in the issued license which follows the statute on which it is based. We cannot apply the rule that where a license contains invalid provisions it constitutes a valid license when purged of such conditions, for the reason that after such purging nothing would remain, except the place and date. Instead of pursuing its statutory authority, the state board of health attempted to usurp the function of the legislature and set up law of its own.

[10,12] However, while there is nothing valid about the issued license, yet the very fact that the board issued authority for the opening and operation of a sanitarium constitutes a finding by the board of proper application for a license and satisfactory evidence of fitness to conduct and maintain the sanitarium. Such finding was a legal prerogative of the board and upon such finding the board was legally obligated to issue a proper license in place of the one actually issued. Assuming that as done which should have been done, to wit, the actual issuance of a proper license, and that such license was subject to revocation as provided by the statute, the revocation here ordered was of a certainty not in regular pursuit of authority. The charges upon which revocation was predicated were based, not on violations of any provision of statute or of any rule or regulation of the board, but on asserted violations of the arbitrary and unauthorized conditions in the issued license. In the "notice of hearing to revoke license" upon which the hearing was based, plaintiff in error was notified that the grounds of revocation charged were:

"It is alleged that such license should be revoked because you have violated conditions 2, 3, 4 and 5 contained therein, to wit:

1- In that surgery has been performed;

2- In that drugs and medicine have been administered;

APPENDIX C.

3- In that contagious and infectious diseases have been admitted and treated;

4- In that the name "hospital" has been used in describing or designating the institution;

At this hearing you may be present, introduce evidence in your own behalf, and be represented by counsel, if you so desire.

Colorado State Board of Health

R.W. Dickson, President
R.L. Cleere, M.D., Secretary."

There was no charge that licensee authorized, or by negligence permitted, surgery to be performed or drugs or medicine to be administered by persons or under conditions prohibited by law or regulation, or that licensee violated any law or regulation in the admittance or segregation or treatment of contagious or infectious diseases, or in its use of the word "Hospital." Even if the evidence adduced at the hearing on those charges established the truth of all of them, as is asserted in behalf of the Board, still no ground for valid revocation was shown. The violation of void conditions could not justify revocation. If proper grounds for revocation had been shown at the hearing, they might not here and now be considered, for the reason that the only matters which the Board could properly consider at the hearing were those included in the notice upon which it was based. Accordingly, we must determine that the court erred in its judgment of dismissal; that the attempted revocation of license by the Board was void; that the license so sought to be revoked was void, and that in its stead at the time of its issuance the Board should have issued a license in accordance with the law under which it acted.

[13] Under Rule 54 of our rules of civil procedure, it is the duty of the court to grant relief to which a party is entitled, even though not specifically demanded in the prayer. Accordingly, the judgment of dismissal is reversed with instruction to the trial court to enter proper decree for the issuance of a license to the plaintiff in error for the maintenance of its chiropractic sanitarium here involved, as of September 27, 1943, conditioned as provided by law, to constitute a permanent authority therefore, until revoked for failure to comply with the requirements of law or rules and regulations of the Board of Health adopted pursuant thereto.

Reversed with actions. En Banc.

APPENDIX D.

Fruits of Our Research

While the principles of chiropractic have not changed since its discovery in 1895, its boundaries have expanded and its techniques improved. Through research at the Spears Chiropractic Clinic and the Spears Chiropractic Sanitarium the scientific contributions made by these institutions have been far-reaching and revolutionizing in the field of healing. To their research departments goes the credit of:

■ Developing a simplified technique which renders chiropractic adjustments completely painless, pleasant and doubly effective. This system is now used wholly or in part by the great majority of the chiropractors of the world and is taught by several of the best schools.

■ Discovering that infantile skull distortion, causing bony pressure upon the brain, is responsible for most cases of cerebral palsy and mental deficiency; and the development of a skull reshaping technique which is proving very effective in correcting these conditions.

■ Discovering and developing a method of reactivating many adult hip and other joints which had been destroyed and made rigid by tuberculosis, arthritis and other disease.

■ Discovering and developing a system of regenerating and reactivating many child hip and other joints which have been destroyed or partly destroyed by Perthe's or other eating or wasting diseases.

■ Discovering and developing a system of hastening healing and relief of disease by manually goading nerves and tissues to excess function or doing many times their normal amount of work.

■ Discovering and developing an unbelievably simple, rapid and effective drugless method of relieving and controlling pain.

■ Discovering in 1939 the cause of leprosy and now generally admitted fact that this disease is neither contagious nor infectious.

■ Developing a hygienic system for fasting for rapidly and effectively ridding the body of toxemia as an aid to the relief of most diseases arising from systemic poisoning.

■ Developing an extremely effective drugless method of relieving chronic alcoholism and its sequelae.

■ Developing a technique by which most types of distressing foot ailments may be corrected painlessly.

■ Discovering several other important and revolutionary facts concerning life, health and disease which are being investigated as rapidly as time and funds will permit. These include unusually effective methods of treating and relieving such "incurable" diseases as arthritis, epilepsy, multiple sclerosis, infantile paralysis, diabetes mellitus, cancer, rheumatic fever, heart ailments, etc.

Leo L. Spears: *Spears Painless System.* (Self-published, Denver, 1950), pp. 6-7

Appendix E.

Statement of Dr. Leo Spears before the U.S. Senate Judiciary Subcommittee on Juvenile Delinquency Denver, Colo., Dec. 14, 1953

Most people are good, regardless of their age. Goodness or badness is usually a matter of judgment or a lack of it. The natural thing for a child or an adult is to be good.

Personal conduct is a matter of personal thinking. While environment, training, education and association undoubtedly have great influence upon the thinking of an individual, I believe physical causes play an important part.

During 35 years of observing and treating human beings, I have learned that abnormal conduct usually has a physical cause. For every mental deficit there is a physical cause or counterpart. Crime is abnormal human reaction which results from some type of mental deficit. Mental deficits are usually correctable only by removal of the physical causes.

Crime is not a disease. It is usually the symptom of a diseased mind which is a symptom of bodily disease or abnormality. The only way to permanently get rid of disease or crime is to eliminate the cause.

Sometime ago, I discovered the cause and methods for correcting cerebral palsy and mental deficiency. Since that time my research has revealed that much of the crime of the country is committed by individuals who are or were problem children. Parents know that problem children are abnormal children. It appears that the cause of such abnormalcy is the same type of distortion that causes cerebral palsy, mental deficiency and related conditions.

What distortion do I refer to? Skull distortion, which creates pressure upon the brain from without. Just to the degree that a skull is distorted beyond the corrective adaptability of nature, it causes pressure upon and distorts the brain and every cell forming it. This unnecessarily causes trouble in the functioning of the mind and the various parts of the body supplied with life force by the depressed or "squeezed" lobes of the brain. This is not a dream. I have sufficient living and documented proof to prove my contentions to the committee or anyone else who may be interested. And my findings, including techniques for remolding distorted skulls to their normal patterns, are in book form.

Everything has a definite pattern. It is pattern that distinguishes species of all plants and animals, including man. And while there are no two things exactly alike, the overall pattern, down to the smallest cell, of all things composing any particular type, breed or specie, are basically the same.

Outside of the slight differences between races, and the male and female, the shapes of skulls and brains of nearly two billion people in the world are basically alike; just as all other parts of the body are alike. As surely as everything has a basic pattern, that pattern must remain unchanged, down to the

155

tiniest cell, for such thing to function normally. Patterns are not accidents. They are responses to creative principles, the very foundation and individuality of creation. Hence, a constantly distorted pattern, whether it be of the skull, brain or any bone, organ or tiny tissue cell, interferes with the functioning of such part.

The human brain is the most complicated, yet the most amazing organ of all creation. The life and functioning of every organ and cell in the body, and of mental processes, are dependent upon its normal functioning.

Each of the brain's 14 lobes [sic] controls certain physical and mental functions. And the result of any brain pressure caused by skull distortion is dependent upon the lobe or combination of lobes, squeezed. For instance, if the pressure is only upon those lobes which control the muscles of the arms and legs, there will be paralysis or other dysfunction of those limbs, but interference with the mind. If the lobes that control mental processes are pressed upon also, there will also be a mental deficiency. If only the mental lobes are squeezed, there will be no muscular disturbances, but there will be mental deficiencies and abnormal mental expressions.

Most people, including doctors, have little or no idea what a normal skull should look like. This means that many skull distortions which cause both physical and mental handicaps are seldom noticed or recognized as causative of physical and mental ailments. Slight distortions often cause enough pressure upon the mental lobes of the brain to make it impossible for the victim to recognize error, adapt himself to social standards, or determine right from wrong. It is this type of individual that usually becomes a problem child, and later a repeater criminal.

What causes skull distortions? (1) Instrumental or other difficult delivery which results in damage to the head. (2) Allowing the new-born, whose head is almost as soft and pliable as bread dough, to sleep in one position during the first few weeks of life, permitting gravity to distort the shape of the head. (3) Rushing or retarding birth by artificial means, throwing a strain or undue pressure upon the head. (4) Maternal pelvic or abdominal abnormalities, causing distorting pressures upon the head during the last few weeks of prenatal life.

How can these things be prevented? (1) Refusal of mothers to allow the use of instruments. (2) Refusal of mothers to permit artificial speeding up or retarding of the normal processes of birth. (3) Greater skill and care on the part of doctors and midwives to prevent head and neck injuries during birth. (4) Mothers carefully inspecting their babies' heads and demanding that distortions or deviations from normal be corrected before the skull has time to harden, or by reshaping the skulls themselves. (5) Mothers being careful to see that their babies are turned often during the first few weeks of life, and never allowed to lie in one position more than a few hours at a time until they are over a year old.

APPENDIX E.

Such measures would not only, I believe, prevent cerebral palsy and extreme degrees of mental deficiency, but would eliminate the possibility of problem children and much of the crime rampant in this country.

And it is time, I believe, that our country should turn its efforts to the prevention of crime instead of the punishment of criminals. I submit that much juvenile delinquency, as well as crime being committed by repeater criminals, can be eliminated and prevented in the future, by proper attention to physical causes of mental abnormalities.

Spears Sanigram, 21 [Jan.] 1955

APPENDIX F.

The Reasons Long Life is Possible

By Dr. Leo Spears

The human body is not a happenstance. It was created on purpose and by design. True "it comes forth like a flower and is cut down; it fleeth like a shadow and continueth not." This is the way of all material things. But the creative forces and natural laws that govern them are omnipotent, omnipresent and eternal.

The body springs from a cell less than one-hundredth of an inch in diameter, which contains nothing of which it is built. Soon it grows into a material entity, of which 62,500 miles of blood vessels are only a small part. It lives and functions until abuse, disease or some other force destroys it.

Some bodies enter the world already dead. Others live various periods, the average life expectancy now being about fifty-nine years. Some live to be one hundred or more.

Since survival is one of life's greatest urges, most people want to live as long as possible. And the body reflects this urge even after the conscious desire for continuance has ceased. So, from the moment of conception to the moment of death, life is a struggle between the forces of creation and destruction. Its longevity is dependent upon how long the creative forces predominate.

Of the nine primary functions of the body, those of growth and repair are most necessary to longevity. Creative processes resulting in growth appear to cease at maturity, but we at Spears Chiropractic Hospital have found that they do not. They only go into partial retirement. To the extent that basic body materials have to be replaced for the maintenance of life, they remain active. But without proper inducement they apparently grow tired and lag in their work. When creative processes are in full predominance over body decay, 140,000,000 cells are created every minute. This means an 8% replacement of basic body constituents every month, or 96% of a new body every year.

Could this creative rate be maintained, the average life expectancy might well be several times what it is today. In fact, one might live almost indefinitely.

This being the case, all we need do to increase human longevity is to find ways and means of keeping the body's creative forces constantly active and operative with a high degree of efficiency. When the creative forces are operating normally, auxiliary functions necessary to longevity seldom lag in their duties. When they do, corrective measures are already available to chiropractors.

Research at the Spears Chiropractic Hospital has already resulted in fairly effective measures for spurring nature into increased creative activity and more rapid body repair – measures which we believe may be of great importance in extending the normal span of human life. These measures are now being used to great advantage in revival of paralyzed limbs and relief of diseased organs.

The body is flexible in its response to demands made upon it. An easy or sedentary existence results in relative physical weakness and ultimate deterioration. To live in bed is to invite rapid decay and early death. Hard physical labor develops strong muscles and bones. Vigorous training for wrestling or boxing increases strength and endurance in every body part.

Self-preservation is the first law of nature and is inherent in all body tissues. The functions of growth and repair are also the greatest servants of this law and are ever at the command of increasing and unusual needs. But these and other functions do not always respond to body needs of their own accord. When they do, they are not always adequate to the occasion.

Artificial stimulants that induce response are only temporary and often injurious. The need is for natural means of inducing the creative forces to remain constantly on the job and in as full force as may be required to keep the body in perpetual health and perfect functioning order.

It is the opinion of Spears researchers that not time but a decline in cell replacement is principally responsible for body attrition known as aging. Aging progresses in exact ratio to any reduction in the creation of replacement cells. When trauma, disease or physical abuse reduces cellular replacement and retards other body functions, aging occurs at a rapid pace. Such deterioration can only be overcome by the natural forces that built the body in the first place and that keep it in repair. In our longevity study, it is our purpose to ferret out ways and means of cooperating with these forces to the end of a longer and happier life for every human being.

Spears Sanigram, 21 [Jan.] 1955

Appendix G.

Statement of Dr. Leo Spears Before the Antimonopoly Subcommittee of the U.S. Senate Judiciary Committee
Washington, D.C., May 14, 1953

I would like to make it plain that I am here as a veteran, seeking freedom of choice in healing matters for the sick, disabled and crippled veterans of this country.

I am a member of the American Legion and the Disabled American Veterans. My hope is to expose the monopoly of medicine in the veterans affairs department of the Veterans Administration, and to call attention of Congress to the misery being caused and the money being wasted by such monopoly. To this end, I have brought along certain articles of proof, and several witnesses whose relief by a nonmedical method of treatment spurned by the Veterans Administration is typical of the relief obtained by many thousands of veterans at their own expense and by public charity after the medical treatment supplied by the Veterans Administration had proven valueless.

I am also here in defense of the right of our disabled defenders to have the same freedom of choice in all matters as other citizens. I do not believe that being veterans should bar them from exercising the same constitutional rights enjoyed by other citizens.

The greatness of this country is built upon the foundations of freedom – freedom of the press, freedom of religion, freedom of politics, freedom of speech, and freedom of choice.

Basically, this means the right of the individual to truth and facts about all things, to worship according to his own beliefs, to vote for whomever he pleases, to speak according to his own conscience and to choose all things according to his own desires and needs so long as he does not infringe upon the rights of others.

The "freedom of choice" guaranteed by our Constitution means nothing unless it is applied to one and all alike. And each must see that his neighbors' be not restricted lest his own be abolished by the same encroachments.

"Freedom of choice" would be a mockery if it applied only to the press, religion, politics and speech. If this country is to be in fact a free nation, freedom of choice must apply to all basic rights, one of the most precious of which is the right to live and be healthy and to choose and to have the system of healing most apt to make these things possible.

"Freedom of choice" would also be an empty phrase were there only one of anything to choose from. "Freedom" implies the right of the creation and growth of a multiplicity of publications, religions, political parties, industries, arts, sciences, and healing methods. And it implies reasonable competition, with government protection, against destructive monopoly. Dr. Benjamin Rush,

APPENDIX G.

Surgeon General of the Continental Army, and one of the signers of the Declaration of Independence, warned: "We have provided for religious freedom, but unless we provide for healing liberty, our best efforts to establish a government of freedom shall prove abortive and the American people shall forever live in bondage." But despite this warning and the obligation of our government to protect humanity against strangling monopolies in all fields of human endeavor, complete healing liberty has never existed in this country. Medical monopoly has not only been allowed to exist almost everywhere, but has often been protected and encouraged by our government, the most tragic instances of which exist in our armed forces and Veterans Administration. The battle for the right of disabled veterans to choose their own system of healing was started back in 1923, when it was first evident that the medical combine had been allowed to get a strangle hold upon the Veterans Administration, indicated by its refusal to furnish state-licensed nonmedical treatment to veterans. February 5, 1924, the Medical Director of the Veterans' Bureau wrote: "The methods of treatment employed by this Bureau are those which represent the consensus of authoritative medical opinion, approved by such representative bodies as the American Medical Association. In view of this, the Bureau does not feel the necessity of adding chiropractic measures to its care and treatment of ex-servicemen."

On March 27, 1953, Dr. J.T. Boone, Chief Medical Director, Veterans Administration, wrote: "There was brought to my attention, the letter you wrote to the administrator on March 13th, 1953, proposing that the Veterans Administration send lay investigators to your institution at your expense to evaluate the results of chiropractic treatment with certain stipulations you specified. For the Veterans Administration to engage in such a project was not favorably considered and your offer is herewith declined."

In other words, the American Medical Association and the medical directors of the old Veterans' Bureau and the present Veterans Administration, have always exercised a monopoly over the treatment allowed to disabled veterans. That monopoly has been strengthened by the years and will continue to grow unless something is done by Congress to break it. It appears that Congress is the court of last appeal for many thousands of disabled veterans who have failed to find relief through the restricted medical means provided by the Veterans Administration.

Because of medical monopoly, thousands of disabled, crippled and suffering veterans are being denied the right of health and happiness which chiropractic alone can provide. This means that those who preserved our freedoms are being denied rights which the rest of us enjoy. And those without financial means are being forced to depend upon charity for health, rehabilitation, and relief which they failed to get through the medical treatment now being provided them by the Veterans Administration.

APPENDIX G.

There was once much ado about veterans selling apples on the street for a living. But few people seem to know that refusal of the Veterans Administration to pay for chiropractic for veterans it is helpless to relieve, is forcing many of our defenders to spend funds their families need for bread and clothes and accept charity made up by churches, veterans organizations and friends for the preservation of their lives and the relief of their miseries.

And what about the cost to taxpayers? Figures that will eventually exceed all other costs of war. Outside of disability payments, it costs taxpayers from $20.00 to $50.00 per day to hospitalize and treat a disabled veteran in government hospitals. The average, with scores of hidden costs, is probably nearer $50.00 than $20.00. But money is unimportant in comparison with the cost in suffering and anguish by our veterans and their families. If veterans were allowed their just right of choice of healing systems and doctors - enjoyed by all but veterans and welfare clients - there would be much less misery and much greater happiness in the world

And there is no criticism of the medical service administered by the Veterans Administration or the great core of conscientious and capable medical doctors serving our veterans. It is seriously doubted that any except the politically minded members of the medical profession endorse such inhuman and unconstitutional treatment of veterans. I say this because it seems impossible that anyone but a political sadist could deny a disabled veteran any reasonable thing and especially the right to freely choose the system of healing that is most apt to reduce his suffering.

In the natural course of things, it seems that we all have some duty to perform, some obligation to fulfill. And sooner or later it becomes our part to make good. It became the part of Columbus to discover a continent; George Washington to father a country; Abraham Lincoln to unite a nation. During the past few years, it has become the part of the young men of this country to sacrifice their jobs, their health and their lives to preserve the freedoms which generations before them had by sacrifices won for this country. It is now the part of this country to end a current war and reconstruct an embattled and discouraged world. If we are not going to reconstruct it on the basis of personal emancipation, personal freedom, and personal liberty in each nation, what is the use of sacrificing human blood and human lives in order to free one nation from the autocratic rule of another?

It is bad enough for one nation to try to usurp the freedom of another nation. But when a certain organization or group unites for the avowed purpose of restricting the liberties of other groups or individuals within its own territory, it is high time for the public to take a hand. Just as surely as this kind of autocracy is permitted by private monopolies, it will finally spread until it finds refuge in the seat of government. And this is exactly what has happened with the medical trust. It has found refuge for its autocratic rule in the Veterans Administration and our armed forces.

In creating the Veterans' Bureau, our law makers did not intend that our disabled veterans should be denied anything that would help restore their health; that the money appropriated for veterans' physical rehabilitation should be used to enrich the interests of any profession; or that any healing art should be given a monopoly in the Bureau. Their evident intentions were that all means and methods be employed that would to restore these men to health. But their good intentions have been cruelly violated by the authorities into whose hands that trust was given.

The autocratic power of the medical department of the Veterans Administration stems from the universal authority of the American Medical Association, whose chief competitor in strength and results is chiropractic. The following citations are typical of the motives and powers of this monopoly:

■ Chiropractic is not made available to disabled veterans or service-men in any government hospital.

■ Despite the many appeals by sick and disabled veterans who have been given up by conscientious and competent medical staffs in Veterans Administration hospitals, not one veteran has ever been allowed chiropractic at government expense on an outpatient or other basis.

■ Chiropractic is not provided or permitted in any federal, state, city or county or private medical hospital in the country. This is taxation without representation.

■ The Blue Cross-Blue Shield and other "voluntary" medical insurance plans generally refuse to pay for chiropractic hospitalization or service. Yet, they are nontaxable competition with some 600 tax paying insurance companies that do.

■ Medical monopoly bars chiropractic voice from practically all health boards in the nation.

■ Not a single one of the many organizations and societies that annually raise money for disease research will allot any funds for chiropractic research.

What reasons are advanced by the Veterans Administration for their refusal to recognize the right of the veterans to have chiropractic at government expense? That it does not have the right to do so under law; that it does not choose to do so. But what are the real reasons? Self-interest; medical monopoly!

This monopoly bases its antagonism on the spurious claim that recognition of chiropractic by medicine would "lower" medical standards. This despite the fact that though chiropractic is only 58 years old and (1) is licensed in 44 states, the District of Columbia, Hawaii and Alaska and (2) its basic educational requirements for licensure are already equal in many states to those of medicine, which 7,000 years ago named 400 diseases and 700 remedies; (3) that chiropractors pass the same basic science examinations required of medical graduates under boards dominated by medicine; (4) that regular four-year professional courses now taught by practically all chiropractic schools are generally equal in subjects and hours to standard medical courses; and (5) that chiropractic schools receive no financial help from anyone, while medical schools are mostly built and operated with tax dollars and private endowments.

Human and scientific babies have to crawl before they can walk. Though medicine is seventy centuries old, less than a century ago anybody could get a medical license after a six-month apprenticeship. Just as there are a few chiropractors today who had but one year of schooling, there are still some physicians who never had more than a year in medical school. But no science should be blamed today for its shortcomings of yesterday.

Here it should be pointed out that the value of any doctor can only be measured by the lives he saves and the suffering he relieves. Disabled veterans are not interested in false ethics or privileged standards. They are not interested in methods of healing or any individual doctors. They know that scholastic degrees do not guarantee competence, and that intelligence and ability are not dependent on a college education; that education often serves only to make crooks more clever; that history is redolent with "uneducated" greats and "educated" fools; that Jesus, the greatest of all healers, had no schooling; that Socrates, one of the world's greatest thinkers and teachers, was self taught; and that two of our greatest presidents, Lincoln and Jackson, never went to school; that merit is the only measure of worth; and that the "uneducated" doctor who cures many is worth a score of educated incompetents. They also know that the fact that chiropractic was discovered by an "uneducated" man is less a disgrace than an indictment of the so-called educated scientists who have overlooked the great chiropractic principles for centuries and who condemn it [*sic*] today.

Chiropractors agree with veterans that had there been no medical failures there would have been no need for chiropractors; and were chiropractic a cure-all, medicine would fall by the wayside. It is very evident that both have a place and both are needed. The fact that disease and suffering are still rampant all over the world is a humiliating indictment of the value of both systems.

Evidently deploring medical monopoly and recognizing the need for chiropractic for disabled veterans, the major veterans organizations started the fight for chiropractic inclusion at government expense back in 1923. It was not long until the American Legion, DAV's, VFW's, all at their national conventions, petitioned our government for the right of their diseased buddies to choose and to have chiropractic on the same basis they are now provided "approved" medical care.

But, despite the fact that thousands of veterans are absolutely penniless today by reason of having sacrificed their business or professions to answer the call of their country when our freedom was in danger, not one appeal for chiropractic has been honored. Many of these men because of their disabilities, are unable to earn a livelihood, much less than pay for treatment of their ills by private doctors.

The time has come when discrimination must be abolished, and when the healing rights of our disabled defenders must be recognized and granted. Several years ago, Senator Tasker L. Oddie, of Nevada, expressed a universal opinion when he said: "The most the government can do is little enough for those who were disabled in the Great War. The American people owe them a debt of gratitude which they can never repay. A sacred trust is on the shoulders of the people and the Congress to fulfill that duty liberally and honestly. The sad truth is that it has not been done."

The veterans know that the American people are anxious to show their gratitude to their boys. They have given freely of their funds that not one disabled veteran might suffer. But their boys are still suffering because the medical monopoly into whose hands the "sacred trust" has been given has, so far as healing choice is concerned, betrayed that trust by its refusal to furnish all meritorious methods of healing for the speedy relief of their sons.

The American people never intended that their money should be spent in the promotion of any method of treatment or in forcing any healing art upon those boys who do not believe in it and upon whom it effects no relief. Their intentions were and still are that nothing be denied the disabled veterans that offers any measure of relief. But their intentions have been nullified by "the consensus of authoritative medical opinion, approved by the American Medical Association."

It seems high time that every individual in this country should ask himself the following questions about our veterans:

■ Should they be denied any right they fought to preserve?

■ Since they defended everything for us, can we justly deny anything for them?

■ Are their lives any less precious now than when we cheered them on in battle?

■ Should monopoly of one system of healing rob them of the benefits of another?

■ Are your taxes being paid for the benefit of a healing monopoly, or the men who are still paying a heavy price for your freedom?

■ Would you rather see them suffer because of discriminatory "ethics" or get well in spite of it?

■ Should the sacrifices they made and are still making for us bar them from any of the rights we enjoy?

■ Should false healing "standards" be maintained at the cost of their health and lives?

■ Is it right to ask our sons to fight and then deny them even one of the rights they fought for?

■ Was the therapeutic department of the Veterans Administration created for the benefit of medicine or for the benefit of diseased and crippled veterans?

■ How much longer are we going to tolerate medical discrimination against any disabled veterans we are obligated by their sacrifices to protect?

■ What confidence can we have in a monopoly whose self-interest is placed ahead of the interests of our beloved veterans?

■ What are we doing about this unconstitutional injustice?

■ What would you think of chiropractors if they sought to deny veterans medical care?

I wish to remind you gentlemen, the Congress and the people of this country, that when our wars were declared, Uncle Sam's call was responded to without quibbling by young men from every walk of life, followers of every form of treatment. But those who believed only in Christian Science didn't say, "Give us Science practitioners or we won't sign up." Nor did those who subscribed to chiropractic say, "Give us our own doctors or we won't fight." They all joined up like the noble men they were, making no demands and asking no favors. Those who didn't know it before they enlisted soon found that they would be given only medical treatment. But they sacrificed their personal beliefs and submitted not only to medical treatment but to vaccinations and injections which they often opposed, without question. Since probably 50 per cent of them did not believe in medicine as a treatment or a preventative, it was a bitter dose to take. But they took it – in the arms and in capsules.

To many thousands of disabled veterans who are eking out a miserable existence, the emergency they faced has ended. When their battle was won, military control and military measures should also have ended for them. When the boys were restored to civilian life, they should have regained their civil rights – all of them! But the pitiful fact is that they did not.

Back in 1952, the child of an unnaturalized family in a Western state became ill. The best in medicine was employed but the child continued to grow worse. Finally a chiropractor was called and the stricken little body was restored to health. At the same time, a hero of the Battle of the Bulge, with a bullet-and-diseased racked body, was in grave condition in a Veterans Administration hospital. Some of the finest specialists in the country were called in, but acknowledged that medicine would not cure him and that he was doomed to an early death. But he was denied the privilege of calling in a chiropractor. For his country he had fought and won. But for him there was no victory. Even after competent and highly honorable medical specialists had acknowledged their inability to do anything for him, the only other road to health was barred to him. But he wanted to get well. So he left the hospital in a wheel chair. An

American Legion Post, his church and a few friends recognized his pitiable plight and provided funds for chiropractic hospitalization and treatment. He got well. But instead of the government paying for the treatment that cured him, it was relieved of the necessity of paying him total disability compensation.

This does not mean, of course, that medicine fails in every case. It is doing a wonderful job. Nor does it mean that chiropractic is always successful. But it does mean that one who is not even a naturalized citizen has more privileges in this country than the boys who gave their health that our freedoms might not perish. The unnaturalized family can choose its own system of healing and doctor. The disabled veteran cannot. And eternity will find the situation unchanged unless Congress rights this wrong before our precious disabled veteran sons pass on to other battle grounds.

Time to our disabled veterans is of the essence. There is nothing eternal except death. Every veteran that passes on who could have been saved by chiropractic is a tack in the coffin of our Bill of Rights. If our government is to factually become a government "of the people, by the people, and for the people," there must be an end to every vestige of government monopoly, not only in the Veterans Administration, but throughout this great land.

We are witnessing continuation of the horrible war in Korea for the sole right of our enemy prisoners to refuse to go home, enemies who only yesterday made it impossible for many of our sons to ever come home. Yet, those who do come home find that are denied an even more precious right of choice then the one granted their enemies. Everywhere the press is making a valiant fight for human rights – that is, for all but the right of disabled veterans to choose their own system of healing. On April 24, the *Denver Post* carried an excellent editorial entitled "Keep Right to Choose for Ourselves." And the right it so nobly defended was pallid and insignificant in comparison with the right of a disabled veteran to live and to be healthy.

When many honest and ethical leaders of medicine publicly admit, as they are constantly doing, the shocking limitations of medical science, we wonder why our lawmakers give medicine full control over the health and lives of the protectors of our rights, with no right themselves of appeal from medicine to natural methods even after medicine has failed to cure them? It must be a lack of knowledge of the facts. But now the facts are out.

And we believe these facts, considered from the cold-blooded standpoint of the dollar alone, are of sufficient significance to warrant immediate Congressional action that will remedy the situation. And the remedy lies only in the enactment of a law compelling the Veterans Administration to give our disabled boys the right to choose their own method of healing at government expense.

Instead of this entailing further expense to the taxpayers, it will mean a great saving in reduced compensation and death claims. It is also an easy matter to work out a plan by which this can be done without disturbing the present government hospitals – simply provide chiropractic through chiropractic hospitals and outpatient service.

When we think of the human side, we vision a challenge to Congress and the nation alike. There is no standard for measuring the benefits chiropractic would bring to those suffering boys, their families and loved ones. And this without harm or extra cost to anyone.

It is paradoxical indeed that the government civil service employees are allowed chiropractic, and that our government pays for chiropractic education for its able-bodied veterans yet denies the disabled the right to have chiropractic care. The answer to this enigma is that government monopoly has no control over government civil service employees or the veterans' educational program.

Every Memorial Day, Old Glory faces the East and bows to half staff. As the memory of bygone and present ghastly and gory war days becloud our vision, we can but hang our heads in grief. But while we pay our fallen heroes their just homage, how many of us are reminded that the noble sacrifice of those fair-faced lads, and those who are still with us, are the full measure of freedom that we are enjoying today? And as we come in daily contact with the diseased, the lame and the blind of those who are yet in our midst, how many of us realize that they are still paying for our liberty in physical suffering and mental anguish? How many of us feel ashamed that one of our living heroes should be denied anything that would add to his health and well-being?

We can but guess the ponderous price our nation would pay to have our dead heroes restored to life and their loved ones; to have the veil of sorrow lifted from their mother's faces. Indeed, no price would be too heavy; no sacrifice too great.

Yet, can the glory of the dead overshadow that of the living? Can any price be too heavy, any sacrifice too great, that would restore them their health and save them yet a while to their loved ones and to our nation?

In closing, I can but appeal to our great president, to this committee and to every senator and congressman, for the constitutional and God-intended right of our living heroes to choose the system of healing that will give them the health and happiness they have so fully earned.

Spears Sanigram, 19 [Aug.] 1953

Appendix H.

Medics "Code of Cooperation" With Nation's Press Revealed

All loyal U.S. citizens support, and fight for, the freedoms on which our form of government is based. Especially freedom of the press.

Yet one wonders whether press privileges in this respect extend to voluntary abridgment of press rights by entering into an agreement whereby all news applying to public health shall be screened by the American Medical Association (AMA), or its local affiliates.

The secret impact, carefully guarded from the public for half a dozen years, is now in the open:

The American Legion's national commander, Arthur J. Connell, "broke" the story Jan. 28, 1954, before the Veterans Affairs Committee in the U.S. House of Representatives. He deplored the existence of a "Code of Cooperation" which provides newspapers, radio and television stations, shall clear "all matters of health or medical news" through established medical channels "before proceeding to publication or broadcast."

The Code reads: "A list of current spokesmen of the State Medical Society shall be supplied to representatives of the press... and shall be kept up to date." No other authority on public health matters is written into the document.

Commander Connell thundered: "This code is in reality a contract which has had the practical effect of suppressing presentation to the public of many facts in the controversy over medical care for America's 21 million ex-servicemen and women." He made this charge in Washington and repeated it in Denver's *Rocky Mountain News*, Feb. 12, 1954.

Text of the Washington release did not state whether Commander Connell concerned himself with the demand of major veterans organization for Chiropractic as a Veterans Administration health service. Indeed, the original cause of Connell's outburst - the suppression by the press of the veterans' case vs. AMA over hospitalization for non-service connected ailments - was almost forgotten in the frantic effort by press and medics to defend their positions.

Spokesmen for Denver newspapers had a variety of comments: They insisted, at first, that Commander Connell was quoting from an out-dated "Code of Cooperation;" also, they claimed that no contract existed. Spokesmen - authorized by the "Code" to speak for the medical profession were quoted at length, accusing Connell of "stretching the truth" and being "totally misinformed." When it became apparent that the Legion commander knew what he was talking about, and had evidence at his fingertips, the Denver newspapers sought to justify their adherence to the "Code" by explaining they had had a tough time blasting information from the "closed-mouthed" medics, and the "Code of Cooperation" eased this situation...

APPENDIX H.

It remedied the situation by putting the medical profession in the censorship saddle! An almost complete blackout of news other than items bearing the medical stamp of approval was achieved.

While the tempest was at its height, there was no interview or quotation from any authority other than press executives and medical people qualified by the "Code" to speak for their profession. No civic-minded citizens, taxpayers or service club leader was ever consulted. No chiropractors, or other members of the healing professions were awarded a line of type.

Though the controversy's pivotal point seemed to be Denver, Colo., there were frequent allusions to the "Code" being effective throughout the nation. This should explain why the press lends itself so readily to medical "news" and excludes stories of patients who owe their restored health to chiropractic...

One of the most notable illustrations of the press's reluctance to credit other than medical science for healing accomplishments was contained in a Denver newspaper's front-page story describing a man's release from the Colorado State hospital through his sweetheart's untiring efforts; and his recovery from insanity through the ministrations of a skilled and sympathetic doctor. The "Code of Cooperation" MAY have been the controlling factor in suppressing the vital circumstance that the patient credited Spears with his recovery. Numerous cases wherein multiple sclerosis and polio victims have walked again after treatment at Spears Chiropractic Hospital rated no space in the press, though news-men privately acknowledge that JUST ONE such recovery claimed by medicine or surgery would be "bannerline stuff."

Favorable news bearing on chiropractic is easily available to the press, but it "goes down the drain" because the "Code of Cooperation" and its censorship board prevail.

Senator William Langer, whose subcommittee (of the U.S. Senate's powerful Judiciary Committee) on medical monopoly held hearings in Washington and Denver to investigate the VA's bar to all health services other than those medically-approved, blasted the press for its suppression of chiropractic news. At that time, Langer did not know about the "Code of Cooperation." He and Commander Connell should compare notes - and probably will. Both are "rolling them down the same alley" in an effort to obtain justice for veterans; and both are confronted by a "controlled press."

Spears Sanigram, 20 [April] 1954

Appendix I.

Failure of Chiropractors to Advertise Is Great Professional Mistake and Growing Human Tragedy

By Dr. Leo L. Spears

Chiropractic is not growing today as it did back in the days when chiropractors were proud of their science, proud of the privilege of practicing chiropractic and proud of telling the world about it.

Whatever the scourge that has induced chiropractors to stop adver-tising, it should be eliminated. While medicine is constantly increasing its propaganda chiropractors are pulling back into their shells and cloaking themselves with quiescence and mystery. This attitude is not only stunting the growth of chiropractic, it is resulting in increasing human misery and loss of life.

The eternal question of patients arriving at Spears Hospital is: "Why, oh why don't chiropractors advertise to let us know what they can do and where they can be found before it is too late?"

Patients come to Spears who have been living within a few blocks or a few miles of one or more good chiropractors for years and didn't even know they were there. Chiropractic's competitors, in the mean-time, never lose an opportunity to praise medicine and talk against chiropractic. With no effort on the part of chiropractors to educate the public to the benefits of their science, what are people to believe? They can only believe what they hear or read.

Almost every newspaper, magazine, television and radio station is constantly pouring medical propaganda into every American home. But seldom do these homes receive chiropractic literature. Yes, it is thought that the medics get their propaganda free. This is not always true. They may not run many paid advertisements, but they spend millions for good articles, radio scripts, speakers, professional promotions, publicity agents and directors. If the truth were known, their propaganda probably costs them more in the end than paid advertising.

It takes money to make money. There is a risk in almost everything. Crops must be planted if there is to be a harvest. Money must be invested in manufacturing plants if we are to have automobiles. And these things must be done to serve the people properly. The medics realize they must keep their wares before the people constantly, at any cost, to keep their offices filled with patients. They realize their returns will be in direct proportion to their investment. It is true they are overdoing their propaganda; that the people are getting tired of their hogwash. But when there is nothing better reaching the people, when there is no other hope presented to them, they have no other course than to follow the signs.

Were it not for the advertising done by Spears Chiropractic Hospital –

advertising for the entire profession – chiropractic could become a lost art. Spears Hospital spent over $400,000 for advertising last year; 99% of the value of this advertising went to the local chiropractor. And this is the way we intended it to go. All our ads direct patients to their local chiropractors first. It is conservatively estimated that our adver-tising sent a million new patients to chiropractic offices in 1953. Less than a hundred chiropractors sent even one patient to Spears Hospital. Only about 300 chiropractors have ever sent patients to Spears during the eleven years this hospital has been in operation. We referred several thousand patients to chiropractors last year - patients who had never heard of chiropractic until they read our ads and came to Spears Hospital or wrote us for the names of local chiropractors to whom they could go. Many of these patients didn't even know the meaning of the word "chiropractic," or that there was one in their locality.

It is a privilege to practice chiropractic. With every privilege there is also a responsibility. And it is the responsibility of the chiropractor to educate. It is a sacred obligation - almost as sacred as the obligation to feed, clothe and care for one's family.

Ethics are all right. But "ethics" which prevent good, constructive, educational advertising, whether local, state or national, is anti-chiropractic and detrimental to the life and health of the people. Just to the extent that chiropractic fails to advertise, "physical medicine" will grow. Our national chiropractic associations should be constantly engaged in educational advertising and publicity campaigns, and encouraging and assisting state associations to do likewise. So long as national and state associations do not broadly advertise or publicize our science, they certainly have no ethical right to criticize those who do. Somebody must do this job.

There is no law that can prevent anyone advertising, so long as the advertising is honest and truthful. Advertising is the life of industry and the life blood of all human contact. The two greatest advertisers in the world are the United States government and the American Medical Association.

The public is not prejudiced against advertising. To the contrary, it depends upon advertising for practically all of its information. Even the churches find it profitable to advertise the Word of God.

TESTIMONIAL ADVERTISING? Yes, indeed! Do you object to any of your patients telling others about what chiropractic and you have done for them? That is testimonial advertising!

It is far more ethical to let your patients tell the world about you and chiropractic than for you to do it. When you use testimonial advertising, you only make it possible for your patients to tell others than their next door neighbors about your work. A testimonial that is good for you is good for the public! It is utterly ridiculous for chiropractors to believe that such advertising is unethical!

APPENDIX I.

We cannot argue with success. Rather than stand back and criticize, isn't it far more logical to follow the lead of those who have succeeded ethically? Who can deny that chiropractors are entitled to the same privileges that others enjoy? And who can deny that the people are entitled to know the truth about chiropractic?

Yes, it is my advice that you sell chiropractic to the world. Do it through your national and state associations if possible - without them if necessary. But advertise! The advertising of one chiropractor benefits all chiropractors - and the people.

How much should you spend for advertising? At least 50% of your entire income until you have more business than you can handle. Then spend no less than 10% of your income to educate the people to the efficacy of the science we love. This is the best way to promote the growth of the chiropractic, save human lives and to prevent suffering.

Spears Sanigram, 21 [Jan.] 1955

APPENDIX J.

Spears Free Clinic and Hospital For Poor Children
v.
Maier

[128 Colo. 263]

Supreme Court of Colorado
Sept. 23, 1953

Judgment affirmed.

Action by a nonprofit corporation operating a chiropractic clinic and sanitarium against a physician for libel in signing and recording a death certificate with a statement on the bottom margin that decedent died from criminal neglect at plaintiff's sanitarium and causing newspaper publication of a photostatic copy of such certificate and defendant's further statement that decedent died after having "laid several days with no care" at such sanitarium. To review a judgment of the District Court of the City and County of Denver, William A. Black, J., dismissing the first count of the amended complaint on defendant's motion, and a judgment on a jury's verdict for defendant on the second count, plaintiff brought error. The Supreme Court, Stone, C.J., held that the action, having been commenced over 3 years after the recording of the certificate, was barred by a one year statute of limitations as to the first count, and that the trial court did not err in permitting doctors of medicine to testify, in the absence of objections to their testimony and in view of an instruction to the jury that the propriety of any act or proceeding of a practitioner of any one of the healing arts in treatment of his patient must be judged only by the standards of practice and principles, tenets and beliefs of the school of healing arts to which he belongs.

1. Libel and Slander 84
Each publication of libel is separate cause of action and should be separately pleaded.

2. Limitation of Actions 55(1)
A cause or right of action for libel accrues on date of publication of libel.

3. Limitation of Actions 55(1)
An action against physician for libel in signing and recording death certificate, with statement on bottom margin that decedent died from criminal neglect at plaintiff's chiropractic sanitarium, over 3 years before commaencement of action, was barred by one year statute of limitations, in absence of allegation or contention by plaintiff that defendant subsequently made or distributed

copies of certificate within limitation period, as certificate was not continuously published because it was open to public inspection and continuously inspected. '35 C.S.A. c.102, § 2.

4. Libel and Slander 25

The fact that many people read a libelous statement is evidence of extent of damage therefrom, but does not establish publication of libel as to each other.

5. Libel and Slander 25

On redelivery, rereading, or other repetition of libelous statement to others than person libeled by further voluntary act of person making statement constitutes republication of libel by him.

6. Evidence 538

A doctor of medicine is not ipso facto an incompetent witness as to any fact in case simply because case involves compliance with chiropractic standards, especially where judgment is sought against such a doctor by corporation operating chiropractic sanitarium for libel; question involved not being witness' competency, but competency of evidence sought to be introduced through him.

7. Appeal and Error 758(1)

Counsel for plaintiff in error owe duty to point out in their briefs specific errors of which they complain.

8. Evidence 547

In action against physician for libel in causing newspaper publication of photostatic copy of death certificate, signed and recorded by him, with statement on bottom margin thereof that decedent died from criminal neglect at plaintiff's chiropractic sanitarium, plaintiff's objection to another physician testifying to anything about decedent, her case or condition in answer to question whether he remembered her case was properly overruled.

9. Trial 105(3), 207

In action against physician for libel in causing newspaper publi-cation of photostatic copy of death certificate, signed and recorded by him, with statement on bottom margin thereof that decedent died from criminal neglect at plaintiff's chiropractic sanitarium, admission of testimony of doctors of medicine was not in error, though chiropractors must be judged only by standards of their own profession, where plaintiff did not object to such testimony and trial court instructed jury that propriety of any act or proceeding of practitioner of any one of healing arts in treatment of patient must be judged by standard of practice and principles, tenets and beliefs of his school of the healing arts.

10. Appeal and Error 215(1), 730(1)

Asserted errors in instructions to jury must be specifically pointed out to both trial court and Supreme Court to be considered by Supreme Court on review of trial court's judgment.

11. Trial 114

Wide latitude is allowed attorney in advocating his client's cause in argument to jury.

12. Appeal and Error 207

Whether remarks of defendant's counsel in argument to jury were improper cannot be considered by Supreme Court on review of judgment on jury's verdict for defendant, in absence of objection to remarks when made or request by plaintiff for instruction to jury concerning them.

$$--\ o\ --$$

Charles Ginsberg, George Louis Creamer, Denver, for plaintiff in error.
Van Cise & Van Cise, Denver, for defendant in error.

STONE, Chief Justice.

Plaintiff, Spears Free Clinic and Hospital for Poor Children, is a Colorado corporation not for profit, which operates a chiropractic clinic known as Spears Clinic, and a chiropractic sanitarium known as Spears Sanitarium. Defendant Maier is a physician. One Susia A. Bowers was received as a patient in the Spears Sanitarium on May 28, 1946, and remained there until the evening of June 3, 1946, when she was removed to a hospital where she was under the care of the defendant. The day after such removal surgery was performed on her, following which she died. On June 7, 1946, the day of her death, defendant made out a death certificate, and, upon the bottom margin thereof wrote: "This patient died from criminal neglect at Spears Sanitarium. Dr. Maier." More than three years thereafter, on Dec. 3, 1949, in an article in a Denver newspaper, a portion of said death certificate containing defendant's above-mentioned statement was photostated, following affirmation of the truth of said statement by defendant to a reporter of said newspaper. Thereafter, on Jan. 14, 1950, his action for libel was brought against defendant.

In the amended complaint, in a so-called first cause of action, it was alleged that defendant signed and placed of [*sic*] public record the death certificate and personally wrote across the bottom thereof the words, "This patient died from criminal neglect at Spears Sanitarium," and that said certificate has continually since reposed in the records of the Department of Health of the State of Colorado with said words inscribed upon it, open to public inspection, and has been continuously inspected, seen and viewed and said words "have been continually and continuously published from and since the said date and are now being so published."

For a so-called second cause of action, plaintiff alleged that the defendant on Dec. 3, 1949, caused to be published in a newspaper, including such marginal statement, and that defendant then further stated to said newspaper that Susia A. Bowers died after having "laid several days no care" at Spears Sanitarium, and caused said statement to be published, and that said statement was false.

Defendant, in answer to the first count of the complaint, pleaded, inter alia, the statute of limitations providing that actions for libel shall be commenced within one year next after the cause of action shall accrue, and not afterwards. In answer to the second count, he admitted the signing of the death certificate and denied the other essential allegations.

Defendant moved to dismiss the first count of the plaintiff's complaint on the ground that it failed to state a claim upon which relief could be granted, and upon hearing subsequent to answer wherein the statute of limitations was pleaded, the motion was sustained and judgment entered upon the pleadings for dismissal of said count. The case came for trial to a jury on the remaining count, where verdict and judgment were in favor of defendant, and plaintiff here seeks reversal.

[1,2] The first stated ground for reversal is that the court erred in granting defendant's motion to dismiss the first count of the complaint. Several challenging legal propositions are argued in the briefs; but, in view of our conclusion, we think we need now consider only that based on the statute of limitations. It is not disputed that each publication of a libel is a separate cause of action. Being such, each should be separately pleaded. Lininger v. Knight, 123 Colo. 213 p.2d 809. Cause or right of action accrues on the date of publication. Plaintiff's amended complaint was filed pursuant to an order of the court requiring it to state, as a separate cause of action, in separate counts each and every act of alleged libel, together with the dates thereof. No special damage was alleged, and plaintiff's case rests on libel per se. The count which was stricken contained a specific allegation only as to one act of libel, to wit, that of placing of public record of death certificate with the libelous words across the bottom, and one specific date thereof to wit, June 7, 1946, which was more than three and a half years prior to the commencement of the action. Under the statute of limitations, action is barred if not commenced within one year "next after the cause of the action shall accrue." Section 2, chapter 102, '35 C.S.A.

[3-5] Even if we were to ignore the order for separate statement and search the pleading of that count for allegation of other causes of action within the period of limitation, we find therein no allegation nor contention that defendant subsequently made or distributed copies of said death certificate or of his marginal statement thereon; rather, the contention is that the certificate itself so deposited in the files of the Registrar of Vital Statistics was open to public inspection and had been "continuously" inspected, and thereby it was "continuously published."

Such is not the law. The fact that many people read a libel is evidence as to the extent of damage therefrom, but does not in itself establish publication as to each reader. So to urge is to confuse the result of libel with the act of libel. A letter is published as soon as it is posted, and in the place where it is posted, if it is ever opened anywhere by any person other than the person to whom it is addressed. Odgers on Libel and Slander, (5th ed.), page 162. It is only the redelivery or rereading or other repetition of the libelous statement to others by further and voluntary act of defendant that constitutes republication by him. Annotation 1 A.L.R. (2d) 384, et seq. It is not here urged that defendant made republication in any such manner until the occurrences of 1949, and these occurrences were set out in the second count of the complaint and the issue raised by them was not stricken. Plaintiff's novel "theory of continuous publication" as here urged would apply equally to any published or written statement continuing of record or in the hands of others, and to hold that the possibility or likelihood of its being read from time to time by other people would constitute "continuing publication" would effectively nullify the statute of limitations,

Plaintiff cites authority to the effect that one is responsible for repetition or other publication by others under his authority or as the natural and probable consequence of his own publication. So admitting, there is no allegation in the stricken count or elsewhere in the complaint of any such repetition or republication by others within the period of the statute of limitations, or at all, and, had there been such allegations, they should have been set out as separate causes of action in separate counts of the complaint. There was no error in sustaining defendant's motion to dismiss the first count of the complaint after the statute of limitations had been pleaded thereto.

[6-9] It is next urged that the "court erred in permitting before the jury testimony of doctors of medicine," since chiropractors are to be judged only by the standards of their own profession. Admitting the latter proposition, the former does not follow. A doctor of medicine is not ipso facto an incompetent witness as to any fact simply because the case involves compliance with the standards of chiropractic, especially where a judgment of $300,000 is being sought against the witness. The question involved is not that of the competency of the witness, but that of the competency of the evidence sought to be introduced through him. Here plaintiff has not set out in its brief, as required by the rule, a single question or answer which is challenged as objectionable on the ground that the witness was a doctor of medicine, nor a ruling of the court thereon. It is the duty of counsel to point out in their briefs the specific errors of which they complain; however, upon reading of the record here, we find part of the testimony as to medical standards was elicited by plaintiff's own counsel, and the remainder was given without objection, except in one

case where a physician witness was interrogated as to whether he remembered the case of Susia A. Bowers, and objection was made "to this witness testifying to anything about Susia A. Bowers or her case or her condition." Patently such objection was properly overruled.

Notwithstanding the failure to object to any such testimony, the trial court carefully protected plaintiff by instructing the jury to the effect that the propriety of any act or proceeding of a practitioner of any one of the healing arts in the treatment of his patient is to be judged by the standard of practice and by the principles, tenets and beliefs of the school of the healing arts to which he belongs, and by no other. No error appears in permitting the testimony of doctors of medicine.

[10] Again, it is contended that the court erred in the giving of certain instructions. Only one of the instructions objected to is set out in the briefs. In itself it was proper, and no objection is shown to have been made to the giving of it or the giving of any instruction. On the contrary, it appears from the record that when the court tendered to counsel for plaintiff instructions proposed to be given, plaintiff's counsel stated, "I have no exceptions and no tenders." Asserted error in instructions must be specifically pointed out both to the trial court and to this court. Here neither appears.

[11,12] Finally, it is urged that "the court permitted improper latitude to the counsel for the defendant, in closing argument." Insofar as allegedly objectionable argument is pointed out to us in the brief, it does not support the objection now made to it, and it does not appear that any objections were made to it in the trial court. We may well say, in the words of President Judge Thompson, in Adams Express Co. v. Aldridge, 20 Colo. App, 74, 77 P. 6,10: "Wide latitude is allowed an attorney in advocating his client's cause, and we are not prepared to say that by the language quoted the bounds of propriety were overstepped. *** But whatever might be said regarding the propriety of the remarks attributed to counsel, there was no objection interposed to them at the time they were made, nor was any instruction requested concerning them; and therefore, even if they might be the subject of censure, the defendant would not be entitled to a consideration here of the question respecting them which is now raised."

The judgment is affirmed. En Banc.

APPENDIX K.

Spears Free Clinic and Hospital for Poor Children
v.
Cleere et al.

[197 F.2d 125]

United States Court of Appeals, Tenth District
May 10, 1952

Action by Spears Free Clinic and Hospital for Poor Children, a Colorado corporation, operating Spears Chiropractic Sanitarium and Spears Clinic, against R.L. Cleere and others, for damages under the Clayton Act for alleged violation of the Sherman Antitrust Act in that defendants allegedly had restrained the practice of chiropractic and had allocated to the medical profession the practice of the healing arts in Colorado. The United States District Court for the District of Colorado, William Lee Knous, J. sustained defendants' motion to dismiss the action, and plaintiffs appealed. The Court of Appeals, Phillips, Chief Judge, held that since the purpose and object of the alleged conspiracy and the means adopted to effectuate it were to restrain the practice of chiropractic and to allocate to the medical profession the practice of the healing arts in Colorado, the effect upon interstate and foreign commerce was fortuitous and remote and not direct and substantial, and did not come within the purview of the Sherman Antitrust Act.

1. Commerce 43

The practice of healing arts in Colorado, including chiropractic, is wholly local in character and mere fact that a fortuitous and incidental effect of alleged conspiracy to prevent maintenance of chiropractic hospital would be to reduce number of persons who would come from other states and countries to such hospital for chiropractic treatments did not create such relation between interstate and foreign commerce and such local activities as to make them part of such "commerce."

2. Monopolies 12(1)

To come within purview of Sherman Act, the restraint of commerce or obstruction of commerce must be direct and substantial and not merely incidental or remote, and the conspiracy or combination must be aimed or directed at kind of restraint which the Act prohibits, or such restraint must be the natural and probable consequence of the conspiracy. Sherman Antitrust Act, §1,15 U.S.C.A. §1.

3. Monopolies 12(1)

In order to show violation of Sherman Act, a specific intent to restrain trade or create a monopoly need not always be shown, but it is sufficient that a restraint or monopoly result as consequence of defendants' conduct. Sherman Antitrust Act, §1,15 U.S.C.A. §1.

4. Monopolies 12(1)

Where the object and purpose of conduct of one accused of violation of Sherman Act is to restrain or monopolize activities or matters purely local in character, such facts may be considered in determining whether the effect on interstate or foreign commerce is direct and substantial or only incidental, indirect and remote. Sherman Antitrust Act, §1,15 U.S.C.A. §1.

5. Monopolies 14

A curtailment of manufacture of articles to be shipped in interstate commerce or lessening of number of persons who travel in interstate commerce, resulting from conspiracy to restrain or monopolize a wholly local, is ordinarily an incidental, indirect and remote obstruction to interstate commerce. Sherman Antitrust Act, §1,15 U.S.C.A. §1.

6. Monopolies 12(1)

Where purpose and object of conspiracy, and of means adopted to effectuate it, were to restrain practice of chiropractic and to allocate to medical profession the practice of the healing in Colorado, the effect upon interstate and foreign commerce was fortuitous and remote and not direct and substantial, and therefore was no violation of the Sherman Antitrust Act. Sherman Antitrust Act, §§1,2,15 U.S.C.A. §§4,15 U.S.C.A. §15.

$$- - o - -$$

Charles Ginsberg and George L. Creamer, both of Denver, for appellant.

Kenneth W. Robinson, James T. Burke and Duke W. Dunbar, all of Denver, for appellees.

Before PHILLIPS, Chief Judge, and STRATTON and MURRAH, Circuit Judges.

PHILLIPS, Chief Judge.

Spears Free Clinic and Hospital for Poor Children, a corporation hereafter referred to as Spears Hospital, brought this action to recover damages under 15 U.S.C.A. §15 for violation of 15 U.S.C.A. §§1,2. On motion of the Spears Hospital the court dismissed the action as to certain defendants. The remaining defendants are the Medical Society of the City and County of Denver, a Colorado corporation, former and present members of the State Board of Health of the State of Colorado, and former or present officials or trustees of the Medical Society. One of the defendants is a licensed dentist, one is a registered pharma-

184

cist, and two are attorneys duly licensed to practice law in the State of Colorado. The other defendants are doctors of medicine duly licensed to practice in the State of Colorado, and are members of the Medical Society. The defendants interposed a motion to dismiss the action on the ground that it did not state a claim on which relief could be granted. The trial court sustained the motion and dismissed the action. Spears Hospital has appealed.

The complaint alleges that the Spears Hospital operates as a chiropractic institution and has on its staff licensed chiropractors, laboratory technicians, X-ray technicians, physiotherapists, nurses and dietitians, that it provides facilities wherein persons are given and furnished, by duly licensed persons, chiropractic treatments, that are permitted by the laws of Colorado; and that "numerous persons from all of the United States, and from many foreign countries" regularly come to the institution for treatment. It further alleges that the defendants combined and conspired to prevent licensing of such institution by the proper authorities of the State of Colorado, to prevent the operation and maintenance of such institution, and to allocate to the members of the medical profession within the State of Colorado the entire practice of the healing arts within the state, to the exclusion and restraint of the practice of chiropractic; and that the defendants did certain acts to prevent the maintenance of the Spears Hospital as a chiropractic institution and to monopolize the entire practice of the healing arts within the State of Colorado in the medical profession, to the exclusion and restraint of the practice of chiropractic.

[1] The practice of the healing arts in Colorado, including chiropractic, is wholly local in character. The alleged conspiracy and the acts alleged to have been done in furtherance thereof had for their purpose and object the monopolization and restraint of purely local activities. No price fixing or price maintenance for professional or other services was involved. There was no intent to injure, obstruct or restrain interstate or foreign commerce. The mere fact that a fortuitous and incidental effect of such conspiracy and acts may be to reduce the number of persons who will come from other states or countries to the Spears Hospital for chiropractic treatments does not create such a relation between interstate and foreign commerce and such local activities as to make them part of such commerce. United States v. Yellow Cab Co., 332 U.S. 218, 23-232, 67 S.Ct. 1560, 91 L.Ed. 2010.

[2] To come within the purview of the Sherman Act the restraint of commerce or the obstruction of commerce must be direct and substantial and not merely incidental or remote. Apex Hosiery Co. v. Leader, 310 U.S. 469, 510, 60 S.Ct. 982, 84 L.Ed. 1311. The conspiracy or combination must be aimed or directed at the kind of restraint which the Act prohibits, or such restraint must be the natural and probable consequence of the conspiracy. Apex Hosiery Co.

APPENDIX K.

v. Leader, 310 U.S. 469, 511, 60 S.Ct. 982, 84 L.Ed. 1311.

[3] A specific intent to restrain trade or create a monopoly need not always be shown. It is sufficient that a restraint or monopoly, within the purview of the Act, results as a consequence of the defendants' conduct. The defendants "must be held to have intended the necessary and direct consequences of their acts, and cannot be heard to say the contrary. United States v. Masonite Corp., 316 U.S. 265, 275, 62 S.Ct. 1070, 1976, 86 L.Ed. 1461.

[4] Where, however, the object and purpose is to restrain or monopolize activities or matter purely local in character, those facts may be considered in determining whether the effect on interstate or foreign commerce is direct and substantial or only incidental, indirect and remote. In Levering & G. Co. v. Morrin, 289 U.S. 103, 53 S.Ct. 549, 77 L.Ed. 1062, the complainants were engaged in fabricating and erecting iron and steel and attempts were made by the unions in the City of New York to compel them to employ only union labor in this work. The complaint alleged that all the steel used by the complainants in the City of New York was transported from other states, and that the success of the respondents' efforts would result in the destruction of the complainants' interstate traffic in steel. The court said, 289 U.S. at page 107, 53 S.Ct. at page 551, 77 L.Ed. 1062: "All this, however, is no more than to say that respondents' interference with the erection of steel in New York will have the effect of interfering with the bringing of the steel from other states. Accepting the allegations of the bill at their full value, it results that the sole aim of the conspiracy was to halt or suppress local building operations as a means of compelling the employment of union labor, not for the purpose of affecting the sale or transit of materials in interstate commerce. Use of the materials was purely a local matter, and the suppression thereof the result of *** a purely local aim. Restraint of interstate commerce was not an object of the conspiracy. Prevention of the local use was in no sense a means adopted to effect such a restraint. It is this exclusively local aim, and not the fortuitous and incidental effect upon interstate commerce, which gives character to the conspiracy. *** If thereby the shipment of steel in interstate commerce was curtailed, that result was incidental, indirect, and remote, and, therefore, not within the antitrust acts ***."

[5] A curtailment of the manufacture of articles to be shipped in interstate commerce or the lessening of the number of persons who travel in interstate commerce, resulting from a conspiracy to restrain or monopolize a wholly local activity, is ordinarily an incidental, indirect or remote obstruction to such commerce. In United Leather Workers International Union v. Herkert & Meisel Trunk Co., 265 U.S. 457, at page 471, 44 S.Ct. 623, at page 627, 68 L.Ed.

1104, the court said: "This review of the cases makes it clear that the mere reduction in the supply of an article to be shipped in interstate commerce by the illegal or tortious prevention of its manufacture is ordinarily an indirect and remote obstruction of that commerce. It is only when the intent or the necessary effect upon such commerce in the article is to enable those preventing the manufacture to monopolize the supply, or control its price, or discriminate as between its would-be purchasers, that the unlawful interference with its manufacture can be said directly to burden interstate commerce."

[6] Here, the purpose and object of the conspiracy and of the means adopted to effectuate it, were to restrain the practice of chiropractic and to allocate to the medical profession the practice of the healing arts in Colorado. It is this exclusively local aim and not the fortuitous and incidental effect upon interstate and foreign commerce which gives character to the conspiracy. The effect upon interstate and foreign commerce was fortuitous and remote and not direct and substantial.

We conclude that in the instant case there was no direct, immediate or substantial effect on interstate or foreign commerce bringing the alleged conspiracy within the scope of the Sherman Act.

We deem it unnecessary to pass upon the question whether the practice of the healing arts, including chiropractic, is trade or commerce within the meaning of §1 of the Sherman Act. (See United States v. Oregon State Medical Society, 72 S.Ct. 690.)

Affirmed.

Appendix L.

SPEARS APPEALING DISTRICT COURT VERDICT IN $11,000,000 SUIT AGAINST BBB AND DENVER POST

In its opening statement, the defense asserted that Spears Hospital "had no standing in court because it operates illegally." (Their) argument was that, as a corporation, the institution could not be licensed to practice Chiropractic; only individual chiropractors, counsel asserted, are entitled to licensure (and the right to practice). This had reference to a moot statute which forbids to the hiring of doctors ... by a hospital as corporate employees. Such services, the defense claimed, can lawfully be rendered only by free agents engaged in specific acts... The judge stated verbally, at least twice during the hearing that he would not concern himself with this question since the issue was not pertinent to the case; furthermore declaring the point of law involved was outside his purview. Yet, in rendering his final, written decision, the judge devoted 15 pages of his 18-page opinion to this very issue, declaring the plaintiff (Spears) "had no status to bring an action in court."

The judge had previously ruled in favor of Spears on this point when he rejected the defense's motion for dismissal of the $11 million dollar suit alleging a plot to put the chiropractic hospital out of business; in addition, he ruled there was prima facie evidence of conspiracy (which he amplified as a "meeting of the minds" on the project) by the defendants, and that there had been a showing of financial damage due to a terrific falling off of business coincidental with the joint activities of (the defendants) to discredit Spears Hospital. The court's verdict completely reversed his earlier-expressed opinion, with the statement that no conspiracy was shown by the testimony, and that financial records revealed no financial loss.

Charles Ginsberg, Spears attorney, commenting on the decision, said: "Injection of an issue that was no issue at all throws a new light on the case. It was a complete surprise that the judge injected the issue in the decision. On two different occasions during the trial he held that the issue could not be injected. He added: "If Spears is practicing illegally, then so is every other hospital in Denver. All hospitals are employing physicians on a permanent basis, the same as Spears. There certainly has been no intent on the part of the hospital... to violate anything, and the authorities have not objected to the (Spears) hospital procedure."

Dr. John Burd of Denver, president of the Colorado Chiropractic Association, expressed himself as "quite surprised with the decision after the course the trial took."

A re-survey of the case is appropriate at this time, when preparations are being made to take this vitally important suit to Colorado's highest tribunal.

APPENDIX L.

Its crucial implications may be weighed by the words of Attorney Ginsberg in his final arguments before the district court: "It would only take a judgment of this court to turn loose a culmination of their vindictiveness - a judgment in their favor."

This reference to the defendant's attitudes and actions dates back to the Denver Better Business Bureau's and *Denver Post's* investigative and publicity teamwork which, had they been successful, would have resulted in a grand jury indictment against Spears Hospital. Weapons in this campaign were BBB's unfavorable reports on Spears Hospital to prospective patients, and the *Post's* news columns hinting broadly that the grand jurors were probing Spears' records for evidence of "quackery." This phase was brought into the open when the grand jury got a court order for delivery to it of ALL Spears' books, accounts and records, compliance with which would have closed down the hospital and created a situation of utter chaos. The order as modified on terms suggested by SPEARS: an audit at the hospital by qualified accountants. *No indictment was returned by the grand jury.*

To protect the institution's reputation, Spears Hospital filed suit for $10 million against the agencies and individuals responsible for these attacks. When the offenses continued, a second suit for $1 million alleging "continuing conspiracy" to destroy Spears Hospital was filed. When this multi-million dollar damage suit came to trial Sept. 12, 1955, after more than a year of delay, astounding evidence and testimony were revealed during the three weeks and two days' time consumed, namely:

(1) Defendants conferred together and agreed to share information on their investigations, with a view of submitting same to the grand jury. (The court called this "a meeting of the minds" on the project.) (2) *Denver Post* reporter who turned detective on "medical quackery" matters, confessed that the ONLY testimony he gave to the grand jury pertained to Spears Hospital. He had gained unlimited access to Spears records on the pretext that he would write an objective story, describing scientific research achievements, and treatment efficiency; instead, he listed cases terminal on arrival or who later died at home and turned the names over to the Better Business Bureau. He made no report whatever on Spears' research... or the multitude of satisfied patients who recovered their health at Spears, and the court forbade the plaintiff to do so. (3) Figures showing that a big decrease in patronage at Spears Hospital necessitated many months of heroic measures to "break even" on operational costs. This diminishing business was coincidental with the attacks by defendants on the institution. (4) No unfavorable criticisms were received from former Spears patients queried by the Better Business Bureau, despite efforts to that end by the BBB and *Denver Post* correspondence and personal contacts. (5) The *Post* reporter who covered grand jury deliberations acknowledged that he might have stated, "I'll put Dr. Spears in jail," in the spirit of "rollicking good fun"

when queried by Attorney Charles Ginsberg on this point. (6) The *Denver Post* admitted 14 months' of investigation against Spears; and the Better Business Bureau began accumulating a file of information on Spears Hospital even before it established offices in Denver. (This, according to Ginsberg, "was all calculated to do injury to the plaintiff.")

Ginsberg's closing argument to the court charged the "wedding" of the Better Business Bureau with the *Denver Post* was "an open and conspiratorial agreement publicized by them as such" with the objectives to destroy the hospital.

He had said earlier: "We meet a strong foe - a powerful newspaper as defendant, serving what it terms to be in its own language 'an Empire' and serving it with imperial purpose and manner. It carries on its imperial purpose in the belief that those who fail to follow its dictates and purposes are to be destroyed. It makes a perfect companion to the Better Business Bureau which is dedicated to a like cause. They are perfectly wedded in a notorious affinity. They have taken upon themselves a power held by law enforcement agencies and the court to police their dictates..."

Answering the *Post's* defense that it had covered the investigation by its employee and the Better Business Bureau simply as news, Ginsberg retorted that such was not the case, but that the defendants "used (the investigation) to try to build up a criminal charge in testimony before the grand jury." He added that he thought it was quite obvious at whose request. "One profession has not chosen to accept with any degree of responsibility the field of Chiropractic, which it deems an intruder and a cult."

In contrast with the *Post's* coverage of its own, the BBB's and the grand jury's investigation of Spears, that newspaper assigned an objective-minded reporter to the recent court proceedings. He reported honestly the legal fulminations on both sides. Ginsberg was quoted accurately, and without bias. The same applied to defense counsel. There were none of the weasel-wording of news to give the text an editorial slant. The screaming, insinuating headlines were also absent. Thus, the *Post* files contain an honest journalistic record of the trial. Was this because the *Post* suddenly became aware of its responsibility to the public?

The words of Charles Ginsberg in his final appeals are prophetic: "It would take only a judgment of this court in their favor to turn loose a culmination of their vindictiveness."

Spears Sanigram, 25 [Dec.] 1955

Appendix M.

In Memorium
Dr. Leo L. Spears

By Charles Ginsberg, LL.B.

Spears Chiropractic Hospital, August 7, 1956

I would infringe on the thoughts expressed by Abraham Lincoln at Gettysburg when he conveyed the purpose of that occasion to a rededication of the people to the purposes of freedom, and so would our departed leader of the Chiropractic profession. I would call upon you now in this hour of memory of our beloved friend to rededicate yourselves to the perpetuation of this institution that was so beloved by him, and to help complete the plans that he had purpose for. Were I a minister, I would dwell upon the thought this great benefactor of mankind, this devoted servant of the interests of health of the people, has found his just reward in consequence of his devoted service to mankind and thereby to God. But not being a minister of the Lord, I shall try to remember him in a practical way.

The instances of this man's life that have been impressed on me and I believe on you and on the community that he served - quite an extensive community - are the people who came to him from all ends of the world seeking his learned and compassionate attention. Leo Spears was a man of purpose whose plans were not limited to his own expectancy. He planned an institution here far and away beyond any reasonable expectancy that he had to be with it. And now Providence has seen fit to remove him and to leave a great work unfinished. Now, his nephews, Dr. Dan (Spears), Dr. Howard (Spears) and Dr. Perry (McClellan), Mrs. Laura Ohlson, and other members of the family are entrusted with this great institution. He has left them a monumental task and I believe, with the preparation he provided, they will be able to carry on to fulfillment all of his plans and certainly all of his purpose.

For thirteen years I walked closely with this man. Walking and working with him was a constant challenge. From the very inception of this institution he became the object of derision by those who didn't understand or were too narrow-minded to appreciate - hateful, venomous attacks, in many instances.

Some thirteen years ago, before it was fully prepared to function, a stranger came into this hospital in the middle of the night seeking help. He had come to Denver in the last stages of chronic disease, only to be turned away by two public hospitals in this city because he could not meet residential status. Then he came to Spears Hospital and was taken in, no questions asked. They hadn't had the opportunity even of examining him when, in the course of that night, the patient died.

Then, unbelievably, the most egregious thing in my experience as an attorney happened. Dr. Leo Spears and his nephew, Dr. Dan Spears, were haled before the courts as common criminals, charged with having committed manslaughter. No more outrageous usurpation of justice had ever occurred! This was widely publicized and widely acclaimed as the obvious accomplishment of a competitive healing art and upon my being called in to defend the Drs. Spears, it was the beginning of a long experience and friendship that continued to this day. It became obvious during the course of this case that the authorities had acted in a manner other than as dutiful agents of the state. There suddenly sprung in them a desire to let go of the charge with some saving of face on their part. Then I was approached with the suggestion that a plea of nolo contendre would be acceptable to them to have the matter terminated. Well, as a matter of duty, I transmitted the prosecutor's offer to my clients. My opinion was asked and I frankly stated - "Well, that would mean a termination of the case. There is always an element of risk in any trial. There is no certainty as to result... even the achievement of justice. This is a means of terminating without that risk."

What was Dr. Leo's reaction to that? "No," he said, "we'll go to trial. If I have committed an offense, I know my many friends will meet me in jail. My patients will call on me there. I am an American citizen who served my country and tried to serve it well. I will not compromise my position. You can go on to jail. If you haven't any confidence in your ability, I have. I know that you will achieve justice."

Then they came back with another offer: charges against Dr. Leo would be dropped and they would accept nolo contendre from Dr. Dan. He (Dr. Leo) wouldn't even consider it. So, they went to trial and received a directed acquittal from the court.

At that time, the state health board had been derelict and negligent in considering the application for a license to operate a hospital. Out of patience with their delay, he opened the institution without their having yet acted. Yes, he was forcing the matter. Then there followed a period when the hospital was actually vacated, its patients removed while the long and tedious process of the law commenced. Again, in the course of the proceedings, a compromise was offered - a permit (not a license) with restrictions and limitations demanded: restrictions against using the name "hospital" and as to what they could and could not treat. On my advice, we accepted what was offered with the view of getting the institution rolling. At this point, a limited permit was better than nothing.

It went along without much disturbance for some three years. Then, Dr. Leo came to me with a matter that had constantly troubled him. He asked me to petition the board of health to modify the restriction against use of the name hospital. "We are entitled to this," he said. I was rather reticent at first, fearing that it might unloose the dormant activity of our tormentors. I advised that we proceed with caution. I interviewed one of the members of the board and asked him to feel out the other members; to find out how they might react to such a request on our part. Within a short time, I was advised that if we filed such a petition, what I feared would occur. It would bring about a notice of revocation of the sanitarium permit. When I reported this to Dr. Leo, he said: "Go ahead, file the petition. We either have rights or we haven't, and no matter what happens, we have to try to establish our rights."

In what was termed a hearing, our petition was denied. That same night, the health board reconvened without our presence and passed a resolution demanding that we "show cause why our sanitarium permit should not be revoked." The warrant was delivered the next morning. That started a long channel of litigation.

At first, at a mock trial this very board from whom we got no consideration decided against us and revoked the permit. We then appealed to the District Court to review their decision. After an extended hearing, I believe over a month, the judge advised that he would take the matter under advisement and write an opinion. He held it under advisement during the fishing season and the winter which followed - about nine months in all. This judge, who functions in the Colorado back country, had been called down to Denver to hear this case because local judges were reluctant. Then he returned, and without a word of explanation and to the amazement and shock of our opposition, stunned them with a decision that they didn't fully comprehend when he made it. The board of health took exception to it, not realizing that the court had actually decided in their favor. Not a word of explanation on the matter that had been argued for months and voluminously briefed.

Our task now was an appeal to the Supreme Court of Colorado. And there by a unanimous decision of the justices, they not only granted what we had asked for, but went far and beyond that. They said there was no reason in law why this institution should not be a Chiropractic hospital; no reason in law why it shouldn't afford its patients not only Chiropractic care under proper professional supervision, but also any other type of treatment that might be required. The perseverance of our friend was justified and at last this institution was on a solid footing of being licensed in accordance with law and with all the rights the law gives to it.

But that was not the end of our troubles. The end there never seemed to be and how well Dr. Leo Spears realized this. It is best expressed in a copy of his will I believe I can give you in resume without having it before me. In substance, it is an appeal to the people of Denver and the state of Colorado to protect this institution that was so dear to him. He expressed no doubt that after his leaving there would be a continuance of purposeful harassment from detractors, and he enlisted the friends of the institution to shelter it against their devices. And so I appeal to you, friends and members of the profession whom he fought so valiantly to serve, to give you a sound basis for your practice and a hospital in which you could function for the needs of your patients. I carry to you this, his last message, and ask that you zealously contribute your end, morally and in any other way you can, to shelter and protect this institution for which our friend enlisted your help on his parting. I hope you bear this in mind, and by your every act repay this dedicated man.

I have referred to these various litigant matters only to depict the true character of the man who built this institution for you and for the world. Not a man who sought the easy way out, but a man who undertook the "impossible" and was determined to succeed.

We have a wonderful hospital here. There is no ownership - it belongs to the people, to you and to the profession. You can see a magnificent new structure rising that will house some 2,000 patients when completed. Leo Spears conceived it, started to build it in the midst of every kind of worry one could be subjected to, confronted on all sides by enemies and people who hate, yet he had the fortitude and courage to undertake this gigantic task and it stands there, not an achievement yet, but still a monument to his dedicated purpose and unlimited vision.

Now, the achievement is for us, his friends. He left this world with no other substance. He left his kin little except good wishes because he had given it all to this institution. He had nothing for himself, nothing even to take care of obligations to the family for whom he cared so devotedly. He had but one mission in life - to serve all humanity. I say to the successors in his mission - Drs. Dan and Howard and the others, and you - I wish you well. I trust that this institution will reach the full issue planned for it by that dedicated soul now departed.

That he has served well not only his profession but the people who came here in search of health is best attested to by the record. In all the proceedings that we've had, never once have we been confronted by a dissatisfied patient. We have had complaints and charges made by our enemies and their agents, but in all the processes in the courts, never have we known of one instance of dissatisfaction.

Our patients dragged themselves to the courts that they might hear what was going on. They were keenly interested, keenly concerned; knowing the truth and not one of them belied the truth. Our enemies are strong. They have wealth and great power. Gaining justice from them is difficult. Courts are human agencies, though they sometimes seem to forget. I recall a suggestion I read years ago, that judges should carry with them to the bench a roll of toilet paper just as a reminder that they are human.

It is always a pleasure when we find expressions that give substance to the integrity of these tribunals. I want to read from a famous decision that I quoted in a brief I recently filed in the Colorado Supreme Court about the rights of people to choose their mode of treatment, and upon the right of a healing profession to express an opinion in its field not to be construed as a warranty. This was the case of The American School of Magnetic Healing v. McNaulty (187 U.S. Supreme Court 84) in which the opinion was written by Mr. Justice Pepper, who said in part: "We may not believe in the efficacy of the treatment to the extent claimed by the complainants, and we may have no sympathy with them in such claims, and yet, their effectiveness is but a matter of opinion in any court. The bill in this case appears that those who had business with the complainant are satisfied with... the treatment and are entirely willing that the money they set should be delivered to the complainants. In other words, they seem to have faith in the efficacy of the complainants' treatment and their ability to heal as claimed by them. If they fail, the answer might be that all human means of treatment are liable to fail and will necessarily fail when the appointed time arrives." How can anyone lay down the limit and say beyond that there is fraud and false pretense? Only the Better Business Bureau believes that!

Dr. Leo Spears was never a guarantor, nor are you or this institution, against the appointed time when all agencies may fail. Even unto himself, when that appointed time arrived he had to answer the call. In the midst of the troubles and strife when he could least be spared that time arrived and he kept the date with our Maker. He has earned his rest.

I am not a minister; I speak reluctantly of those matters beyond human knowledge. But if there be a compensation for good, a compensation for a concern of mankind and humanity; if there be a place anywhere for one who has dedicated himself and strived a lifetime to the attainment of such good purpose, I believe our dear friend finds comfort.

There is nothing novel in persecution... the Bible bespeaks that. And there is nothing novel in the spirit so greatly much possessed by Dr. Leo Spears... of forgiveness of your enemies. He wrote numerous wills on occasions when he thought himself slipping and in all of these he spoke of forgiveness and kindness for those who tormented him and this institution. That was not novel; he did so in his lifetime. In all my travels with him I was always amazed that he could meet well, cordially and pleasantly those who had spoken ill of him. And I say there is nothing novel in that because was it not Christ who said, "Forgive them, they know not what they do?" I thank you.

(Text from author's collection)

Appendix N.

The Spears Free Clinic and Hospital for Poor Children
v.
The Denver Area Better Business Bureau et al.

[312 P.2d 110]

Supreme Court of Colorado
June 10, 1957

Actions to recover damages for civil conspiracy to destroy plaintiff's business were consolidated for trial. The District Court, City and County of Denver, Robert H. McWilliams, Jr., J., entered judgment dismissing the actions, and plaintiff brought error. The Supreme Court, Knass, J., held that the evidence justified finding that plaintiff had failed to establish that defendants, or any combination of them, had conspired with intent to damage plaintiff's business and had actually damaged such business.

Judgment affirmed.

1. Appeal and Error 1010(1)
Where trial is to the court, the determination of controverted facts rests with presiding judge, and such determination, when supported by competent evidence, will not be disturbed on appeal.

2. Conspiracy 19
In consolidated actions to recover actual and exemplary damages for civil conspiracy to destroy plaintiff's business, evidence justified finding that plaintiff had failed to establish that defendants, or any combination of them, had conspired with intent to damage plaintiff's business or had actually damaged such business.

3. Conspiracy 19
In action to recover damages for civil conspiracy, plaintiff has burden of proving essential elements of a civil conspiracy.

4. Conspiracy 1
To constitute civil "conspiracy" there must be two or more persons, an object to be accomplished, a meeting of minds on the object or course of action, one or more unlawful overt acts, and damages as proximate result thereof.

5. Conspiracy 1
For purpose of entering into civil conspiracy, a "corporation" is a person.

6. Conspiracy 19
In consolidated actions to recover damages for civil conspiracy, evidence sustained finding as to credibility of witnesses.

Charles Ginsberg, Denver, for plaintiff in error.

Philip S. Van Cise, Edwin P. Van Cise, Denver, for all defendants in error.

E. Ray Campbell, Denver, for defendants in error, The Denver Post, Inc., Robert Byers and Charles Buxton.

J. Peter Norlund, Denver, for defendants in error, Colorado State Medical Society and Harvey T. Sethman.

KNASS, Justice.

The parties are aligned here as in the trial court. From a judgment of dismissal entered at trial, plaintiff is here on writ of error.

The pleadings comprise more than 400 folios and the reporter's transcript more than 4,300.

Plaintiff commenced two separate actions for damages based on alleged civil conspiracy, which were consolidated for the purpose of trial. In the first action the Better Business Bureau, referred to as "BBB"; its director Bell, together with numerous individuals and corporations, were named as defendants. Later other companies or corporations and named individuals were brought into the case as defendants. The second suit named as defendants the same individuals, corporations and companies made defendants in the first case.

In essence the gravamen of the two complaints was the defendants willfully conspired to destroy plaintiff's business by giving misleading information about plaintiff; promoting litigation against it; advising persons indebted to plaintiff not to pay their bills; announcing that defendants had assembled incriminating evidence concerning plaintiff; distributing defamatory literature and otherwise destroying public confidence in plaintiff. Plaintiff sought $5,000,000 actual damage and a like sum as exemplary damages in each action.

Issue was joined, affirmative defenses of justification were interposed, the truth of any statements made by defendants was alleged, together with a defense that the acts of plaintiff were ultra vires in connection with the practice of chiropractic, and other matters including on behalf of The Denver Post a defense that the plaintiff had from time to time invited The Post to make complete and thorough investigation of the acts of plaintiff, and that in response thereto assigned a reporter to make such investigation, and that the articles in The Post were "fair comment" on matters of public interest. The Medical Society and Sethman, its executive officer, alleged that they knew nothing about any investigation made by the BBB. A supplemental answer on behalf of defendants was filed amplifying the defense of unlawful practice of chiropractic and medicine on the part of plaintiff, and added the defense that plaintiff had illegally administered drugs and practiced surgery.

Trial was to the court and a wide latitude permitted in the introduction of evidence. The trial judge dismissed plaintiff's actions predicating his decision on two grounds: (1) "That the plaintiff corporation has failed to establish by a preponderance of the evidence that the defendants, or any combination of them, did conspire with the intent to damage the business of the plaintiff corporation and did actually damage that business." (2) "That the business of the plaintiff corporation is being, or has been in the past, conducted in a manner contrary to the laws of Colorado, and therefore the plaintiff corporation cannot successfully maintain this particular type of an action wherein the plaintiff corporation seeks to be recouped for alleged damage to the said business."

[1] Counsel for plaintiff contends that a consideration of all the evidence warrants "the conclusion that the findings of the trial court was contrary to the preponderance of the evidence." The issues were fairly and thoroughly explored in the trial court, and, as stated, great latitude was permitted in the introduction of evidence. We have repeatedly held that where trial is to the court, the determination of controverted facts rests with the presiding judge, and when supported by competent evidence will not be disturbed.

[2-5] From the record before us we are satisfied that the evidence justifies a finding by the trial court that plaintiff failed to establish that defendants, or any combination of them, conspired with intent to damage the business of plaintiff, or did actually damage that business. The burden is upon the plaintiff in actions of this type to prove five elements essential to the maintenance of such action.

In Lockwood v. Bockhaus, 129 Colo. 339, 270 P. 2d 193, 196, these essentials are stated as follows:

"To constitute a civil conspiracy there must be (1) two or more persons, and for this purpose a corporation is a person; (2) an object is accomplished; (3) a meeting of minds on the object or course of action; (4) one or more unlawful overt acts; and (5) damages as the proximate result thereof. The burden of proving these essentials by a preponderance of the evidence is upon him who asserts the claim under such circumstances."

[6] It is claimed that the witness Walter T. Cooper, Ph.D., N.D., D.P.T. made a case for plaintiff when he testified that some two or three months after the Denver grand jury investigation of practices by various individuals and corporations in connection with the healing arts and the treatment of human ills, defendant Bell, director of the BBB, stated to Cooper "that Spears [then head of plaintiff corporation] was an S.O.B. and a quack anyhow, and he should be put out of business" and that "they'd do everything they possibly could to put

him out of business." This statement was categorically denied by Bell and in his findings the distinguished trial judge said, "This Court, in determining the credibility which is attached to the various witnesses, chooses to disbelieve Cooper and believe Bell." There is ample competent evidence in the record to sustain the finding of the trial court.

A full and complete hearing was had and an opportunity afforded all parties to present evidence, and the cause was decided on its merits. No contention is made that the trial court improperly admitted or excluded any evidence.

The foregoing is determinative of this case, hence we need not consider the question whether the plaintiff corporation in view of its corporate activities in connection with the practice of chiropractic, may maintain an action of this nature.

The judgment is affirmed. En Banc. Holland, J., dissents.

Index

INDEX

INDEX

CLOSE SPEARS, STATE DEMANDS

Illegal Practices Laid to Clinic

...tion on Spears
...calls Long Row
...ith City, State

By ROBERT STAPP
...ver Post Staff Writer.

...is worth 8 million dollars. It consists of the sanitarium proper, the ...largest chiropractic sani... has been jousting with ...state agencies almost entirely through in... for the past twenty-five...

Clinic Declared Target Of Jealousy, Prejudice

Dr. Dan Spears, chief of staff of the Spears sanitarium, declared Friday afternoon that the institution had been "singled out" for attack by the state welfare department, but that he would nullify this action concerning these charges, he said.

Speaking, in the absence of his brother, Dr. Leo L. Spears, who is in New York city, Dr. Dan Spears issued the following statement:

"Dr. Cleere has not visited this...

Charges Unfounded Say Spears Attorneys

Attorneys for the Spears sanitarium Friday branded as "wild, fantastic and utterly unfounded" allegations that unhealthful conditions prevail at the institution.

A statement issued by the law firm of Dickerson, Morrissey and Zarlengo, in conjunction with Attorney General's office, said that ...Stare Health Director Roy L. Cleere with acting from "personal pique" and attempting to prejudice the state supreme court in its consid...

officials' charges, the attorneys asserted:

1—That patients suffering from scarlet fever entered the sanitarium before entering the sanitarium. That the state board of health was notified immediately. That the board took charge of the patients, quarantined them in the patient... set up his own isolation technic.

2—That the sanitarium prepares...

Sanitary Setup 1957 Hit; Metzger Probe Slated

By BERT HANNA
Denver Post Staff Writer.

State officials moved Friday to shut down the Spears Chiro... juvenile sanitation as an overnight hospital, following charges...

hardly any formulas and that those it does prepare are submitted to the board of health for approval.

4—That the sanitarium administers medicine and chiropractors use no prescription—in pencil or otherwise.

4—That all nursing records are kept in accordance with rules of the sanitarium and that we are inspected regularly by state officials.

Spears' Lawyers Charge Metzger Acts in Bad Faith

By JACK MOHLER
Rocky Mountain News Writer.

Charges of "bad faith" yesterday were leveled at Attorney General John Metzger by attorneys for Dr. Leo L. Spears who is fighting to keep his chiropractic sanitarium open despite a district court license revocation ruling in 1946.

The charges were made in a dismissal of a petition filed Dec. 2 by Metzger which called for an immediate ...

SPEARS CLOSING URGED

THE DENVER POST—Dec. 2, 1949

Spears Suit Reviewed By Board

By Denver Post
Special
COLORADO SPRINGS, Dec. 12.—
THE DENVER POST—Dec. 12, 1949

health matters and to tackle the two-point legal problem of the...

Sanitarium Attack 'Ambush,' Spears Says

ROCKY MOUNTAIN NEWS

Dr. Leo L. Spears yesterday termed the state's effort to close Spears sanitarium an "ambush by my age-old enemies."

In his first, public comment since state and city health officials outlined charges last week, Spears berated the public to "come and see for itself whether this attack is inspired by jealousy or by an honest desire to protect the public."

Spears returned Sunday from New York City, where he was to lecture to New York chiropractors Thursday night. After being informed of the new charges by telephone...

Practices At Clinic Held Illegal

A demand for action to close the Spears Chiropractic sanitarium as an operating hospital was laid before the state board of health Friday.

Spears' new action and charges against Metzger were filed Friday.

The move was initiated by Dr. Roy L. Cleere, state health administrator, who is "trying to prejudice the Supreme Court in the present...

Clinic Hit In Outbreak Of Disease

THE DENVER POST—Dec. 2, 1949

acute cause of scarlet fever and a serious...

...ropractic Board
...ps Action on Spears

...as a result of mistreatment...
Fitzsimons General hospital administration had denied the patient's request for chiropractic treatment.

REVOKED.

In a hearing, before the state medical examiners, the board was not justified in its rulings, and up held the ruling and upheld revocation. Spears appealed to the United States supreme court, but the high tribunal refused to hear the case.

...head of chiropractic, Peterson Thursday that...ion asserted. "We have often in...